Champions for Peace

Champions for Peace

Women Winners of the
Nobel Peace Prize

JUDITH HICKS STIEHM

ROWMAN & LITTLEFIELD PUBLISHERS, INC.

Lanham • Boulder • New York • Toronto • Oxford

ROWMAN & LITTLEFIELD PUBLISHERS, INC.

Published in the United States of America
by Rowman & Littlefield Publishers, Inc.
A wholly owned subsidiary of The Rowman & Littlefield Publishing Group, Inc.
4501 Forbes Boulevard, Suite 200, Lanham, Maryland 20706
www.rowmanlittlefield.com

P.O. Box 317, Oxford OX2 9RU, UK

British Library Cataloguing in Publication Information Available

Library of Congress Cataloging-in-Publication Data

Stiehm, Judith.
    Champions for peace : women winners of the Nobel Peace Prize / Judith Hicks Stiehm.
        p. cm.
    Includes bibliographical references and index.
    ISBN-13: 978-0-7425-4025-5 (cloth : alk. paper)
    ISBN-10: 0-7425-4025-1 (cloth : alk. paper)
    ISBN-13: 978-0-7425-4026-2 (pbk. : alk. paper)
    ISBN-10: 0-7425-4026-X (pbk. : alk. paper)
    1. Pacifists—Biography.   2. Nobel Prizes—History.   3. Women and peace—History.
4. Peace—Awards—History.   I. Title.

    JZ5540.S74 2006
    303.6'6—dc22

                                                                    2006001754

Printed in the United States of America

⊗™ The paper used in this publication meets the minimum requirements of
American National Standard for Information Sciences—Permanence of Paper for
Printed Library Materials, ANSI/NISO Z39.48-1992.

Historians too often praise reckless and arrogant leaders who send troops to wage war.

This book is intended to encourage and to honor those who seek to avoid war without relinquishing the pursuit of justice.

Contents

❧

In the Tradition of Lysistrata— Women Champions for Peace

Lysistrata may have begun women's actions for peace. In the fifth century BC she mobilized women from a number of Greek city-states to force men to end the Peloponnesian War. The method was the withholding of sexual favors—and, importantly, the women also seized the Athenian treasury. No more money was available to support the war.

Sadly, Lysistrata is fiction. Indeed, she is the heroine of an eponymous comedy written by a man, Aristophanes, for an all-male audience and with men playing all the roles, even the most seductive. But because the play is produced regularly, it seems certain that at least a portion of its audiences may be inspired by the possibility that women can indeed work together to create peace, or at least to bring an end to a particular war.

The stories of the twelve women listed below who have won the Nobel Peace Prize, the very stories that are recounted in this book, are similarly inspiring.[1]

The stories are instructive as well. They tell us that there are many different ways to champion peace, and that one need not be rich or famous to make a contribution. Three winners of the Nobel Peace Prize have been Americans. Others have been from Europe, the Middle East, Asia, Africa, and Central America. They have been young, middle-aged, and old. They have been of titled nobility, and they have been subsistence farmers. They have held doctorates, and they have also been barely schooled. What they have had in common is a vision, a commitment to action, and a willingness to persevere in the face of criticism and, in some cases, imprisonment.

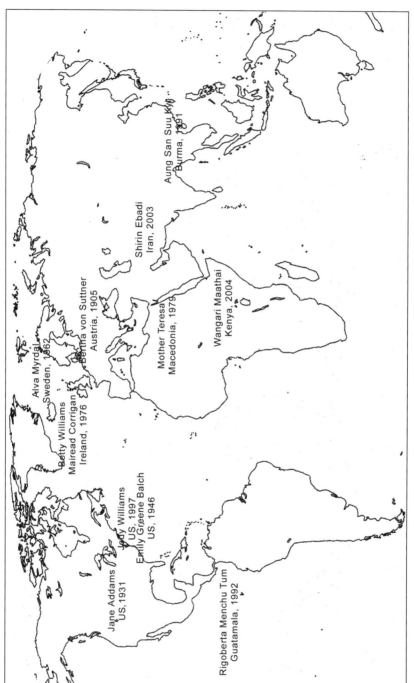

Women Winners from around the World. Drawn by Stacy West

Working for peace does not mean that the consequences of one's work are predictable, or even that there will be agreement as to whether or not peace has been achieved. For example, some argue that simply ending an armed conflict results only in *negative peace*. They contend that while that kind of peace may be preferable to war, for peace to be sustained, it must be *positive*. It must be based on justice both between nations and within a nation.

Alfred Nobel, a Swedish industrialist and the inventor of dynamite, thought that his new explosive was so destructive that nations would have to forego war. To encourage conciliatory behavior, he provided in his will support for a prize to be awarded annually to "the person who shall have done the most or the best work for fraternity between nations, for the abolition or reduction of standing armies and for the holding and promotion of peace congresses." A committee appointed by the Norwegian legislature (the Norwegian Nobel Committee) was charged with selecting an annual winner. Over the years, these committees have not found this an easy task, nor have they closely adhered to the criteria set forth by Nobel. Clearly, they have concluded both that there are many different ways to contribute to peace and that peace is more than the absence of armed conflict.

The first Nobel Peace Prize was awarded in 1903, but the difficulties involved in selecting a winner are demonstrated by the fact that nineteen times since then, in almost one year out of every five, no prize was awarded. This sometimes occurred while a major war was in progress, but no award was made in ten other years as well.

A review of Nobel Peace Prize citations suggests that while the criteria have evolved over time, the selection committees have made awards to six distinct types of recipient: (1) international organizations; (2) successful national officials working in an international context while pursuing legal solutions to conflict; (3) peace activists working in an international context, some with, but many without governmental approval; (4) individuals nonviolently seeking justice, freedom, security, or rights as a preliminary to peace; (5) leaders who have used or sanctioned the use of force but who have agreed to a peace settlement; and (6) altruists who render exemplary service to others.

About one-fifth of the prizes went to organizations rather than to individuals.[2] Organization winners have been spread over the past century, and the International Committee of the Red Cross has won three times. Two organizations shared the prize with their leader. One of these leaders, Jody Williams of the United States, is a woman. Roughly half of the prize-winning organizations were devoted to relief, to the assuaging of misery. Thus, peace per se was not their primary mission, and some critics would even argue that the efforts of these organizations, in aiding refugees for example, can actually prolong war. Other organizations did pursue peace, but none through the exercise of power. Some had a particular focus, for example, the prevention of nuclear war or the support of prisoners of conscience.

About one-third of the individual laureates were national officials who worked in an international, legal context.[3] This kind of winner was particularly typical in the first half of the nineteenth century. A number of these prizes were awarded before women even had the vote, and many before women held high office. Still, there is one woman in this group of national officials, Sweden's Alva Myrdal.

Peace activist winners of the Nobel Peace Prize have been slightly more numerous than national politicians who pursued an international, legal agenda.[4] Some of the activists were esteemed and encouraged by their governments, others were not. In fact, some suffered arrest, prison, torture, or exile. Six women are in this category: Austrian Baroness Bertha von Suttner, Jane Addams and Emily Greene Balch of the United States, Northern Ireland's Betty Williams and Mairead Corrigan, and American Jody Williams, who shared her prize with her organization—the International Campaign to Ban Landmines.

All winners of the prize by nonviolently seeking justice, freedom, security, or rights as a preliminary to peace won after World War II.[5] Most of these individuals challenged established powers, while rejecting the use of force. Most sought justice within their homeland, but received support from many nations. The women in this group are Aung San Suu Kyi of Myanmar (formerly Burma), Shirin Ebadi of Iran, and Wangari Muta Maathai of Kenya.

A smaller and a more controversial category encompasses individuals who formerly were willing to use or to sanction the use of force but who finally agreed to a peace settlement.[6] Five times since 1973, the prize has gone to pairs of such opponents. In the eyes of some, these prizes went to war criminals; others saw them as traitors. One woman, Rigoberta Menchú Tum, whose family fought and suffered grievously in her country's civil war, is included in this group although she had no official role in that conflict and commanded no combatants.

Two individuals won for exemplary care and service: Albert Schweitzer in 1952, and Mother Teresa in 1979. Both were greatly admired, although it is not clear how their work related to peace.

It must be noted that women have had a long history of working for peace; and some scholars argue that women's gender role has given them a viewpoint about conflict that is different from that of men. Some of the women Nobel Peace Prize winners, for example, Addams, Balch, and Jody Williams, have indeed worked within a tradition of peace activism. Many, including von Suttner, Mother Teresa, Myrdal, Menchú, Ebadi, and Maathai, as well as Addams and Balch, have been quite clear about their identity as women and have worked hard for and with other women. Others, including Betty Williams, Mairead Corrigan, and Suu Kyi, have been thrust into peace work because of circumstances and without a significant gender consciousness.

In learning the stories of these women Nobel Peace Prize winners, the reader will find their courage and perseverance immediately evident. The stories evoke pride, but also suggest that following in their footsteps is not an impossible dream. These women were not groomed for a Nobel Peace Prize. They did not pursue or expect to win one. Indeed, Peace Nobelists are not champions in the Olympic sense, that is, individuals who best all others, sometimes by a millisecond or a tenth of a point. In fact, their efforts are not always successful. Instead, these winners are examples. They illustrate what an individual can do. In their acceptance speeches, they inevitably note that they accept the Nobel Peace Prize on behalf of many unrecognized others.

Each of us has the capacity to be one of those others. The stories that follow show that women have undertaken important tasks over the last hundred years and in a variety of circumstances. Their resources and personalities have varied widely, but even if their work began only with the planting of a tree or by insisting on regular garbage collection, their local actions led them to the understanding that peace and justice must be global in order to be positive.

I believe that we have the responsibility as well as a capacity to change our world, and that this responsibility and capacity goes beyond self-interest. It is relatively easy to mobilize women as mothers and against nuclear weapons, terrorism, or other forms of violence perceived as threatening. But our peace work is not serious when it cares only for our own safety or even for preventing violence against women. Most violence is done by men, and much, if not most, is done to men. Further, much if not most is done by governments claiming to be protecting their citizens. Peace work requires attention to men, their interests, and their gender roles. It also means ensuring that governments do not simply incorporate men's roles when they should be representing and fulfilling the wishes of all their citizens.

Let us turn now to the story of Bertha von Suttner, the woman who successfully persuaded Alfred Nobel to create a prize for peace.

Notes

1. Seventy-nine men have won Nobel Peace Prizes. In addition to the twelve women discussed in this book, women have won ten prizes in literature, six in physiology and medicine, three in chemistry, two in physics, and none in economics. Marie Sklodowska Curie of France won in both chemistry and physics, and her daughter won in chemistry.

2. Organization winners include

1904	Institute of International Law, Belgium
1910	Permanent International Peace Bureau, Switzerland
1917	International Committee of the Red Cross, Switzerland
1938	Nansen International Office for Refugees, Switzerland
1944	International Committee of the Red Cross, Switzerland
1947	American Friends Service Committee, United States; Friends Service Council, United Kingdom
1954	Office of the United Nations High Commissioner for Refugees, Switzerland
1963	International Committee of the Red Cross and League of Red Cross Societies, Switzerland
1965	United Nations Children's Fund, United States
1969	International Labour Organization, Switzerland
1977	Amnesty International, Great Britain
1981	Office of the United Nations High Commissioner for Refugees, Switzerland
1985	International Physicians for the Prevention of Nuclear War, United States
1988	United Nations Peacekeeping Forces
1995	Pugwash Conferences on Science and World Affairs (shared)
1997	International Campaign to Ban Landmines, United States (shared)
1999	Médecins Sans Frontières (Doctors Without Borders), Belgium

3. Winners include

1903	Sir William Randal Cremer, Great Britain
1908	Klas Pontus Arnoldson, Sweden; Fredrik Bajer, Denmark
1909	Auguste Marie Francois Beernaert, Belgium; Paul Henri Benjamin Balluet d'Estournelles de Constant, Baron de Constant, de Rebecque, France
1911	Tobias Michael Carel Asser, the Netherlands (shared)
1912	Elihu Root, United States
1913	Henri La Fontaine, Belgium
1920	Léon Victor Auguste Bourgeois, France
1921	Karl Hjalmar Branting, Sweden; Christian Lous Lange, Norway
1925	Sir Joseph Austen Chamberlain, Great Britain; Charles Gates Dawes, United States
1929	Frank Billings Kellogg, United States

1934 Arthur Henderson, Great Britain
1936 Carlos Saavedra Lamas, Argentina
1937 Lord E. A. Robert Cecil, Great Britain
1945 Cordell Hull, United States
1953 George Catlett Marshall, United States
1957 Lester Bowles Pearson, Canada
1959 Philip J. Noel-Baker, Great Britain
1968 Réne Cassin, France
1971 Willy Brandt, West Germany
1974 Eisaku Sato, Japan
1982 Alfonso García Robles, Mexico; Alva Myrdal, Sweden
1987 Oscar Arias Sánchez, Costa Rica
1990 Mikhail Sergeyevich Gorbachev, Soviet Union
2001 Kofi Annan, Ghana
2002 Jimmy Carter, United States

4. Activist winners were
1901 Jean Henri Dunant, Switzerland; Frédéric Passy, France
1902 Élie Ducommun, Switzerland; Charles Albert Gobat, Switzerland
1905 Baroness Bertha von Suttner, Austria
1907 Louis Renault, France; Ernesto Teodoro Moneta, Italy
1911 Alfred Hermann Fried, Austria (shared)
1922 Fridtjof Nansen, Norway
1927 Ludwig Quidde, Germany; Ferdinand Edouard Buisson, France
1930 Lars Olof Johnathan (Nathan) Söderblom, Sweden
1931 Jane Addams, United States; Nicholas Murray Butler, United States
1933 Sir Norman Angell, Great Britain
1935 Carl von Ossietzky, Germany
1946 John Raleigh Mott, United States; Emily Greene Balch, United States
1950 Ralph Bunche, United States
1958 Georges Henri Pire, Belgium
1961 Dag Hjalmar Agne Carl Hammarskjöld, Sweden
1962 Linus Pauling, United States
1974 Seán MacBride, Ireland
1975 Andrei Dmitrievich Sakharov, Soviet Union
1976 Betty Williams, Northern Ireland; Mairead Corrigan, Northern Ireland
       (Although peace activists, these winners worked for peace within their
       own country.)
1980 Adolfo Pérez Esquivel, Argentina
1986 Elie Wiesel, Romania/France/United States
1995 Joseph Rotblat, Poland/Great Britain (shared)
1996 Carlos Filipe Ximenes Belo, East Timor; José Ramos-Horta, East Timor
1997 Jody Williams, United States

5. This category includes
   1949   Baron John Boyd Orr of Brechin Mearns, Great Britain
   1951   Léon Jouhaux, France
   1960   Albert John Lutuli, South Africa
   1964   Martin Luther King Jr., United States
   1970   Norman Borlaug, United States
   1983   Lech Walesa, Poland
   1984   Desmond Mpilo Tutu, South Africa
   1989   The Fourteenth Dalai Lama, Tibet
   1991   Aung San Suu Kyi, Burma
   2000   Kim Dae-jung, Republic of Korea
   2003   Shirin Ebadi, Iran
   2004   Wangari Muta Maathai, Kenya
6. The following fall into this category
   1906   Theodore Roosevelt, United States
   1919   Woodrow Wilson, United States
   1926   Gustav Stresemann, Germany; Aristide Briand, France
   1973   Henry A. Kissinger, United States; Le Duc Tho, North Vietnam
   1978   Mohamed Anwar el-Sadat, Egypt; Menachem Begin, Israel
   1992   Rigoberta Menchú Tum, Guatemala
   1993   Nelson Mandela, South Africa; Frederik Willem de Klerk, South Africa
   1994   Yasser Arafat, PLO; Shimon Peres, Israel; Yitzhak Rabin, Israel
   1998   John Hume, Northern Ireland; David Trimble, Northern Ireland

Champions for Peace

Bertha von Suttner. Courtesy of the Norwegian Nobel Institute

❦

CHAPTER ONE

Bertha von Suttner: Noble Woman and Nobel Friend

The Way Things Were

The second half of the nineteenth century was an era of empire and war, of sultans, tsars, emperors, and kings—and of empresses, and queens. The frequency of war and its increasing potential for efficient devastation stimulated both an arms race and an international peace movement. Sadly, the movement was unable to achieve its goals, and by 1914 most of Europe was embroiled in what was then known as The Great War, World War I.

By 1850 the Ottoman Empire, which had ranged across North Africa to the Caspian Sea and from the Persian Gulf to Budapest, had lost two wars to Russia, and other wars to independence-minded Greeks and Egyptians. The empire's domain had drastically contracted. Further, other nationalities were seeking their independence, and already independent countries had their eye on lands still held by the empire. (The Ottoman Empire was frequently referred to then as "the Sick Man of Europe.")

Russia's expanding empire reached from the Baltic to the Black Sea and included parts of Poland and the Ukraine, Belorussia, Bessarabia, the Crimea, and Finland. Russia had also assumed the role of "policeman of Europe" by helping to quell liberal movements at home and abroad and by repressing revolutions in Poland and Hungary. The future promised continued and, perhaps, increasing power for Russia.

The ruling house of Austria, the Hapsburgs, began as rulers of the Holy Roman Empire in the early fifteenth century. By the nineteenth century, Austria was the most powerful state in Europe, extending through much of what is today Poland, Czechoslovakia, Lombardy, Venetia, and Dalmatia. Although several revolutions had to be quashed, Vienna remained both the political and the cultural center of Europe.

Many historians describe the late nineteenth century as peaceful, but from 1850 to 1914 the Ottoman, Russian, and Austrian Empires were almost constantly involved in small and relatively short wars. The Crimean War (1853–1856) pitted Russia against the Ottoman Empire (Turkey), England, France, and Piedmont-Sardinia ostensibly over the guardianship of holy places in Palestine. Florence Nightingale's work in developing the practice of nursing is, perhaps, the most important result of that war. In the Franco-Austrian War of 1858–1860, Austria lost Lombardy. In 1864 Austria was involved in a war over Schleswig-Holstein, followed almost immediately by a losing war with Prussia. The cost to Austria was Venetia, which went to Italy, and expulsion from the German Confederation. Austria then formed a dual state, the Austro-Hungarian Monarchy, while Prussia turned on France, took Alsace and Lorraine, and by 1871 had unified the German states into a fourth empire.

Russia and the Ottomans went to war in 1877. This resulted in independence for Romania, Serbia, and Montenegro, and administrative control of Bosnia-Herzegovina for Austria, who won it through diplomacy and not arms. The Ottomans won a war with Greece in 1897 but lost Crete, the cause of the war. Russia went head-to-head with Japan over control of Manchuria and Korea and was soundly defeated; the 1905 Russian Revolution was the result. Next, Austria annexed Bosnia-Herzegovina, and Italy seized Libya from the Ottomans. Two more wars were fought in the Balkans in 1912 and 1913. In the first, Russia supported Bulgaria and Serbia, and the Ottoman Empire was expelled from Europe (except for Constantinople); also, Albania gained its independence, thus preventing Serbia from gaining a coastline. In the second war, Bulgaria fell out with Serbia then lost the war and territory. One year later, World War I was precipitated by the assassination of an Austrian archduke by a Serbian nationalist. A four-year war with at least 10 million dead ensued.

Not only were there a lot of wars, but warfare also changed significantly in the years preceding World War I. France introduced the mass citizen-army to the world. Other nations followed by conscripting large numbers of men. Prussia, in particular, developed a highly professional officer corps supported by conscripted troops and trained reserves. Mercenaries dwindled; so did small, traditional armies led by noblemen.

New and deadlier weapons were produced. Rifles capable of shooting fifteen rounds a minute were developed, while the new machine guns could fire six hundred rounds a minute. Navies now boasted steel ships and U-boats.

Italy ushered in aerial bombardment. Chemical weapons were produced. The telegraph made rapid communication possible, while railroads made rapid troop and supply movement possible—and widened war's reach.

Prussia led the way in military modernization and professionalism. It created a general staff that developed detailed war plans, engaged in war games, and prepared detailed maps. It also created a war college where a book on military strategy and tactics, *On War* by Carl von Clausewitz, would become the bible. Clausewitz's creed—that war is but an extension of policy and that it requires the unified commitment of the government, the military, and the people—was widely accepted.

In sum, ambitions for empires, which encompass large and heterogeneous territories, were in direct competition with dreams of independence, which necessarily involve fragmentation and homogeneity. Everywhere in Europe populations were becoming militarized on behalf of one of these purposes. Everywhere militaries were becoming more capable of more destruction. Those who were committed to the building of militaries claimed that strength was the way to peace. Those who created deadlier weapons asserted that the weapons' very existence would create such a powerful deterrent to war that these weapons, too, would be guarantors of peace. In particular, Alfred Nobel, the Swedish inventor of dynamite, believed (or hoped) that that would be true of his invention. This, then, was the chaotic world into which Bertha von Suttner was born.

Baroness Bertha Sophie Felicita von Suttner (née Countess Kinsky von Chinic und Tettau)

Bertha von Suttner was born a member of the Austrian aristocracy. The place was Prague and the year was 1843. But there was a problem. Her father, a retired royal and imperial lieutenant field-marshal and actual chamberlain (a general, like three of his brothers) died before her birth, and because her mother was a commoner, Bertha could not be received at court and was never fully accepted by the Austrian nobility. The long name suggests privilege, and by any standard she was privileged, but she was also marginal.

In her *Memoirs*, von Suttner describes her life. Schooled by governesses, she learned English, French, and piano at a young age. *Jane Eyre*, *Uncle Tom's Cabin*, and the novels of Victor Hugo were in her library. So too were the works of Plato, Hegel, Fichte, and Kant. Elvira, a cousin who periodically lived with Bertha and her mother, was an intellectual with a goal of becoming a famous poet. In contrast, young Bertha's vision of the future focused on romantic marriage.

Elvira's mother considered herself a clairvoyant, so she and Bertha's mother decided to profit at the gaming tables from the aunt's "second sight." Thus the four, the two mothers and Bertha and Elvira (ages twelve and thirteen, and chaperoned at all times), repaired to Wiesbaden to make their fortune. Apparently the excitement of the gaming affected the clairvoyant powers of Elvira's mother, for both women lost their stake and then some. A later trip to Wiesbaden coincided with Austria's war in Italy, but Bertha, by then sixteen, took little notice of the war. In her *Memoirs* she notes that she accepted it as something existent but indifferent to her, as one accepts the eruption of a volcano on a distant island. The families were more affected by their large financial losses, which forced the four of them to leave Vienna for the countryside and to practice economies.

At eighteen, Bertha reentered Vienna and "the world." She was snubbed at her coming-out ball and rebounded with an engagement to a fifty-two-year-old millionaire that was quickly broken after his first kiss. Her life then became that of an international belle with her attendance at salons, balls, promenades, and receptions in Vienna, Rome, Baden, Venice, and Homburg. When Austria went to war with Denmark over Schleswig-Holstein, Bertha again took note, but she experienced neither a surge of patriotism nor a sense of horror. There was no one she knew personally involved in the war. It mattered little to her.

At Homburg she entered into friendships, first with the Princess of Mingrelia, who had once led her own troops against Russia, and then with her children Niko and Salome. Although the princess was twenty years Bertha's senior, her friendship and support would later prove important. More money was lost at the tables, however, and Bertha and her mother again retreated to the countryside.

Again Austria went to war, and for the third time, twenty-three-year-old Bertha scarcely noticed. Her life was untouched. Her mother urged her to train as an opera singer, and Bertha decided she would dedicate herself to the arts. She and her mother then moved to Paris so Bertha could receive proper training. There the relationship with the Princess of Mingrelia was resumed, and Bertha's commitment to the arts and to her voice lessons waned as her taste for high society waxed.

A young Australian whose father owned "a whole street in Melbourne" wooed the young countess, and for a day she experienced the feeling of having "incommensurable wealth" as she and the young man shopped for jewels and a home. A betrothal banquet was prepared, but the eighteen-year-old fiancé did not appear, and it turned out the millions and the street in Melbourne were fiction.

Love and society having brought humiliation, Bertha and her mother moved to Milan so Bertha could again take up the study of music. When the Franco-Prussian War broke out, Bertha, now twenty-seven, noticed because a friend's husband was a French officer. But she only noticed; she continued her custom of never reading newspapers, although she was an avid, a compulsive reader of books.[1] She devoured all of Shakespeare, Goethe, Schiller, Lessing, and Victor Hugo, who particularly captivated her. She read Dickens, Byron, Shelly, de Musset, and Tennyson. In French she perused Sand, Balzac, Dumas, Racine, Augier, and more.

But she did not confine herself to fiction and poetry. She read ethnography, chemistry, and astronomy as well. Her favorite field, notwithstanding her disinterest in politics, was philosophy. Hard stuff to work through on one's own! In her diary she recorded the reading of Kant, Schopenhauer, Hartmann, Strauss, Feuerbach, Pascal, and Comte, saying, "These and many others, all of whose names I cannot here enumerate, were my intellectual comrades, in whose company I led a happy double existence." The philosophy of Mill and that of Marx seem to have escaped her—or perhaps they were too "political." There were other works available that would have a great influence on her in the future, but they had not yet claimed her attention. In particular, these were the works of Darwin, Buckle, and Spencer. She notes her thirst for knowledge about the nature of man and society. She also notes that her curiosity about how things "are" never led her to think about how they might be.

Von Suttner is an example of an excellent and energetic mind being exercised in isolation. She had no teachers, professors, fellow students, or coffeehouse intellectual friends. She is also an example of a person who continues to develop as an adult. Indeed, in looking back at her years of unconcern for politics and war, she drew the lesson that people must be educated about both, rather than blamed for not already thinking about them, and that education never comes too late.

The Franco-Prussian War was a landmark event in modern European history. France was humiliated and lost Alsace and Lorraine. More importantly, the German states were unified under Prussia. The new Prussian empire would become a formidable threat to both Russia and Austria-Hungary, but von Suttner was still relatively oblivious, though at the end of the war she happened to be in Berlin (still pursuing a vocal career), where she witnessed the return of the victorious Prussian troops and experienced it as "a lofty, historic festival of joy."

At age twenty-nine von Suttner had yet another romance. This time it was with another student of music, a German prince. A younger son with no inheritance in his future, he planned a career in the United States under an assumed name. An engagement was announced with all parents approving. The young man then sailed for the United States to launch his career, died aboard ship, and was buried at sea.

Still single at thirty and with her mother's resources reduced to a widow's pension, von Suttner decided to give up singing and to become financially independent, that is, to take a job. At that time her only option was essentially a position as governess, tutor, or companion. She chose a position with the von Suttner family in their *palais* in Vienna as a companion to the four von Suttner daughters, age fifteen through twenty. The family also included three sons. Two were married; the youngest, Arthur, twenty-three, lived in the *palais*.

The living at the *palais* was grand with many servants, three drawing rooms, an opera box, and a castle in the country. Von Suttner's friendship with the Princess of Mingrelia had continued. The princess was then building a new castle. (The old one had been destroyed by the Ottomans in a war that brought Mingrelia under Russian protection.) It was planned that Bertha would join her there when the castle was completed, presumably in three years' time. What was not planned, and was socially impossible, was the fact that Bertha and Arthur, seven years her junior, had fallen in love.

When the baroness discovered the relationship, Bertha announced that she would leave, but asked for a recommendation for a position far away from Vienna. An advertisement was produced:

> A very wealthy, cultured, elderly gentleman, living in Paris, desires to find a lady also of mature years, familiar with languages, as secretary and manager of his household.

The ad had been placed by Alfred Nobel. A self-taught chemist, Nobel was a wealthy bachelor at forty-three. He led an international but lonely life, living grandly in Paris near the Arc de Triomphe.

After several exchanges of letters, Bertha accepted the position and went to Paris. She was greatly impressed with Nobel, who told her of his hope of producing "a substance or a machine of such frightful efficacy for wholesale destruction that wars should thereby become altogether impossible." Impressed though she was, in only a few days the young countess had sold a piece of jewelry, bought a train ticket to Vienna, and surprised Arthur, who had been sending her daily messages of love. A secret wedding was arranged, and the pair then eloped to the Caucasus. Their plan was to have the Princess of Mingrelia secure a position in the Russian court or state service for Arthur.

Thus began nine years of Georgian exile. The princess's palace was still not ready, so the newlyweds stayed in Gordi until it became evident that there would be no position for Arthur in either the court or government service. The couple were now on their own, so it was necessary to move to the nearest town, Kutais. There they scraped by, teaching languages and music.

Again war between Russia and the Ottoman Empire broke out—but this time it could not be ignored. The Caucasus was sure to be invaded; even Kutais was threatened, and many of its sons departed for the front. With lessons disrupted, Arthur managed to provide some income by sending articles to Austrian and German newspapers. Bertha tried her hand too (writing under a pseudonym), and was pleased to be both published and paid. Still, no opportunities presented themselves for Arthur, so the couple moved to Tiflis. There, each worked during the day. Then having dressed for dinner, they joined the local aristocrats in the evening. Over the course of nine years, the couple lived in a variety of Caucasus towns, Bertha teaching while Arthur built a career as a self-taught architect. Both continued to write, and Bertha expanded her repertoire to include realist novels.

In 1882 and after almost a decade, Arthur's parents decided to make peace and to invite the couple back to Vienna. By then both von Suttners were making a living by their writing. On their return they became members of the authors' union and entered the city's literary circles, but lived outside Vienna in the family castle, Harmannsdorf. Bertha's work became more ambitious, and *Das Maschinenzeitalter* (*The Age of Machinery*) was sent to the printer with the admonition that it was to be published anonymously, for Bertha feared that its scientific and philosophical subject matter would go unread if published under a woman's name. The work was designed as a series of lectures about the current day, but as though presented at some time in a more progressive future. In these Bertha criticized the current school system, prudery, discrimination against women, the church, nationalism, and "the most reprehensible crime," war.

That winter a visit to Paris renewed Bertha's acquaintance with Nobel, with whom she had been in correspondence ever since her brief employment by him. The von Suttners also entered into the life of the Paris salons, where the question of war with Germany was much in the air. And there was something else, too. It was at this time that Bertha von Suttner first learned of the establishment of the International Peace and Arbitration Association in London. Hodgson Pratt, its president, had also organized branches in Stuttgart, Berlin, Milan, and Rome, and in Sweden, Norway, and Denmark. Von Suttner was so enthralled by the association that when the proofs for *Das Maschinenzeitalter* were delivered, she added a section on it.

At midlife, this impetuous, enthusiastic, talented, self-disciplined insider-outsider was about to write what would become one of the most widely read novels of the era. But it would not be Art. It would be propaganda, and it would be written to capture the hearts as well as the minds of her readers. It would portray life in its worst reality. Like Nobel's dynamite it would, Bertha van Suttner hoped, put an end to war.

The book was *Die Waffen Nieder*, variously translated as "Away with Weapons," "Ground Arms," or "Lay Down Your Arms." Its form was a purported autobiography based on a woman's diaries—a woman who, unlike von Suttner herself, had been personally affected by the wars of the era. This required research, and that research confirmed and strengthened von Suttner's antiwar feelings. As she noted, "I can certify that the sufferings through which I led my heroine were actually experienced by me while I was working on it." With confidence, she sent it to the journal that regularly published her work. It was returned. The journal's editors feared readers would "take offense." After other rejections, von Suttner decided to publish the work as a book rather than as a magazine serial. Her publisher waffled; he proposed a new title; he proposed that a respected statesman read it to remove anything disturbing. Von Suttner held fast. The whole point was to unveil the horrors of war. The book was intended to criticize existing culture and institutions. It was meant to speak for those who feared to or could not speak for themselves.

The timid publisher finally relented, and was rewarded. The two-volume novel was first published in 1889, and hundreds of thousands of copies sold as *Die Waffen Nieder* was translated into a dozen languages. Copyright laws not being what they might have been, this did not result in a fortune for the author, who needed it (Arthur's family fortune had by then largely disappeared). Still, Bertha was especially pleased by two of the letters she received from readers. One was from Leo Tolstoy.

> I admire your work very much and think that the publication of your novel is a good omen. The abolition of slavery was preceded by the famous book written by a woman, Mrs. Beecher-Stowe; God grant the abolition of war follow your book.

A second was from Alfred Nobel.

> I have just finished reading your admirable masterpiece. We are told that there are two thousand languages—1,999 too many—but certainly there is not one in which your delightful work should not be translated, read and studied. . . . Nevertheless, you make a mistake to cry "Away with Weapons" because you yourself make use of them . . . the charm of your style and the grandeur of your ideas.

Literary circles were not kind, but the book had not been intended for them. It had been intended to advance the work of the peace movement by adding to the diplomatic and dignified discourse of educated male leaders the passion of an aroused public that von Suttner believed to have progressed beyond the views set forth by newspapers and newsmakers.

What follows is an outline of the book's tale that I have included in order to let the reader experience at least a taste of von Suttner's famous work.

Die Waffen Nieder (Lay Down Your Arms)

The book's central character, Martha, daughter of a retired officer, marries a military officer. While granting respect to scholars, poets, and explorers, Martha, reflecting the military culture of her time and place, believes that only "winners of battles" deserve "real admiration." Thus, on the birth of her son, she enthusiastically agrees with her husband that their son must become a soldier, "the noblest profession of all."

Her doubts begin, however, when her husband describes the duties of a soldier's wife, whose place is "at our household hearth. It is to protect this, and guard it from any hostile attack, to preserve peace for our homes and our wives, that we men have to go to battle." Martha is confused. There is no menace to their hearth, just some "tension between two [political] cabinets." She understands that if her husband goes to war, it will actually be for adventure and ambition. Her questioning begins. What if we lose? The mere mention of this possibility is "unpatriotic." What about the slain, the crippled? "Glory recompenses all." Why is the Austrian side marked by virtue, honor, duty, courage, and the other by cruelty, guile, hatred? Her father, his friend (nicknamed Minister "To-Be-Sure"), and her aunt describe, first, war's glories, and next, the duties of the wife and the solace religion can offer her. Their voices are heard throughout the novel, repeating and repeating their positions—voices heard during every war and in the prelude to it. Martha's views, however, change over time. Her doubts arise from the purely personal and become stronger with the departure of her young husband for the front. There he is slain, and soon thereafter the war is lost.

Twenty-year-old Martha retires from society for four years. During that time she enlarges her horizons and is particularly impressed by Buckle's *History of Civilisation in England*, which argues that as nations progress, war and the love of war diminish. Although the seeds of an antiwar position have been planted, Martha is now ready for a new husband. She finds one in an older officer, who is introduced to her so that he might tell her the story of her first husband's death. (The latter is described as dying "in the full intoxication of war.") The officer, Frederick von Tilling, wins Martha's heart at a dinner party filled with banal conversation by refusing to express a view about Darwin until he has read

Darwin's book, and by his view that worthless, cruel, and self-seeking people are victims of their circumstances and education and are not inherently bad.

Although Martha's new husband has no love for or illusions about war, he remains an officer, for he has no other profession or way to support Martha. Also, he feels compelled to adhere to convention and the rules of honor even when they are not congruent with his beliefs.

A war with Denmark looms. It will soon be followed by one with Prussia, Austria's ally in the previous war. In a series of well-scripted conversations, Martha begins to realize that the motives given for war "are nothing but phrases—phrases and pretexts." Still, she recognizes within herself a spark of patriotism, that love that ordains "the most horrible work of the deadliest hatred—War." Von Suttner's volume is filled with energetic dialogues and passionate monologues developing an antiwar position. They make good reading aloud, and they would not have been pleasing to those prosecuting a war or to those of conventional religious belief. She strives for a wide audience, but grieves that the public surrenders so easily to war, for "when the sword is once drawn nothing more is necessary than to shout 'Hurrah,' and press hotly on to victory." Besides that, "all that is necessary is to invoke the blessing of heaven on war."

Von Tilling is called to service. His letters home provide grisly descriptions of war's butchery and tell of a fellow soldier's pride and excitement in being able to kill "without being a murderer." Martha begins to realize that every war "contains within itself the germ of a succeeding war." With this war over and having fulfilled his duties, von Tilling decides to leave the military, but Martha's fortune has been lost. Von Tilling remains an officer, now solely because of need.

War begins yet again. Toasted by Martha's father and seen as inevitable by her Aunt Mary, it is seen by Martha as barbarous. Martha views the argument that one pursues peace by preparing for war as false. She finds equally false the multiple professions of "defense" while a nation's multiple other reasons for going to war are proclaimed. (She notes that no nation ever admits to being engaged in "aggression.") Her husband dutifully heads for the front. Martha broods, which her father declares "sinful." Austria loses several battles. The letters of Martha's husband describe the horrors of war as experienced by those who fight and distinct from the view of the generals and from what is reported by the newspapers. "Never assert that war ennobles men," he writes. Horses are shot, puppies killed, and a twelve-year-old executed.

Then Austria loses a crucial battle, and the letters stop coming. Martha decides to go to the front herself. She describes the returning wounded in the train station. On her trip to the front she is given a full narrative of the most recent battle by a doctor who was there. Once she is there, we receive a third gruesome description of war from Martha's own observations, augmented with descriptions by a doctor, a nurse, and an inspector of field hospitals. Here is an excerpt.

> In one single barn alone sixty of these poor wretches were crowded. Every one of their wounds had originally been severe, but they had become hopeless in consequence of their unassisted condition . . . almost all were gangrenous. Limbs crushed by shot formed now mere heaps of coagulated blood covered with filth, in which the mouth was represented by a shapeless black opening, from which frightful groans kept welling out. . . . The living were lying close to dead bodies which had begun to fall into putrefaction, and for which the worms were ready.

Von Tilling has been wounded. He and Martha are reunited; the Prussians arrive and commandeer their home. Martha's sister instantly falls in love with one of the conquerors. The Prussians depart, and cholera breaks out. Servants die. Both of Martha's sisters die. Her brother dies. Her father dies (of a heart attack) and has a deathbed conversion in which he curses war.

Montesquieu has pointed out that it is easy enough to portray a hell that all can recognize—boiling oil, screeches, terror—but that it is hard indeed to describe a heaven that all will praise. What kind of music would heaven provide? What food? What recreation? And so it is with Die Waffen Nieder. Its critique of war, its description of the horrors of war, and its analysis of men's willing participation in war all ring true. But then comes the more difficult part—to prescribe a strategy that will provide for an end to war, that will enlist leaders and citizens in this effort, and that will inspire them to take the same risks and make the same sacrifices for peace as they make for war.

Von Tilling leaves the military. Martha has received a new inheritance, and von Tilling is content now to live on this inheritance; he is also ready to enlist in "the peace army." The couple visits a military cemetery on All Souls' Day, and the Austrian emperor appears. Martha imagines his grief and remorse and the social and political pressures that brought him to declare a war. She also skewers a clergyman's efforts to comfort a grieving mother whose son has died in the war.

Recognizing that one cannot command a living institution like an army to simply cease to exist, the peace army in which von Tilling enlists focuses on arbitration. There is more positive advocacy for peace as well, advocacy that acknowledges the difficulties and impediments to peace. But von Suttner has one more wrench in store for the reader. Austria is at peace, but the von Tillings have gone to Paris for the World Exhibition. War breaks out between France and Prussia, but the von Tillings elect to stay in Paris rather than to travel during hostilities. France falls; the French emperor surrenders; the Republic is proclaimed; and disorder and disarray prevail. Martha's German-speaking husband is arrested on the street by Communards, quickly tried, and executed. Martha is again a widow. The novel concludes with her grown son's speech, an homage "to the future" when "manhood is to raise itself into humanity." His son, he proclaims, will never become a soldier.

Von Suttner continued to write novels, but she never achieved anything so powerful as *Die Waffen Nieder*. In fact, her interest and energies shifted to peace activism. Still, she was compelled to continue her writing because the family's means were strained.

Peace Activist

Nearing fifty, Bertha von Suttner turned to organization and propaganda after a visit from English pacifist Felix Moscheles. He had asked to meet von Suttner and was stunned to be introduced to her husband, who he had assumed was dead. He had taken *Die Waffen Nieder* to be autobiographical! At the time the von Suttners were vacationing in Venice. When Moscheles expressed his wish to form a section of the International Peace and Arbitration Association there, Bertha said she would speak to the marquis at whose home she would be attending a ball that evening. Lo and behold, organizing began. The marquis called a meeting, some one hundred people came (all men save Bertha von Suttner and Moscheles's wife), and an organization was formed. Publicity created discussion both pro and con in support of the organization (with many women con); it also provoked mockery, and in some a "stolid, obstinate, indifference."

In addition to this Peace Association and others, a European Interparliamentary Union had been formed consisting of members of parliament who wished to resolve international disputes by arbitration. Von Suttner's Peace Association friends urged her to help organize a parliamentary delegation from Austria to attend an Interparliamentary Union conference to be held in Rome that fall (1891). She did, but of course, could not be a delegate herself. So she then organized a private Austrian Peace Society, to which she could belong. Having done so, she became chairman of the newly created, two-thousand-member society, a position she held until her death. This gave her an official role in the international meeting of the Peace Societies also to be held in Rome that fall. (Creating organizations ran in the von Tilling family: that spring her husband had formed the Union for Resistance to Anti-Semitism. In both cases, organizing began with a passionate appeal in the press.)

Bertha von Suttner embarked for Rome, protected by "that naïveté which consists in ignorance of difficulties and hindrances, and which helps forward every hazardous undertaking better than deliberation and experience."[2] Her friend, Ruggero Bonghi of Austria, was not allowed to preside at the Interparliamentary Union's conference because of his professed sympathies for France over its loss of Alsace and Lorraine, but he was chosen to head the meetings of the Peace Societies.

Ironically, these meetings were begun with a march played by a military band and an honor guard of uniformed men. Von Suttner gave a public address to the Peace Society meeting. One news account said, "It was not the first time that one of the sisterhood had quacked on this spot, and this time it was not even a matter of saving the Capitol," referring to geese that had once aroused Rome to a threatened attack. Peace activists must always expect criticism and ridicule; none are exempt. Interestingly, von Suttner did not experience stage fright during her address, although stage fright had plagued her as a singer.

Soon after the conference, a young man from Berlin asked von Suttner to be the editor of a newspaper he wished to publish. His name was A. H. Fried, and the paper was to be called *Die Waffen Nieder*. Its importance is shown by the fact that Fried, too, would later win a Nobel Peace Prize. Now began what would be a constant scramble for support from aristocrats and the wealthy. Endorsements and cash were both needed.

The following year the Peace Societies met in Bern, where they had established an international office. Von Suttner and two others introduced a motion for a Confederation of European States that would be bound to settle issues through arbitration. It was adopted. But debate was vigorous, and a variety of other proposals were put on the table. Von Suttner took the position that proposals that were intended to mitigate and to regulate war diverted the organization from its main purpose and were not acceptable. "If the goal lies in the south one ought not to pave the way to the north." *Pacifism* had not yet made its appearance as a word, but von Suttner was clearly staking out that position.

Alfred Nobel had visited the conference and invited the von Suttners to visit him in Zurich when it was over. He was dubious about the efforts of the conference, but invited Bertha to try to persuade him of the value of its work. If persuaded, he said, "I will do something great for the movement." Nobel was attracted to socialism and believed that when he died his fortune should not go to relatives but to the community. He continued to believe that war might be ended if horrific weapons made armies capable of mutual annihilation.

With joy and optimism Bertha noted the founding of a Peace Society in recalcitrant Berlin. With sorrow she missed the 1893 Peace Societies meeting in Chicago for lack of funds. With pleasure she noted the settlement by arbitration of a dispute in the Bering Straits.

The next year the Interparliamentary Union's fourteen member nations met in The Hague, and Bertha von Suttner and her husband were invited as guests. There the English proposed an international arbitration tribunal. The Germans dissented, calling the proposal "absurd," and predicted it would "never" come to pass. It did, and only five years later. Russia, though, was not invited. Russia had no parliament.

One near success for the arbitration movement was the Anglo-American Arbitration Agreement. The English queen and the U.S. president signed on, but the agreement failed by three votes in the U.S. Senate. In 1897 von Suttner managed an audience to present a petition to the Austrian emperor himself. He said he would consider it. The countess (by marriage reduced to the rank of baroness) who had not been eligible to be presented at court as a young women, found that in middle age she could conduct business there.

Meanwhile, wars rolled merrily along. China was defeated by Japan. The Ottomans persecuted the Armenians. Spain repressed the Cubans. Italy invaded Ethiopia, urged on by the press but criticized by peace activists, including women, who lay on train tracks to prevent the movement of troops. The take-home messages for von Suttner were (1) the short memory of the population required constant reeducation, and (2) the decisions of the fifty or sixty men who engaged in "high politics" had to be combated with the support of the newspapers. Peace, von Suttner realized, was not something that could be "settled." It must be worked at. "The people" must be constantly educated; then they must speak and they must be heard.

Nobel's death in 1898 revealed that those who he most respected were not "winners of battles" but discoverers, healers, writers, and peacemakers. In particular, he chose to advance peace not by leaving money to a particular group or strategy but by creating an annual prize for "the person who shall have done the most or the best work for fraternity between nations, for the abolition or reduction of standing armies and for the holding and promotion of peace congresses." Sweden was assigned responsibility for the selection of the science and literature prizes, Norway for the peace prize.

That same year the Russian tsar invited European nations to attend a peace conference. Responses were generally positive, although some, for example, Germany's Social Democrats doubted others' sincerity. The German emperor's response was said to have been "Peace will never be better assured than by a thoroughly drilled army ready for instant service."

Nevertheless, the first Hague Conference was held in 1899. Von Suttner, the only woman at the opening ceremonies although millions of women had signed petitions that were presented to the conference, conducted a salon and plunged into activities designed to keep the proceedings focused on disarmament and arbitration. Such conferences involved lengthy formal proceedings, but they also involved banquets, cruises, religious ceremonies, balls, receptions, gossip, lobbying, intrigue, reunions, private dinners, and musicales. Von Suttner was everywhere.

Russia and the United States advanced disarmament and arbitration proposals. The Permanent Court of Arbitration was established, but Austria, Germany, France, and others did not support disarmament. Nevertheless, a number of agreements were made concerning the rules for conducting war—particularly rules related to neutral shipping and the protection of noncombatants. Rules against aerial bombing, submarine mines, and poison gas were ratified here, but were later violated in World War I. It was also following this conference that the peace movement began to use the term *pacifism*. A second Hague Conference, again called by Russia, was held in 1907. It endorsed a world court, but this endorsement did not receive the necessary ratifications.

Bertha von Suttner. Reproduced from the Collections of 15307
Library of Congress LC-05262-107347

In 1901 the first Nobel prizes were awarded. The Nobel Peace Prize went jointly to Frédéric Passy of France and Jean Henri Dunant of Switzerland. Von Suttner was pleased with Passy's award. He was founder and president of the French Peace Society and later became the first president of the Interparliamentary Union. Dunant for his part had founded the International Committee of the Red Cross almost forty years before, but von Suttner was not pleased with his award. She believed that efforts to ameliorate war only made it more palatable. She was a committed pacifist. The 1902 death of her husband—"My Own," she called him—caused von Suttner great personal grief. It was accompanied by the complete collapse of the von Suttner fortune, which resulted in the forced sale of Castle Harmannsdorf. And world peace was marred by the Boer War, Germany's aggression in China, and the Russo-Japanese War, which ended in revolution in Russia. Further, von Suttner's newest literary efforts were being poorly received. Ever resilient, von Suttner continued her whirlwind existence. A German newspaper poll reported that she was seen as "the most important woman of the present" (second was the queen of Romania and third was actress Sarah Bernhardt). Von Suttner hobnobbed with Prince Albert of Monaco, traveled to the United States where she met with President Theodore Roosevelt, learned to ride a bicycle, and on her sixtieth birthday received a testimonial including substantial funds contributed by pacifists from around the world.

In 1905 the Nobel Peace Prize came to Bertha von Suttner. The monetary award was gratefully received but rapidly eaten up by debts and gifts to relatives. Women's groups in particular honored von Suttner. (Jane Addams would be the next woman to win the Nobel Peace Prize, but not for a quarter of a century.) Financial relief was finally offered in the form of a pension from Andrew Carnegie. Perhaps best known for his funding of libraries, Carnegie, a pacifist, funded an endowment for peace, the Hague Peace Palace, and supported the U.S. peace movement.

International renown did not make von Suttner a heroine in Vienna. "Fat Bertha" and "Jew Bertha" were among the names in casual use. While she lent moral support to women pursuing equal rights, and to social democracy, she saw the end of all wars as "the one Great Thing." Her concept of war included class war, wars over nationality, and wars over religion.

At age sixty-nine she embarked on a six-month speaking tour in the United States, traveling from coast to coast. Here the papers called her "Peace Bertha" and "the angel of peace." She met with such dignitaries as William Randolph Hearst, William Jennings Bryan, and William Howard Taft. She saw a football game, addressed the National Education Association, and a suffragist convention. Perhaps the highlight of her visit was her July Fourth speech in San Francisco where women had recently won the vote. She proclaimed:

> Ladies and Gentlemen, Voters of California. . . . The one half of humanity that has never borne arms is today ready to blaze into this living palpable force (the Principle of the Brotherhood of Man). Perhaps the universal Sisterhood is necessary before the Universal Brotherhood is possible.

She died in 1914, a week before the assassination in Sarajevo launched World War I.

The Legacy

Von Suttner was an Austrian aristocrat. The multicultural nature of Austria's empire, coupled with Bertha's youthful travel to the resorts and casinos of Europe, gave von Suttner an international perspective from the start. Living for nine years in Asia added to her broad view of the world. She thoroughly enjoyed nobility's pleasures—the opera, balls, receptions, and salon conversation—and she had a sense of the elegant, enjoying the latest fashion, good food, good looks, and courtly ways. Even though her finances were frequently precarious, she managed to live in both style and comfort. She also believed in the value of social events and graces for the advancing of her cause—thus her insistence that she must maintain a salon in The Hague during the 1899 peace conference.

Rank did provide access, but von Suttner did not feel bound by the conventions of her class. She trained for a career in opera, married a man seven years younger than she, eloped to another country, and even though married, she made her own money. Her futuristic book *Das Maschinenzeitalter* was critical of most of the institutions of her day. She did not pander.

There were then few ways for women to participate in public life. Voting was still mostly a dream, and there was certainly no place for a woman in political office. Even nursing was considered dubious. Von Suttner's power came from two principal sources: her self-assurance and her pen—and her assurance was rooted in her very nineteenth-century belief that society was progressing. Darwin, Spencer, and Buckle all said so. Bertha von Suttner and her fellow peace activists committed themselves, therefore, to assisting that advance. Her confidence also meant that she was untroubled by criticism, mockery, unflattering cartoons, and snubs. Her pen also served in two ways. It helped to provide an economic base, first when the young von Suttners were cut off from their families after their secret marriage, and later when they were reconciled but the family fortune was lost. More importantly, however, her writing mobilized large numbers for the peace movement and made her one of the Europe's best-known figures.

Die Waffen Nieder was specifically intended to appeal to the reader's emotions—to get beyond the debates of learned and powerful men. And it was intended for a mass audience. It was not written for the critics, but for the many middle-class readers who enjoyed a good story. It was simultaneously didactic and passionate, and it was read. Von Suttner believed that she spoke for what the people wanted—or for what they would want if they thought about it, if they had the facts, and if they understood what war really meant. She was in sympathy with many of the movements of her day and clearly commiserated with the poor. However, she was uncritical of the economic system and was as opposed to class war as to any other kind of war.

Once she turned to organizing and campaigning for arbitration and disarmament, her writing usually took the form of journalism. She also found herself doing what any activist must do—raising funds. In her case, this was not accomplished by soliciting subscriptions from the many but by seeking the assistance of wealthy patrons like Alfred Nobel. Similarly, her hopes for the future hinged on changing the policies of emperors, not on overthrowing them. She hoped enthusiastic and organized populations could influence the rulers of Germany, Austria, and Russia, leading them to commit to peace. In particular, she had hopes that the Russian tsar who had called both of The Hague peace conferences could win over his fellow rulers, even though he ruled with a heavy hand at home.

She proudly carried the white flag of peace, while criticizing both those who were engaging in an arms race in the name of peace and those who sought to ameliorate the conduct of war. She cited Teddy Roosevelt, a fellow Nobel Peace Prize winner, as an example of the former. Her anger at the prize given to Jean Henri Dunant is an example of her dislike of the second. But to her, the guilty were not just the rulers and their agents. Those who passively accepted preparations for war and those who were sad but resigned were guilty too. They needed persuasion. They had to be given hope. They had to take a stand, if only through petitions. And it could be done!

The peace race and the arms race were being conducted simultaneously. Those devoted to peace emphasized arbitration with some success, and the idea of a world court was seriously entertained. Their efforts at disarmament, though, were not successful. Some hoped for an eventual world government. The fact that countries had already formed a variety of alliances gave hope

Two-euro coin of Bertha von Suttner. Taken by the author

that these alliances could, in turn, be allied with each other, and eventually form a single, peaceful government.

Sadly, the alliances worked in the opposite way. The assassination of one nobleman in Sarajevo dragged virtually all of Europe into one of the worst wars humans had yet known. Von Suttner's worst nightmares came true. But many of her dreams were resurrected after that terrible conflagration. The League of Nations was a first step toward the development of influential—if not powerful—international legal institutions. Then within decades Europe would be embroiled in the Second World War, which would be followed by the founding of the United Nations, a better but still imperfect effort.

In *Die Waffen Nieder*, von Suttner describes young Martha wishing that she could have been Joan of Arc, a female hero in war. Instead, von Suttner herself became a female hero for peace. Her attraction and influence are demonstrated by the fact that years after its publication, the Nazis found it necessary to ban *Die Waffen Nieder*. Today, Bertha von Suttner's face appears on the Austrian 2-euro coin.

Notes

1. Bertha von Suttner, *Memoirs of Bertha von Suttner* (Boston: Gina, 1910). She enumerates her reading in the first volume, 174–76.

2. Bertha von Suttner, *Memoirs*, 357.

Jane Addams. Courtesy of the Norwegian Nobel Institute

⌒ᴗ

Jane Addams: "The Greatest Woman Who Ever Lived"

Time and Place

Jane Addams (1860–1935) was born before the U.S. Civil War and lived through the Gilded Age, World War I, and the early years of the Great Depression. Although she and Bertha von Suttner (1843–1914) shared the planet for more than fifty years, they did not share efforts on behalf of peace. Von Suttner died before World War I started; Addams's peace advocacy reached its peak only after that war had begun.

Von Suttner lived among the European nobility who moved with ease between Paris, Berlin, Rome, and Vienna, and who vacationed in spas and at private estates. Empires were in command, although three of them (the Russian, the Ottoman, and the Austria-Hungarian) were actually in decline and would disappear after World War I, and a fourth (the Prussian) would suffer a humiliating and punishing defeat in that war. In contrast, Addams grew up in what some called "the Far West." That was Cedarville, Illinois, a village that was not even incorporated when her father settled there in the 1840s. At that time Illinois may have been thought of as a frontier, but it was more one of opportunity than of hardship. Freeport, only five miles away, was a bustling railroad town, and Cedarville, like many other agrarian communities of its day, prospered. Its inhabitants worked hard and were committed to democracy. Those with advantages tended not to flaunt them. The less well-off were treated as equals; it was important not to be "stuck up."

Then there was Chicago 120 miles to the east. It was rapidly rebuilt after the fire of 1871, and by 1890 covered more than 180 square miles. It was second only to New York in population. Two-thirds of its 1890 population had been born abroad and came to Illinois seeking opportunity—not as farmers, but as workers. Most found work. They worked for Pullman building railroad cars, for Armour processing meat, for McCormick making reapers. *Democracy* may have been a Chicago watchword, but Chicagoans did not experience much equality, for the latter part of the nineteenth century was one of an unvarnished capitalism that was little tempered by tradition or noblesse oblige. Huge fortunes were made in oil, steel, and the railroads as the U.S. economy grew to be the world's largest. At the same time, one of two Chicago children died before the age of five, and labor's anger was demonstrated by the 1886 Haymarket bombing.

The economic boom that followed closely on the heels of America's Civil War began only months after Jane Addams's birth. Her father, an unaffiliated Quaker, was an abolitionist. Elected to the Illinois State Senate as a Whig, he later attended the Ripon Conference that founded the Republican Party. He was also a friend of Abraham Lincoln, and both he and Jane passionately believed that under Lincoln the United States had embarked on a "tremendous" experiment in self-government, one that constituted "the most valuable contribution America has made to the moral life of the world." In Hull-House's first year, Jane would give copies of Carl Schurz's "Appreciation of Abraham Lincoln" to every member of the boys' club.[1]

Jane Addams's father did not go to war himself, but he raised money to outfit a regiment and assisted in recruiting. Tiny Cedarville sent sixty-three men to the conflict. Jane, then, grew up in the turbulent era of Reconstruction in the South, and of manic urbanization and industrialization in the North. Debate and political organizing were alive and well. Farmers mobilized through the Grange; Susan B. Anthony campaigned for the vote for women (Addams's father supported education but not suffrage for women); and labor groups made efforts to organize. While Cedarville remained a small, stable, and largely harmonious and prosperous community, Jane's father was engaged in the larger world. He spent the legislative sessions in Springfield more than two hundred miles away, and he followed the international news. He was especially enamored of Mazzini's efforts to unite Italy into a republic. Young Jane, strongly influenced by her father, enjoyed personal security and the democratic ethos of small town America, but she was not ignorant of the dramatic changes going on elsewhere.

Preparation

Jane's father was a well-off miller and civic leader. Still, he regularly rose at 3 a.m. to work with his mill hands. He had such a reputation for sincerity

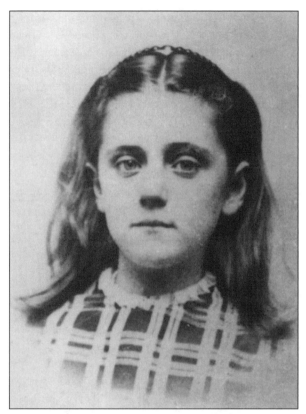

*Jane Addams. Courtesy of the University of Illinois at Chicago, The
University Library, Special Collection Department, Jane Addams
Memorial Collection, JAMC neg. 2*

and integrity that it was said that not only did he never take a bribe, he was
never even offered one. He was not a church member, but the Addams family
regularly attended services, and he believed he had a duty to the community
and its well-being. Jane's mother died in her ninth pregnancy when Jane was
two. Jane was then the youngest. She had four older siblings: a brother, Weber,
who would periodically be committed to mental institutions; a sister, Martha,
who died at sixteen of typhoid fever; Mary, who mothered young (Laura) Jane,
known in the family as Jennie; and Alice. Three other siblings died of cholera
before Jane was born.

Jane was not robust. She had Pott's disease, which resulted in curvature
of the spine, and at various periods in her life she would be an invalid. As
the youngest and most frail, she received special attention from other family

members. Her father played the dominant role in her life, although his remarriage when she was eight provided a stepmother whose enjoyment of luxuries differed from the values to which Jane was accustomed. Still, Jane's new mother cared for her stepchildren and particularly encouraged their reading—both alone and aloud together. Jane was particularly fond of Louisa May Alcott and Charles Dickens, although her father disapproved of the reading of fiction and required the reading of history as part of her studies.

Jane attended the local school and learned the variety of domestic skills expected of girls and young women at the time, but she was not especially interested in them, in fashion, or in coquetry. She did worry about predestination and death, but science and nature were her special interests—ones she shared with her stepbrother, George, who was the same age.

Jane wanted to go to Smith College, which had opened only three years before, and thought that she might become a doctor like her other stepbrother, Harry. Her father was unwilling to let his last child go so far away, however, and insisted that she attend nearby Rockford Female Seminary as her sisters had done and where he was a trustee. George was to go to Beloit College. For the first but not the last time, Jane experienced a conflict between what she called "family claims" and her own wishes. She did as her father preferred.

Jane's Rockford Seminary class began with twenty-five, mostly local, students. Only seventeen graduated. The seminary's stated mission was "to teach the great Christian lesson that the true end of life is not to acquire the most goods . . . but to give oneself fully and worthily for the good of others." Life at Rockford was austere and the school's myriad rules were meticulously enforced. A daily one-hour walk and attendance at chapel were required. Addams mostly complied with the rules of conduct, but she maintained her intellectual independence, for example, by refusing to make a declaration for Christ. And she did acquire an education. She was particularly influenced by Carlyle's assertion of the importance of great individuals and by Ruskin's view that the state must work to end human suffering. She further developed her sense that one must make "a social effort," and she articulated a consciousness of women's capacity and of their right to be different from men and independent in thought and action. As a junior she was the only woman to participate in a statewide oratorical contest. She came in fifth. Young William Jennings Bryan was second. In her graduating essay, titled "Cassandra," she bemoaned the Greek woman's fate—to be right but not believed.

Jane's plan after graduation from Rockford was to attend Smith College in preparation for medical school. Her father opposed the idea but then died suddenly, leaving her an inheritance of some $50,000. Jane, her stepmother, and her sister Alice then moved to Philadelphia, where Jane and Alice enrolled in the Women's Medical College of Philadelphia. (Alice was married to a doctor and did not plan to finish the degree but hoped to learn enough to be of assistance to him.) Jane found she did not like the subject matter, her stepmother discouraged her ambition, and the dean of the college thought the ideal role for her students was that of medical missionary—a prospect Jane abhorred. Back pain and depression set in—eight years of it. Jane's twenties were unhappy and without clear direction.

After treatment for neurasthenia and for her back, and after assisting her brother Weber's family when he had to be institutionalized, Jane rallied enough to embark on a two-year European tour (1883–1885). The entourage included four young women and two adults; one was Jane's stepmother. The group energetically pursued European culture in all its forms. Jane simultaneously reveled in what she was seeing and learning and felt uneasy about the expense of their travels. She wondered too about the disconnection from worthwhile, nurturing activity experienced by the current generation of college-educated women. Upon returning home, she was again absorbed in helping family members and in serving as a companion to her widowed stepmother—particularly in Baltimore during the winter society season.

In 1887 she began a second European tour—this time with two women friends, Ellen Starr and Sarah Anderson, whose trips she partly financed. The culmination of their tour was a visit to London's Toynbee Hall, a settlement house based on a new philosophy of charity. That philosophy sought to elevate the poor rather than simply to succor them. Its basis was allowing the poor to participate in a community in which all were treated with respect and as equals. Privileged and educated young men lived in Toynbee Hall in a London slum. They held outside jobs but participated in a wide range of activities, clubs, and classes with the neighborhood poor. Almost thirty, Jane had found her purpose. She decided to create a similar settlement in Chicago. Hers would adhere to the Toynbee model, but with two important exceptions: the residents of her settlement would be women, and the settlement would not be specifically based on Christian doctrine.

Twenty Years at Hull-House

In her remarkable book *Twenty Years at Hull-House*, Addams chronicles the founding and growth of her social experiment, Hull-House. That experiment was so successful that the Chicago City Council once proclaimed her "the greatest woman who ever lived."

The work began with her arrival in brawling Chicago in January 1889. Her first step was to introduce herself and her plans to anyone who would listen. This meant the clergy, elected officials, reporters, and the very active club women of Chicago. These were largely women of wealth and influence, many of whom were already involved in various kinds of charity work. Again, Addams's vision was new. It was one in which people of different economic classes would live and work and learn together. They would be equal as members of the Hull-House community and would enrich each other's lives. The purpose was mutual growth, not service by the privileged. The community would also include people of different nationalities and languages. Thus Addams intended to bring together people of diverse customs and beliefs, people who were rich and who were poor, and people with college degrees and those who were illiterate. It was an effort to bring the social democracy of a homogeneous, small, western town to a raw and turbulent city of immigrants. Even if they did not totally disappear, neither Addams's depression nor her back trouble interfered with her new undertaking.

The first concrete step was to find a house. It had to have rooms for meetings and lectures—and rooms for the women who would live there. Addams wanted the house to be an always-welcoming home. Its door was never to be locked, and all who crossed its threshold were to be welcomed in an attractive and comfortable parlor.

While Addams used some of her own funds to found Hull-House, it was Helen Culver, a liberal real-estate dealer, who first leased the building to her and then donated it and several nearby lots to the enterprise. Jane and Ellen Starr, whom Addams had first met at Rockford Seminary, were the first occupants. They immediately began a kindergarten, clubs for girls and clubs for boys, a library, book clubs, drawing and sewing lessons, English classes, and more. Within two years the house was being used by one thousand people a week. The intent was to provide intellectual stimulation; to provide access to the beautiful in literature, music, and art; to offer a moral environment; and in short, to provide a center "for a higher civic and social life." The house was located on Halsted Street between an undertaker and a saloon. Addams described the neighborhood as one where the streets were "inexpressively dirty," the schools "inadequate," sanitary legislation "unenforced," the paving "miserable" (and sometimes entirely lacking), and the homes "unconnected" (to the sewer system).[2]

Addams and her fellow residents found themselves much involved in their neighbors' lives—in the joys they experienced or in the sorrows, for example, of a beaten wife, an unwed mother, an arrested juvenile, a woman giving birth unattended, or a family provider dying unexpectedly. In an essay titled "The Subjective Necessity for Social Settlements," Addams laid out her philosophy at a time when settlements were rapidly being established across the country—often by other young, college-educated women. The "necessity" was for an outlet, for an activity that would permit individuals (especially women) to fully use their emotions, talents, and minds in advancing "human brotherhood" and in fulfilling the claims of the "submerged tenth."[3] One root of this necessity, Addams believed, was a commitment to social democracy. Another was the revival of nondoctrinal, early Christian beliefs that were nonresistant and based on love of all human beings. A settlement, she said, requires a "spiritual force" that has "the overmastering belief that all that is noblest in life is common to men as men."

Jane Addams. Courtesy of the University of Illinois at Chicago, The University Library, Special Collection Department, Jane Addams Memorial Collection, JAMC neg. 17

To make that belief concrete, she argued that a settlement must be adaptable, flexible, tolerant, and responsive. If what is needed are public baths, build them. If what is needed is safe exercise for boys, build a gym. If what is needed is a rooming house for young women, build that. If what is needed is a place for conversation, create a coffeehouse. If coal is expensive, organize a cooperative. If spirits need elevation, build an art gallery. Again, the purpose of these various activities was one: to advance human moral development by advancing community.

Hull-House residents approached their work as nurturing women. They gave special attention to children and their needs, and Addams carefully studied all that was known about child development and delinquency. Residents gave classes in nutrition, hygiene, and child care. But many of the women who came to live at Hull-House were not satisfied with an ethic of care or of self-help. They saw that particular problems were often part of a general problem; and while Addams, in particular, could illustrate injustices and tragedies with wrenching personal stories, she and her friends began to see that democracy required more than social equality. It required collective action, political action, and, further, it demanded that its political goals be accomplished without the power of women's votes.

By 1895 Hull-House had twenty-five residents. (All residents were carefully selected and had to serve a probationary period.) Among these twenty-five were Florence Kelly, Julia Lathrop, Dr. Alice Hamilton, Louise de Koven Bowen, and author Charlotte Perkins Gilman. Bowen would become a longstanding and generous financial supporter of Hull-House. Hamilton would become the first woman to serve on the faculty of the Harvard Medical School. Kelly and Lathrop would help to propel Jane and the other Hull-House residents into public advocacy. Lathrop also became an expert on child delinquency, while Kelly's research was crucial to the passage of protective labor legislation in Illinois, and she was even appointed to administer the law before it was declared unconstitutional. Hull-House residents then turned to lobbying for federal legislation. A lesson Addams learned from these efforts was that if legislation is too advanced, if it moves beyond popular opinion, it will ultimately fail, as will legislation that lacks consistent enforcement.

As Hull-House evolved it captured the attention of philanthropists, intellectuals, and academics, particularly those at the new University of Chicago and those associated with the Society for Ethical Culture. It also welcomed labor organizers, especially those like Mary Kenney, who worked on behalf of women workers.

The depression of 1893 created misery and labor unrest in the Hull-House neighborhood. Soon Addams found herself a member of a six-person commission charged with getting George Pullman to submit his workers' complaints to arbitration. The commission failed, a strike brought the nation's railways to a halt, federal troops broke the strike, union leader Eugene Victor Debs went to jail, and Addams was launched into public controversy—something she did not relish when it involved debate from ideologically fixed positions. She thrived on discussion, however, and particularly enjoyed the weekly Hull-House meetings of the Working People's Social Science Club, where socialists and anarchists of all stripes engaged in vigorous dispute.

Many of Addams's previous supporters were dismayed by this forum offered to "radicals." Addams responded that discussion would not be suppressed because Hull-House was "subsidized by millionaires," nor would it be "bullied by workingmen." Thus, while sympathetic to workers, she found she could not subscribe to a socialist any more than to a capitalist or a Christian doctrine. She described two lessons learned from several failed efforts to bring arbitration to labor disputes: (1) unions could be as corrupt as politicians and businessmen, and (2) labor needed to organize, and not just locally and nationally, but internationally as well. Still, results, not ideas, were what were important to Addams, and she judged that in the Chicago of the 1890s, "actual attainment" came from "men of affairs rather than from those given to speculation."[4] To create change one must deal with those who hold power.

Addams's most local campaign was to get the neighborhood garbage collected. Her first step was to get herself appointed ward garbage inspector—a political appointment with a yearly salary of one thousand dollars. Her energy, organizational skills (she put three hundred children to work collecting newspapers and cans), and persistence changed the neighborhood. Her next effort was to remove the ward's powerful and corrupt alderman, Johnny Powers. She failed, but learned another important lesson—receiving jobs can be more important to people than the integrity of the provider.

A bout with typhoid fever and an effort at recuperation led to a third trip abroad in 1895. Addams spent time in London studying the variety of public and private efforts then being advanced to put an end to poverty. She also traveled to Russia because she was interested in meeting Leo Tolstoy, who was then putting his Christian philosophy into practice by living and working as a peasant—even when his wife and other members of his household were not. Tolstoy believed each person should work to produce all he consumed. He was not impressed with Addams. First he criticized the outsize sleeves of her dress, which he said held material enough for a child's garment. Nor was he impressed by the fact that she was supported by a farm worked by others. After this encounter, Addams vowed to spend two hours a day working in the

Hull-House bakery—to do "bread labor"—when she returned. The plan soon fell by the wayside as the press of affairs again consumed her.

Addams's new frontier was the press. She wrote for magazines like the *Atlantic Monthly* and for academic journals like the *American Journal of Sociology*. Others wrote about her. She became a celebrity and was welcomed at the White House by President William McKinley. And visitors came to her. Teddy Roosevelt came, Queen Marie of Romania came, Sidney and Beatrice Webb came, and Peter Kropotkin came. She was sought after as a speaker and she traveled through much of the country on lecture tours. And perhaps most importantly, she wrote *Democracy and Social Ethics* (1902), *Newer Ideals of Peace* (1907), and *Twenty Years at Hull-House* (1910). Much of the narrative I've given here comes from the last, and the reasoning of the second will be discussed in the next section, but the analysis offered in Addams's six essays in *Democracy and Social Ethics* merits elaboration.

Her argument was that democracy is not a matter of counting votes and following the majority's wishes. Democracy assumes the value of every individual and the interdependence of all. It requires an education and a decent standard of living for each individual. It also requires an emotional as well as an intellectual commitment, and it is the essence of a developing social ethic concerned with the whole, an ethic Addams believed was replacing an earlier ethic based on relationships between individuals.

With sensitivity Addams described how the relationship between "the charity visitor" and her beneficiary would be altered by a democratic ethic of natural sympathy. She discussed at length how "filial relations," particularly those between educated women and their parents, were being changed as women accepted citizenship in the world instead of confining their understanding of their duties to family obligations. She addressed the servant problem and the appropriateness of the work of caring for the young, the old, and the infirm, but the inappropriateness of caring for healthy adults. She reflected on the reasons why able young women would choose factory work over work in a private home—and then described the deficiencies of factory work, too. For example, Pullman's refusal to arbitrate, she said, was rooted in the old ethic of the individual, but his enterprise was social and, therefore, called for a social resolution—one that took into consideration the consent of the many as well as the conscience of the individual.

Addams recognized that progress inevitably entailed compromise, and that it was usually initiated by the few. Still, she believed it could only be sustained by the consent of the many. Perhaps her most insightful discussion considered political reform. It was not merely a matter of honest officeholders and fairly counted votes, she contended. Democracy required that the end, the

Jane Addams. Courtesy of the University of Illinois at Chicago, The University Library, Special Collection Department, Jane Addams Memorial Collection, JAMC neg. 58

general welfare, be the central concern. She thought this was something that reforming businessmen and academics too often forgot. Corrupt politicians, she said, did not forget this. They knew that moral facts overrode moral ideas. Thus, politicians' numerous good deeds, from Thanksgiving turkeys to city jobs to funeral expenses, were experienced as moral facts, as a city version of village kindness. Politicians' favors improved people's lives, and so the people appreciated the politicians. Addams's democracy, then, was not based on an individual's pursuit of self-interest. It rested on the recognition that each of us belongs to the whole and that democracy involves the actual experience of taking care of each other. Sometimes Addams sounds like an idealist, but she was a realist in that her views were derived from wide experience and from committed action. She did have one enduring faith, however. It was in the direction of change. Things were improving, she believed, and would continue to do so.

Addams served on the Chicago Board of Education, where she was frustrated by the businessmen's emphasis on efficiency, the media's colorful and distorted reporting, and the teachers' insistence on their own interests. She was active on the national political scene, too, supporting Teddy Roosevelt's run for the presidency as a Progressive in 1912, and stumping for women's suffrage as vice president of the National American Woman Suffrage Association, which was pursuing a state-by-state strategy. Her popularity diminished, however, when she made public statements calling for equality under the law for anarchists and for trying to discover *why* some of them turned to violence. Her popularity would fall further in 1915.

War and Peace

Addams was thinking about peace before there was war.[5] As early as 1907 she thought she could detect a "gradual development of the moral substitute for war" amid Chicago's cosmopolitan populace. For her, Chicago was a microcosm. If order and democratic government could be achieved there, it might be achieved internationally. She recognized that the standard arguments against war, arguments based on either prudence (reasoned self-interest) or pity, did not suffice. What was needed was an affection based on companionship, on shared experience, on concrete, mutual knowledge. A second requirement was the understanding that while government protection against foreign nations and crime was important, citizens must also be protected from disease, ignorance, and exploitation. Government, she believed, had a responsibility for the "normal needs of every citizen." In the United States, she argued, government had assumed that responsibility only in the field of education. As it assumed other responsibilities once considered solely domestic, responsibility for health for example, government would need to utilize women who routinely provided such care in the domestic sphere. Thus, democracy and peace would necessarily involve the incorporation of women in public life.

Addams was bemused by the fact that imperial Germany had gone much further in providing for its citizens than had the United States—that if one measured a government by the standard of living of its citizens, the United States would not place first. She contended that the problem was the U.S. Constitution, which was based on "that old Frankenstein, the ideal man of the eighteenth century," and which was grievously outdated. Assuming the standpoint of "the humble people," she noted that America's founders did not trust the people, and that Americans were clinging to a past that provided no machinery for "simple democratic expression." Society's spotlight on the financially successful meant that the experience, talents, and knowledge of most citizens (especially new immigrants) went unrecognized and untapped. Still, while the worker was her "everyman," Addams saw socialists as "new scholastics" who divided the world into classes, and some union organizers as exploiters who used collective bargaining to gain power. Social peace, she believed, required more than the pursuit of interest; so did international peace.

Addams thought the macrocosm was moving in the direction of peace, however. She noted the different organizations campaigning for arbitration of conflicts between nations. She noted the existence of the world court. She noted that workingmen were holding international conferences, that even poor people now traveled internationally, and that newspapers reported the same stories around the globe. Internationalism was becoming a fact.

In 1912 she gave a seconding speech for Teddy Roosevelt's presidential candidacy on the Progressive ticket. As a delegate, she voted for a platform that included the building of two battleships, consoling herself that the platform's social-welfare and industrial-regulation planks were crucial building blocks for peace. She was more distressed by Roosevelt's plan to fortify the Panama Canal. Indeed, she noted that "'peace' was forever a bone of contention" between Roosevelt and her, and that he always remarked that surely *he* was the American authority on peace since it was *he* who had been given the Nobel Peace Prize (for mediating the Russo-Japanese War).

William James was the first to argue that what was required for peace was "the moral equivalent of war." As a psychologist he understood war's attraction. He understood that honor, sacrifice, solidarity, and loyalty were all of profound importance even if they couldn't be measured or precisely analyzed. Addams appropriated the concept and used it frequently in her speaking and writing before World War I. She held that young men did not go to war to kill, but to die—that they went for honor and with high ideals—and that one cannot expect people to give up ideals without giving them new ones.

In June 1914 a Serbian nationalist killed an Austrian duke in Sarajevo. Although the United States first remained neutral in the conflict, Austria-Hungary, Germany, and the Ottomans were soon at war with Russia, Britain, France, Serbia, Montenegro, Belgium, and Japan. Ten to twenty thousand died every day. Technology had made killing monstrously efficient. War had been motorized, and airplanes had introduced a whole new way of war.

Addams sprang into action. With other social workers, she helped organize a Union against Militarism, led an Emergency Federation of Peace Forces in Chicago, and within six months had become the chair of a newly organized Women's Peace Party that enlisted forty thousand women and brought three thousand of them to its first meeting in Washington, D.C. The Women's Peace Party had been inspired by the public speeches of Mrs. Pethick Lawrence of England and Rosika Schwimmer of Hungary, women from opposite sides of the struggle, who called, sometimes singly and sometimes together, for American women to urge their government and other neutrals to call a conference that would propose terms for peace. The initiative called for "continuous mediation," and the goal was to offer a concrete, positive step that could be taken by the combatants, all of whom professed to want to end a war that each claimed was purely defensive. The Women's Peace Party set forth an eleven-point platform, which also called for arms limitations, nationalization of the manufacture of weapons, peace education, removal of the economic causes of war, a peace commission, and suffrage for women.

Just as she thought women had something special to offer politics because of their long history of nurturance, Addams believed women, because of motherhood, had a special contribution to make toward peace, and that, in fact, a small first step had been made long ago when women forced an end to child sacrifice. She recognized, though, that a majority of women in the affected countries supported their nation's war effort.

Several months after the Washington meeting, the Women's Peace Party was invited to the International Congress of Women at The Hague, the scene of many efforts to encourage cooperation and the rule of law between nations. Forty-seven American women set sail, discussing all the way across the Atlantic the history of the peace movement and terms for resolving the current conflict. Their ship was stopped by the British in the English Channel. Perhaps for the first time the delegates began to understand that theirs might not be a popular position. The English press was hostile and ridiculed them as "Peacettes." To many of those outside such organizations, to speak of peace in time of war is to undermine the troops, to be unpatriotic, even to be treasonous.

A thousand delegates came to The Hague from twelve countries. Both belligerents and neutrals were represented. Questions about the cause of the war were set aside. Discussion focused on two things: (1) possible terms for ending the war, and (2) prevention of future wars. Addams was elected president, and in her closing address she expressed hope that the young women present might see the creation of an international organization that would make war "impossible" because nations would have created an "ordered" way to resolve conflict. She reminded them that Grotius, Kant, and Tolstoy were called dreamers and cowards for putting law above force, and that women should not hesitate to protest and to propose policies, "feeble" as their efforts might seem to them.

The Hague meeting would give birth to the Women's International League for Peace and Freedom (WILPF), and Addams would be elected its president, a position she would hold for a decade. Emily Greene Balch would become its executive secretary, and her story and that of the league will be told in the next chapter. Here I would like to focus on Addams's other work, particularly in the United States, where she fastened her hopes on arbitration to be led by President Woodrow Wilson, who would win reelection on the slogan "He kept us out of war," and whose Fourteen Points speech reinforced her hopes. However, soon after his election, Wilson declared that the United States should have the largest navy in the world, and within a month of his inauguration, he called for a declaration of war.

During the time between the beginning of the war in 1914 and the U.S. entry in 1917, Addams spoke and wrote in many venues in opposition to the war. In July 1915 she reported to a large audience in Carnegie Hall on the International Congress of Women at The Hague and on her experiences visiting the battlefront. The United States was still neutral, but the recent sinking of the *Lusitania* had stimulated anti-German feelings. The title of her temperate speech was "The Revolt against War." One important point she made was that the support, the "temper," for war was mostly fed by events that occurred during the war—not by events prior it. Late in the speech, Addams described talking to young soldiers from both sides of the conflict who expressed their reluctance to kill, even though many said they were willing to sacrifice themselves. She went further and said that in all countries, soldiers were given stimulants before they were ordered to charge with bayonets. The audience applauded enthusiastically, but the newspapers and then much of the public interpreted her comments as dishonoring soldiers by suggesting they were cowards and drunks. Addams made several efforts to correct press accounts, but they were to no avail. Almost overnight she went from paragon to public enemy. She and her allies were quite unprepared for the media and the public's intolerance of pacifists and of critics of the war. Addams was publicly booed. Speeches were canceled. She began another period of semi-invalidism.

As a committed pacifist, Addams was disappointed not only by her government's decision to enter the war but by the many peace activists and suffragettes who enthusiastically accepted Wilson's leadership. Even during the war, Addams continued her peace advocacy. She testified before the House of Representatives Committee on Military Affairs, opposing the Bill to Increase the Efficiency of the Military Establishment. She argued that the very existence of large, standing armies was conducive to war, that newspapers were misleading, and that men were more emotional than women because of the responsibility they assumed for defense, and that men could even "panic" when there was, in fact, no enemy. She spoke against conscription and against offering military protection for U.S. investments abroad. She spoke on behalf of self-governance for "oppressed and dependent nationalities." She argued that science and economics had already been internationalized and that national governments needed to develop a system to permit peaceful change. She asserted that pacifists were not unpatriotic, that they were not cowards, that they were not isolationists, and that peace could not be secured without justice, without the "inner consent" of citizens. She was forthright and consistent and deeply frustrated by the media's lack of or negative response. It seemed to her that the press was engaged in a "concerted and deliberate attempt at misrepresentation."[6]

Addams became a member of the national committee of the new Fellowship of Reconciliation, which provided support to conscientious objectors and drew the attention of the Secret Service. She also engaged in work for the Department of Food Administration, which worked at production and conservation of food at home and its distribution abroad. As soon as the fighting stopped in spring 1919, Addams went to Europe, first at the invitation of the Red Cross and then with the American Friends Service Committee, to assess conditions created not just by the warfare but by the Allies' blockade. She found grievous hunger: children alive but unlikely to ever fully recover from their deprivation. Her energies then turned to food relief. And again she created controversy, this time by calling for food for German and Austrian children as well as for those of the Allies. She was distressed, too, that the blockade continued against Russia and Hungary even after the Armistice because the Allies disapproved of their political regimes.

After the war, diminished in health and influence, Addams soldiered on. She found that domestic reforms related to labor and to immigration were hampered by the fear generated by the Russian Revolution. "Reds" had replaced anarchists as the tool wielded by fear-mongers, and Addams soon joined the national committee of the newly established American Civil Liberties Union (ACLU). She entreated the United States to join the World Court, and she opposed both the military training required at all state universities and a U.S. plan to develop chemical weapons. She lamented that the very word *international* had become suspect to many, and that the WILPF was described as a danger by the Daughters of the American Revolution and condemned by the American Legion and by Reserve Officers' Training Corps (ROTC) leaders.

She was saddened too by the conformity she found on college campuses, and perplexed by college women who were quite attentive to their new liberties and powers but who seemed to have given up on the social and economic reforms so important to Addams's generation. Still, she was sustained by her international work with women both in the WILPF and in other organizations such as the Pan-Pacific Women's Congress, first held in 1928 in Honolulu under her presidency.

Addams's hope for a peaceful resolution to international conflict and the development of moral relations between nations were quickly dashed by the League of Nations, led, as she noted, by the same diplomats who had presided over the death of 10 million soldiers and an equal number of civilians. Its first and great failure, to her, was its refusal to ensure that every human being (or at least all participants in the recent war, i.e., the inhabitants of Europe, but not necessarily those of India and China) had food. She could not understand how the league could fail to respond to the most obvious and basic agony—hunger. Even two years after the war was over, a report to WILPF found that only 20 percent of Austrian children were even "approximately normal."[7]

A Rewarding and Rewarded Life

Addams was almost sixty when the war ended. Nevertheless, her work on behalf of peace and nurturance continued until her death in 1935. She traveled extensively including an around-the-world trip. She praised democratization where she saw it, criticized militarism where it reigned, and expressed her admiration for Gandhi and his campaigns in South Africa and India. She wrote too, and during this time published *Peace and Bread in Time of War* (1922), *The Second Twenty Years at Hull-House* (1930), *The Excellent Becomes the Permanent* (1930), and *My Friend, Julia Lathrop* (1935). She retained a devoted following, even if her previous near-saint status was not reclaimed. She was feted on the fortieth anniversary of Hull-House in 1929, on her seventieth birthday in 1930, and was awarded the Nobel Peace Prize in 1931. Ironically, she shared it with Nicholas Murray Butler, a supporter of peace education but also a supporter of World War I. Addams's international standing was shown by the tribute paid her on her seventy-fifth birthday. This included speeches delivered by radio from London, Paris, Moscow, and Tokyo.

Addams's health seemed to fail her when her vision failed, and when she did not see a rewarding course of action that would enable her to invest all her energies, emotion, and intellect in work that advanced democracy and, by extension, peace. After her seminary graduation, Addams had languished until she conceived the idea of creating Hull-House. She then seemed to acquire super-human physical and emotional strength. After her efforts on behalf of resolving World War I without having the United States participate in that war, and after the virulent attacks on her for her positions on free speech, the war, and pacifism, her health failed again. Still she carried on, although with diminished energy. (She was, after all, sixty and aging.)

Addams was remarkable for the consistency and coherence of her commitment to democracy. She was remarkable too for her insistence on practicing her beliefs and for her confidence that society in neighborhoods, in cities, and in nations was evolving toward a democracy that would lead to a new morality based on the rule of law rather than force. Thus, she was both an idealist in her belief in progress, and a realist who learned from concrete experience. She didn't trust abstraction; she listened attentively to people with the widest range of experience—Chicago's juvenile delinquents, international heads of state, and starving peasants. She was wary of those who claimed to have all the necessary answers, whether they were moguls, ministers, socialists, or academics. She opposed any analysis that separated people into antagonistic groups, whether worker and capitalist, or men and women. But at the same time she firmly believed that women had something special to offer the political world, whether at the level of the ward or in international government. She was certain that women's culture of care would improve the governments then under the sway of a rhetoric claiming that society most benefited when it unleashed competitive man.

Addams was a pacifist. And she was a pacifist in time of war, a time when that view was held by only a few and when even many former pacifists changed or suspended their beliefs. How did this democrat feel when she found herself at odds with elected leaders, with the learned, and with most of her fellow citizens? At first she found herself "faint-hearted," not eager to declare her position. She was partly comforted by her belief, however, that change was often initiated by an individual whom others called "a crank and a freak and in sterner moments . . . an atheist or a traitor."[8] But while timidity and society's scorn were problems for her, she saw another snare to be avoided. That was to become dogmatic herself, to succumb to self-righteousness. Holding such unpopular views created stress for a pacifist who was also a pragmatist and thus persuaded that beliefs must be vindicated by practice. Life was also stressful for a democrat who believed in government by the consent of the people.

Perhaps the most striking thing about Jane Addams, about Jane of Cedarville, is how relevant her message remains, and how many of us still seek to discover the concrete action that we can take that will advance democracy and peace.

Notes

1. Addams's *Twenty Years at Hull-House* is an American classic. See her discussion of Lincoln's importance, *Twenty Years at Hull-House* (New York: Signet Classic, 1961), chap. 2.

2. Addams, *Twenty Years at Hull-House*, 64.

3. Addams's philosophy is outlined in chapter 6 of *Twenty Years at Hull-House*.

4. Addams, *Twenty Years at Hull-House*, 128.

5. A good source for Addams's thinking about democracy and peace is her collection of essays in *Newer Ideals of Peace* (New York: Macmillan, 1907). Also, one should examine Allen F. Davis's edited collection of Addams's essays, *Jane Addams on Peace, War, and International Understanding, 1899–1932* (New York: Garland, 1976).

6. See Jane Addams, *Peace and Bread in Time of War* (New York: Garland, 1972), 134.

7. Addams, *Peace and Bread*, 234.

8. Addams, *Peace and Bread*, 141.

Emily Greene Balch. Courtesy of the Norwegian Nobel Institute

❧

CHAPTER THREE

Emily Greene Balch: The Dismissed Professor

Balch's World

Emily Greene Balch was born in a small town, Jamaica Plain, Massachusetts, in 1867. Culturally though, she is best described as a Bostonian—and a sophisticated Bostonian at that. She lived until 1961, so she grew up in the period following the U.S. Civil War, saw the United States begin its imperial career with its victory in the Spanish-American War, witnessed U.S. participation in two World Wars, experienced the beginning of the cold war between the United States and the Soviet Union, and grieved over the increasing involvement of the United States in Vietnam. Eighteen different presidents—from Andrew Johnson to Dwight D. Eisenhower—governed during her lifetime.

Although the Civil War ended in 1865, the nation was deeply divided and much of the South was under Northern domination—even military rule—until President Rutherford B. Hayes (who fought for the North during the war) withdrew the troops, and ten years of Reconstruction ended. During the war, Balch's father served first as an army private and later as secretary to Massachusetts Senator Charles Sumner, a passionate abolitionist. An aunt went south to educate newly freed Negro children.

The last quarter of the nineteenth century saw the industrialization of the United States and the end of the frontier, that beacon of opportunity for many generations. Oil, steel, and the railroads were the economic foundation of a Gilded Age that produced immense fortunes and degrading poverty. Labor began to organize; indeed, Massachusetts passed the first eight-hour workday legislation in 1874. Other reformers organized too, first as (largely agrarian)

Populists, and later as Progressives. In 1898 (Balch was then thirty-one), the United States annexed Hawaii, the Philippines, Puerto Rico, and Guam, and took control of Cuba. Further, the United States soon announced its Open Door policy, ensuring access to China's economy and establishing itself as a global power with global interests.

The United States participated in both The Hague peace and disarmament conferences so energetically supported by Bertha von Suttner. When World War I broke out anyway, President Woodrow Wilson adopted a policy of neutrality and ran for his second term on a peace platform. Soon after winning reelection, he went to war against the German, Austria-Hungarian, and Ottoman empires. While the war was in progress, he issued his Fourteen Points, which were designed to ensure peace and democracy in part by creating the League of Nations. After the war many of his points were ignored or overridden at the Paris Peace Conference, and the Senate rejected U.S. participation in the league.

The United States turned inward after the war. In the 1920s it enjoyed a spectacular boom; in the 1930s, an equally spectacular bust. In contrast, Balch turned outward. She became active on the international rather than the national scene.

Between 1921 and 1938 the United States did participate in a series of conferences designed to limit naval armaments. Further, U.S. Secretary of State Frank B. Kellogg was instrumental in achieving the 1928 Kellogg-Briand Pact in which fifteen nations, including Germany and Japan, renounced war as an instrument of national policy. Sixty-two nations ultimately joined the pact. However, the pact did not deter Japan from moving into Manchuria, Italy into Ethiopia, and Germany into Austria.

World War II began in 1939. The United States did not enter until two years later, but once France had become occupied, it became clear that the United States was not neutral. In fact, a peacetime draft was begun in 1940, aid was extended to Great Britain and the Soviet Union, and Japanese assets were frozen.

Roosevelt, Churchill, and Stalin coordinated strategy for the war and for the postwar period at a series of meetings. Among their most important agreements was the decision to require an unconditional surrender by the Axis powers, and the decision to create the United Nations with a Security Council in which the major powers would enjoy a veto. Other decisions involved the division of Germany into occupied zones, war-crimes trials, denazification, and the building of democratic institutions in Germany. On August 6 and 9, 1945, the United States dropped atomic bombs on Japan. The war soon ended, but an entirely new debate began about the relationship between weapons and peace.

World War II did not did not bring peace to the world. The U.S.-Soviet Union cold war began almost immediately. The Korean War followed. A hydrogen bomb was exploded. Castro won Cuba, and the Cuban Missile Crisis ensued. Most importantly, the United States slowly escalated its involvement in Vietnam into a full-blown war. Emily Balch died three years before the Gulf of Tonkin Resolution was used by President Lyndon Johnson as permission to engage in full-scale war; the escalation that followed would have sorrowed but not surprised her.

The Education of Emily Balch

As an activist and scholar, Balch was involved with America's newest immigrants. Her own ancestors, though, came to the United States as early as 1623. John Balch was one of a party that came not to find religious freedom but to establish a new and, hopefully, prosperous settlement. That first settlement collapsed, but Balch and four others soon founded what would become Salem, Massachusetts. His descendants did prosper, and by Emily's time they were educated Whigs and Unitarians or Episcopalians. (The men were mostly educated at Harvard.) Emily Balch's maternal ancestors arrived in 1633; they too prospered and stayed close to their New England roots.

Girls were not taught to take a back seat in the Balch family, which included one son and five daughters. Indeed, her lawyer father proposed taking Emily into his profession, and her mother was a woman of exceptional energy who, as a young woman, had ventured to Mattoon, Illinois, to teach school.

At nine Emily began reading adult books like Prescott's *Conquest of Mexico* and Motley's *Rise of the Dutch Republic*. Reading aloud was a family pastime; *Gulliver's Travels*, *Middlemarch*, the *Arabian Nights*, and Kipling's *Plain Tales from the Hills* were among the fare. Books were central to her existence, and she recalled that many stories she read had "a heroine who had a mission." She once wrote, "This theme of the person with a mission which came to be the subject of so much raillery, has also genuine and useful overtones."

The Balch children did not attend Sunday school but had a private Bible class that approached the Bible historically and "in a liberal and scientific spirit." Their church was the local Unitarian church, and Balch described its minister Charles Fletcher Dole as "the chief of all the influences that played upon my life." His message was one of service: of service to goodness, of service to goodness regardless of cost. The pledge she made to herself as a girl—to serve—was to govern her actions for the rest of her life. Although the Sabbath was not perfectly kept (swinging and sandbox play were allowed),

Emily Balch about ten years old. Courtesy of the Swarthmore College Peace Collection

the family recited hymns together on Sunday evenings. Apparently they were not sufficiently musical to sing.

Although women had been admitted to Oberlin College in the 1830s, and Harvard (where Emily's father was an overseer) had an annex for women, going to college was not a routine matter for women in 1886. Still, Emily and a friend decided that they wanted a college degree. Her friend's father, a professor at Harvard, refused to be embarrassed by having his daughter attend the Harvard annex, so the girls decided on the newly-opened Bryn Mawr, a Quaker school for women near Philadelphia. By completing her work in three years, Balch graduated in Bryn Mawr's class of 1890.

Bryn Mawr offered a high quality and challenging curriculum. Among the first faculty selected by Dean Carey Thomas, who would later become

President Thomas, were Edmund Wilson and Woodrow Wilson. Balch was first drawn to the classics and to literature, but in her third year she switched her major to economics, which she studied with Franklin H. Giddings. This was an unusual choice for a woman, but Emily's social conscience was developing in an environment when the excesses of the Gilded Age had stimulated calls for reform. Each day it seemed to become increasingly clear to Emily that the existing economic system was, simply, unjust.

In her January 1888 review of the previous year and her composition of resolutions for the next, Balch wrote, "I long for reverence, humility, purity, truthfulness, simplicity, strength, wisdom, love, providence, gladness, regularity," and "I hope I shall not get lost in study or pursue it for pleasure beyond its best measure for my purpose, unknown to me as yet"[1]—an ambitious and heartfelt, but hardly carefree commitment. The concept of "a mission" was clearly central to Balch's vision of the future, and her studies, however enjoyable and important, were seen as a means, not an end.

At graduation Balch was awarded a fellowship for a year's study in Europe. Although she did not believe she deserved it, she accepted the honor when the college president insisted. On the advice of her economics professor Franklin Giddings, she decided to study in Paris, where the university was reputed to be more friendly to women than other universities. College had been completed, but in some ways Balch's education was just beginning.

In Paris she found an academic sponsor and prepared a study titled "Public Assistance of the Poor in France." She did so using only books and secondary sources. Thus, she read endless tomes composed primarily of statistics, but her research did not include visiting a slum, or talking to poor people or even to government officials. She was not satisfied with her work, but she became fluent in French and began to grasp the value of comparative studies.

On her return to Boston, she decided she needed practical experience and volunteered with the Boston Children's Aid Society. She worked primarily with Italian children in Boston's "notorious North End," and among other things she prepared a guide titled "Manual for Use in Cases of Juvenile Offenders and Other Minors in Massachusetts," perhaps stimulated by the incarceration of one of her charges. She also served on the board of trustees of Marcella House for "pauper, neglected and criminal children." These children, she noted, "had not so much as a separate claim to a single garment, nor, if I am not mistaken to an individual toothbrush." This provided a dose of reality; it also increased her understanding of realpolitik, for as she gained familiarity with the workings of municipal government, she saw that it "fed the reformers with one hand and the ward politicians with the other."[2]

The next summer she attended a summer school on applied ethics held in Plymouth, Massachusetts, by the Ethical Culture Societies. There she met Jane Addams (then thirty-three), who had founded Hull-House three years earlier. Her Wellesley professor, Giddings, was also in attendance, and so were two women Emily would work with later: Katharine Coman, a member of the Wellesley faculty, and Vida Scudder who would become a member. This summer program may have been the impetus for Balch to begin even more concrete action. That consisted of helping to found a settlement house, Denison House, in Boston. She accepted the position of headworker at the settlement, but violated one tenet of the settlement house movement by not living in the house. Instead, she lived in her family home.

Soon after the founding of Denison House, the country experienced the panic of 1893. Workers became desperate, and the settlement house soon found itself involved with the unemployed and with the labor movement. As a result, Balch formally joined the American Federation of Labor, which she believed was concerned not just with increasing wages, but with the creation of "juster and more humane social relations everywhere." The settlement house workers gave special attention to women workers, including telephone operators, sewing-machine operators, and tobacco strippers (for the manufacture of cigars).

Balch also joined with a circle of Boston reformers who tackled a full range of urban problems such as immigration, corrupt government, and sweatshops. Her persistent commitment to service, though, always rested on the belief that activity must be based on knowledge, on information, on facts. After offering classes at Denison house on social and economic issues, she concluded that teaching provided more "leverage" for change than settlement housework. Accordingly, she returned to school. She attended the Harvard annex for a semester, and the new and progressive University of Chicago for a quarter, where she studied economics and what would become the field of sociology. Balch was now twenty-eight. She had earned a college degree five years before, had acquired a good deal of practical experience, and had also acquired bits and pieces of advanced study. Her life was a comfortable one, but she believed that she needed a period of extended, formal study before she would be ready to move from the role of student to that of teacher. Her father offered to finance a year of work in Berlin. She accepted.

Emily and her friend Mary Kingsbury were the exceptions among their fellow students at the University of Berlin. They were Americans, and they were women in a university that did not routinely admit women. To study there they had to obtain a variety of permissions, including permission from each and every faculty member whose class they wished to take.

Emily Balch reading in the garden at Bryn Mawr. Courtesy of the Swarthmore College Peace Collection

The atmosphere in Berlin was very different from that in both the United States and France. Germany was a proud and new (twenty-five years old) empire with a dominant military and a powerful professional bureaucracy. German philosophers, like Fichte and Hegel, had taught reverence for the state. Others, like Marx, had introduced communism and socialism to political debate and organizing. The many Russian students at the university were hoping to bring home ideas and strategies to change their government. Kingsbury married one of them.

Balch was not at all sympathetic to German foreign policy, which she saw as one of using force to "bully and shoulder" Germany's way to preeminence, all in the name of advancing selfish national interests. She believed Germany hated England "because she is the other big boy and has what they want." She was more sympathetic to the socialist and pacifist arguments of Wilhelm Liebknecht, who was a member of the German legislature, but no friend of the state that had once exiled and more than once imprisoned him.

Balch was pleased with her academic work at the university and with the community of students of which she and Mary were part. She was unable to finish her doctorate while in Germany and hoped to finish a thesis on her return to the United States. That did not work out, but the lack of a doctorate did not prevent her from having an academic career.

One more important event contributed to Balch's education. At the end of the school year, she and Kingsbury went to London where they attended the 1896 International Socialist Workers and Trade Union Congress. Among the eight hundred delegates from twenty countries who attended were socialists Liebknecht, August Bebel, Jean Jaurès, Clara Zetkin, Sidney Webb, and Bernard Shaw. The first two days were taken up with a debate over a previous decision to exclude all anarchists. Economic arguments were core to the discussion and to resolutions subsequently passed, but the delegates gave equal attention to calls for the various instruments of democracy—a free press, free speech, freedom of association, universal suffrage. The international commitment of the congress was shown by demonstrations for peace and against things like standing armies and secret treaties. Balch, who had certainly been exposed to poverty in her work in Boston, described in writing home the profound poverty so visible in London. "It is pretty sickening," she said.

Balch returned to the United States on the same ship as Katharine Coman. The journey gave them the opportunity to renew their acquaintance. It also resulted in Coman's offering Balch the opportunity to work at Wellesley that fall. Wellesley, a women's college, was then just twenty years old. Near Boston, it possessed a beautiful campus set on a lake. It also had the added attraction of permitting Balch to again live at home. Even though Balch had not finished her doctorate, she was invited first to work half time and soon thereafter to move into a regular faculty position.

More than forty years later in her 1938 antiwar essay "Three Guineas," Virginia Woolf championed education for women, but it was *not* to be the same education as that which educated men for profit and war. She also advocated professions for women, but professional women were not simply to fall into the procession of distinguished men who held false loyalties—loyalty to nation in particular. Nor, Woolf said, should women join men's organizations even if those organizations were for a good cause. Women could better serve through their own society, through, Woolf believed, an "Outsider's Society." Balch, of course, could not have read this essay, which had not yet been written, but her choices in education, in her profession, and in her associations seem to make her an exemplar of Woolf's message.

The Professor

At schools and universities then as today, many new faculty anxiously (or eagerly) replicated the teaching they had received, strove for the approval of their faculty peers, and took care not to disturb their institution's administrators and trustees. Not Balch. Her self-defined mission was to give young women a mission. She created her own courses—courses on socialism (students read Marx), on labor problems, on social pathology. She offered a course on immigration and one on statistics. She had her students do fieldwork that included volunteering at Denison House. She organized field trips to poor houses, insane asylums, and prisons. The content of Balch's courses was certainly novel in women's education of the time and rare in universities in general. Coman, a student of economic history, was Balch's department chair, and she encouraged rather than discouraged Balch. By this time Vida Scudder, a member of the Socialist Party, had joined the English faculty and there were other socialist faculty members as well. Thus, Balch was not flying solo in the attention she gave to social ills.

Balch not only involved her students in off-campus activities, she too participated in community efforts of various kinds. She and Vida Scudder organized a three-day conference titled "Socialism as a World Movement"; she investigated a labor strike for the Boston Twentieth Century Club; she advised her sister, who was assisting a strike of street-car workers; she served on the Massachusetts Factory Inspection Commission and the Massachusetts Minimum Wage Commission; she gave talks; and she gave Wellesley visibility—a visibility not everyone approved of.

One of her more important activities was to help found the Women's Trade Union League. (Another founder was male, and men were invited to join.) The original leaders were, like Balch, not workers but "allies" of the workers, that is, middle- and upper-class women devoted to social justice. Among the issues the league sought to address were child labor, piece work, a minimum wage, and social insurance. The league pioneered many programs, including school lunches, day nurseries, and worker education. In these efforts Balch played an important role by providing the data that underpinned the league's policies and advocacy.

Perhaps Balch's most important (and comprehensive) research resulted in a volume titled *Our Slavic Fellow Citizens*. The United States was, of course, a nation of immigrants. Until the 1840s, most of these immigrants had been English and Scotch, with some Germans, and most had been Protestant. The upheavals of 1848 and the Irish Potato Famine brought a flood of German and Irish families. Later between 1880 and 1909, there were 17 million new arrivals. Perhaps a quarter of these came from Italy, and another fifth were Slavs. By 1900, only half of the U.S. population was made up of those who had two parents who had been born here. The new immigrants tended to settle in cities, were often at the bottom of the economic scale, were thus living in visibly deplorable conditions, and often did not speak English. Also, many were Catholic, Orthodox Christian, or Jewish. The "old stock" American population often saw them as a problem. But Balch saw them as deserving of sympathy and interesting. She decided to do a comprehensive study of a group that was large but not well-known—the Slavs. She took two years of leave from Wellesley, one paid and one unpaid, to do it.

Her subjects were largely from Bertha von Suttner's homeland, Austria-Hungary. She studied the members of this new wave of immigration both in the United States and "at its source"—an ambitious and unique endeavor. Her focus was the immigrants' "social character." She did not examine crime rates or poverty—subjects of concern to many critics of policies that permitted the entrance of such large numbers of immigrants. Among the critics of these policies were her former mentor Franklin Giddings and Henry Cabot Lodge, leader of the Immigrant Restriction League of Boston.

Her study found that the group loosely known as Slavs encompassed some eight nationalities, seven languages, Roman Catholic, Jewish, and Orthodox Christian religions, and several alphabets. Seventy percent of those coming to the United States were from Austria-Hungary, and many supported independence for their homelands (e.g., Croatia and Bohemia) even as they, and especially their children, were becoming Americans. Balch pointed out that most of these Slavic immigrants to the United States were peasants, but peasants who had been self-sufficient landowners, and who were experiencing downward mobility as their lands were subdivided by each new generation. High taxes and required military service were also motives for their emigration, but Balch discounted the idea that agents who profited from organizing emigration were a causal factor. Her conclusion was that their immigration was simply "a part of that great leveling and fusing activity which is one side of the historical process." She went on to say that "modern transportation and communication combine in wiping out local differences, spreading among distant peoples the reciprocal knowledge of one another, and evening up their levels," and she quoted French sociologist Gabriel (de) Tarde: "Civilization of the prevailing type is becoming planetary." Thus more than a century ago, Balch (and Tarde) anticipated today's globalization.[3]

While she saw this process as inevitable and beneficial, Balch was sensitive to the cost of lost culture, the pain of those left behind, and the difficulties of those facing the unknown in a place where they did not speak the language. She noted the special pain of women who lost their village social life and whose children grew up to be "alien and contemptuous." The men, she observed, were more likely to find freedom and a respect that was "new and very dear to them"—in spite of the varieties of discrimination they experienced.

Balch spent her sabbatical year visiting Bohemia, Slovakia, Galicia, Slovenia, Croatia, and the Dalmatian coast. She took photos and recorded the special characteristics of each distinct culture, including folklore, modes of dress, the nature of the housing, and their characteristic food and drink. While generally appreciative of each culture, she observed that one tended to passivity and drunkenness, another produced wanderers. In some places religion created conflict; in others, language. She noted that sometimes families emigrated, but that often men and single women would go first, and that their remittances played an important part in their homeland economies. Balch also paid attention to those who returned—observing how they had changed and how they were received.

Balch then spent a year studying Slavs in the United States. It proved impossible to study them by nationality here, so she studied them by geographical location. She stayed in city tenements, in mining camps, farms, and in settlement houses. She found that many of these midcentury emigrants first found their way to Texas but that they didn't stay because of their distaste for slavery. (Until 1848, many of the Slavic peasants had themselves been bound to the land.) Another concentration of Slavic immigrants was found in Wisconsin and in Illinois, but by 1880 the largest concentration was found in New York. A substantial part of the New York and Illinois immigration was Jewish. The earlier immigrants wanted land, which explained their move to the upper Midwest. The second wave, who were poorer and less skilled, tended to move to Pennsylvania coal mines, to New England farms, and to large cities where they lived in "colonies" and worked at low-paying jobs in poor conditions.

In this half of the study, Balch also detailed the household life of the immigrants. This detail included music, celebrations, clothing (women exchanged kerchiefs for hats), food, and women's work that often included wage work as well as the raising of large families and the taking in of boarders.

She described the development of national societies, lodges, gymnastic clubs, and native-language newspapers. She discussed intermarriage (with native-born Americans), which tended to occur between Slavic men and native-born women, and at both the top and bottom of the social scale.

Balch acknowledged the mistreatment of immigrants and their own focus on the making of money, but concluded her study by urging that Americans work with their "new neighbors." She said, "We must learn to connect our ideals and theirs; we must learn to work together with them for justice, for humane living conditions, for beauty, and for true, not merely formal, liberty." In this way, "we may preserve every difference to which men cling with affection, without feeling ourselves any the less fellow-citizens and comrades."[4]

Her stay in Prague had been enhanced by a friendship she developed with Thomas Masaryk; her experience there also led Balch to her 1906 decision to publicly declare herself a socialist. This she did even though she disbelieved most of Marx's fundamental assumptions. After World War I, however, she relinquished the designation. The label had become too congruent with Marxism; and her observation of governments had not given her confidence in their ability to manage economic systems fairly.

World War I broke out in 1914, an event that would change Balch's life and lead her to international work for peace. This work began with her participation in the American Union Against Militarism, which later became the American Civil Liberties Union (ACLU). It was followed by her participation in the Women's Peace Party and then in the International Congress of Women at The Hague. Forty-two American women had been summoned to this Lysistrata-like action, including Jane Addams, who would preside at the conference, and Sophonisba Breckenridge, the first American woman to earn a doctorate in political science. The impetus for the conference came from women already organized on behalf of suffrage. But sadly, socialist men had succumbed to nationalism; the workers of the world were not united for peace.

Teddy Roosevelt denounced the women and their efforts. An English paper called them "Pro-Hun Peacettes." En route to The Hague by ship, Balch read Kant's "Perpetual Peace" and von Suttner's *Lay Down Your Arms*. The delegates were wise and experienced women who did not expect to change the world. As Balch said, "We do not suppose that we have power or knowledge or importance. We just mean to do what we can and hope to stir little waves of thought and feeling . . . and so add our little momentum to the great whole that is rolling up against war and advancing reason and good feeling between nations."[5]

Balch had a sabbatical year just before the United States entered the war, and she devoted herself to peace work. When the United States entered the war, she took an unpaid leave to continue that work.

During the war she gained national visibility through her writing and lectures. She also became a member of the Fellowship of Reconciliation, a pacifist organization, and of the People's Council of America, which had a pro-labor and pro-peace position and also offered support to the revolution going on in Russia. The positions taken by these organizations were not popular.

Unfortunately, the end of the war coincided with the expiration of Balch's most recent five-year appointment at Wellesley. As part of the reappointment process, Balch prepared (for the Wellesley president) a statement outlining her sympathy with the goals of President Woodrow Wilson, but stating that in her Christian belief she did not support war and that she believed that the right of association was fundamental to democracy. Like Balch herself, this statement was clear, unvarnished, and reflective. The trustees of the college, however, responded through the Wellesley president that though they recognized her "essential nobility of spirit," they wished to postpone consideration of her reappointment for a year. Many on the faculty were incensed, but the next spring the trustees voted not to rehire Balch. At the age of fifty-two, Balch was unemployed. Her mission to teach, and her vocation of helping young women to "train themselves," of helping them to "critically examine the social order of which they were a part" and to make themselves "serviceable," had come to an end.

Balch went quietly. She made no issue of academic freedom. In 1925 she began living in a small house attached to another house belonging to friends in Wellesley. In 1935 the Wellesley president who had been prevented from rehiring her years before, invited her to give the college Armistice Day address. Balch was "pleased."

Peace Activist

The story of the International Congress of Women at The Hague is more Addams's story than Balch's, although it was Balch who wrote of it in *Women at the Hague*. She also helped edit the detailed proceedings of the conference and accepted membership in a delegation that was to carry its message to a number of heads of state and foreign ministers. Perhaps the most important resolution passed by the conference was one put forth by Julia Grace Wales, a professor at the University of Wisconsin. It was a call for "continuous mediation without armistice." In particular, nonbelligerents were called upon to convene a conference to offer mediation.

After the conference, one delegation led by Jane Addams went to the war capitals: London, Berlin, Vienna, Budapest, Rome, and Paris. It also met with Pope Benedict XV and with the foreign minister of Belgium. A second delegation that included Balch, Wales, and Rosika Schwimmer traveled to Russia, Denmark, Norway, Sweden, and Berne. Later Addams and Balch both had meetings (separately) with President Woodrow Wilson and Secretary of State Robert Lansing. Remarkably, the delegations were successful in obtaining face-to-face meetings with the power brokers of the era and in having substantive discussions with them. They also mobilized women on behalf of their proposal for continuous mediation. In one three-day period, women sent twelve thousand telegrams to the White House calling for a conference of neutrals.

President Wilson was unswayed, but Henry Ford supported the women's idea, chartered the Ford Peace Ship, and paid for an unofficial Conference for Continuous Mediation in Stockholm. Balch did not sail with the Peace Ship, but she did serve as a member of the conference for some months. The press mocked the enterprise, and Ford bailed out within a year.

An important part of Balch's prewar work consisted of collecting, editing, and publishing a wide variety of proposals for ending the war. These came from many sources including President Woodrow Wilson, the Pope, some nine socialist organizations, President Charles Eliot of Harvard, and a number of peace organizations. The documents were published as *Approaches to the Great Settlement*, which is an important resource for understanding the period.

Back in the United States, Balch allied herself with the Women's Peace Party, which was uncompromising in its pacifism. She also worked with younger and more radical activists, thereby lending respectability to the American Neutral Conference, which evolved into the Emergency Peace Federation and then into the People's Council of America. The council's activism and left-wing views provoked physical as well as verbal attacks—some of them from returned veterans. Balch stood fast in her pacifism, though, while Ford and many of her religious, labor, and suffragette friends turned their efforts to support for the Allies. When President Wilson called for a declaration of war, the Senate voted 82 to 6 in favor, and the House 373 to 50. During the latter vote, Balch watched in dismay from the House gallery.

Balch was especially active during the war in writing and lobbying on behalf of conscientious objectors. In an exchange with Bishop Richard Cooke in the *Christian Advocate* she stated the case for the objector's patriotism and commitment to liberty and democracy. She further argued that the objector might be doing something more difficult than the reluctant compliant when he made himself "a byword and a hissing." She described the loneliness of the objector and the self-doubts that arise when the objector wonders whether he is in danger "of priggishness . . . in his claim to deeper moral insight than his elders and betters and those who have given and are giving their lives in war." She concluded, "His is not an easy path. Let us at least be fair enough to recognize that he believes that he is serving not himself but us."[6]

Balch herself had a strong Christian faith, but it was not founded on theological exploration or sectarian fellowship. After the war though, she became a member of the London Yearly Meeting of the Society of Friends. Later, in a lecture at Bryn Mawr she explained, "It was not alone their testimony against war, their creedless faith, nor their openness to suggestions for far-reaching social reform that attracted me, but the dynamic force of the active love through which their religion was expressing itself."

The Armistice was signed in 1918, but peace was not made until 1919. The official peace conference was meeting in Paris at the same time that the International Congress of Women held its second meeting, in Zurich. For many of the women, the congress was a bittersweet reunion. They had worked together for peace four years before at The Hague. Now, when they met with the war over, women from the blockaded countries illustrated war's ravages by their starved bodies. Though their countries had been at war, the women unanimously called for an end to the blockade and also unanimously critiqued the new Treaty of Versailles (Balch was largely responsible for a meticulous analysis of its many provisions). They criticized the honoring of secret treaties, the disarmament of only one set of belligerents, and, importantly, the extraordinary reparations the treaty demanded. They concluded by formally organizing themselves as the Women's International League for Peace and Freedom (WILPF), choosing Jane Addams as international president, and Emily Balch as international secretary-treasurer, a full-time position that was to be located in the same place as the League of Nations, in Geneva. In setting its agenda, WILPF passed resolutions on race equality, Jewish rights, mass deportations, and conscientious objectors. It also opposed the use of force by revolutionaries, however just their cause.

WILPF's Geneva office gave Balch a salary and a close view of the new League of Nations. She understood the league's deficiencies and that governments "were not in earnest" in wanting to use it to prevent aggression and to maintain peace. But her view was that great benefit could be derived from its many cooperative, international activities that dealt with specific issues such as education, narcotics, and the white slave trade. Again, Balch and others had access to officialdom; some WILPF members were even sent to the league assembly as their countries' official delegates.

Balch had responsibility for organizing the WILPF third international conference in Vienna in 1921. One item on the agenda required WILPF members to take an absolutist position on pacifism. That proposal did not pass; the more inclusive position taken was one in which members vowed to work resolutely for peace and against war. Balch's work included editing a journal, *Pax International*, and organizing a series of international summer schools. She relinquished her position in 1922 at age fifty-five but continued her work— including, again, editing the proceedings of the peace congress held that year in Washington, D.C.

Balch's travels (often financed by wealthy women friends) continued to be wide-ranging. In 1925 she traveled through Algeria, Tunisia, and Libya to Istanbul. She also traveled to Athens, Bucharest, Belgrade, Budapest, and Vienna, spreading the WILPF gospel especially to students and journalists. In 1926 WILPF asked her to lead a commission to study conditions in Haiti, which had been under U.S. military control since the Marines had been sent in more than a decade before. It was, essentially, a study of nation-building (or nonbuilding). Titled "Occupied Haiti," the report by "six disinterested Americans" (five women—two members of WILPF, two "colored women," a representative of the Fellowship of Reconciliation—and Paul Douglas, later Senator Douglas) representing the Society of Friends Foreign Service Committee. The report's principle recommendation was that "a well-considered and carefully planned program of progressive steps toward self-government" be put into place. A series of specific recommendations included ending "preventive imprisonment" and showing the same respect to Haitians as would be shown to "people of a white race." An economic analysis, a discussion of land tenure, and recommendations for education (including raising the salaries of teachers from $6 to $15 a month) were included. Balch made her report directly to President Calvin Coolidge. Four years later, President Herbert Hoover sent an official delegation to Haiti, and this delegation made very similar recommendations. Its recommendations were carried out. That delegation was aided by a memo from Balch concerning the difficulties of obtaining "true Haitian feeling," which was concealed by timidity, hatred, fear, and French ways of thinking.

Balch did not slow down in her sixties as the world sank into depression and then exploded into war. In 1929 she was chosen with two others as joint chair of WILPF. She traveled to Palestine in 1930 and to Germany in 1931, which she compared sadly to her student days there more than a quarter of a century before. She again served as WILPF international secretary in Geneva, urging her own government and others to anticipate and plan for action in the event war should break out. Meanwhile, she prepared proposal after proposal for dealing with such hot spots as Manchuria, and Spain. She wrote about disarmament, reconstruction, and internationalization of aviation, the Mediterranean, and the Antarctic. She also worked hard to bring refugees to the United States.

World War II created a dilemma for Balch: she found she could no longer hold to absolute pacifism. The guidance she gave her fellow U.S. members of WILPF was to continue to work in peace education, to advocate for co-operative world organizations, and to work for human rights. She did not, however, consider it WILPF's charge to provide relief and assistance to those harmed by the war. On her seventy-fifth birthday in 1942, the address she gave, "Towards a Planetary Civilization," held out hope for a world without national armies and with a unity based on moral standards and devoted to "the common good."

While opposed to the concept of unconditional surrender and to world government, Balch believed the plans for a United Nations might be bene-ficial. The failure of the League of Nations she attributed not to any specific deficiencies but to the self-interestedness of the nations that had sent repre-sentatives to its meetings. She now hoped for two things: (1) a declaration of individual and group rights that would apply internally, and (2) a mechanism for preventing rather than just punishing aggression.

Balch did not urge appeasement as the cold war developed, but she urged, as she always had, reason, goodwill, and a willingness to take risks. She well understood that human fear and self-interest were great hindrances. In 1957 at age ninety, she recalled her address in Zurich in 1919: "Only by initiative, self-sacrifice, and intelligence in a spirit of honest good will" can we create a new world order where people can live and work together on a basis of consent and cooperation rather than coercion. Americans, Balch believed, must overcome their own dogmatism, and others must forgive America for being so powerful yet "not worthy."

Balch won the Nobel Peace Prize in 1946. Among those nominating her was the president of Wellesley, Mildred McAfee Horton, who had commanded the Women Accepted for Voluntary Emergency Service (WAVES) during World War II. Balch said the ceremony was a bit like going to her own funeral.

Lessons Taught

Balch was a serious woman. She regularly engaged in self-criticism, and she constantly sought to improve. She was disciplined, balanced, and temperate, but she was also an intellectual. She thought ideas and programs should be based on logic and solid information, and she was quite ready to engage in the most tedious study and analysis in order to provide a sound basis for belief and action. She was committed to principles but engaged in the concrete. Thus, she urged her students to study economics and science as well as the humanities, and to get practical experience too. Again, she was reflective; she was rigorous; she was realistic; she was always open to the need to revise her thoughts. What would be lesson number one, according to Balch? Use your full intelligence.

Balch's strong commitment to service meant that thinking was not enough. Action was required. One had a responsibility to society even if that society rarely afforded its women advanced education, denied them political office (even the vote), and made no room for them to make a fortune. And once she had determined that a course of action was wise and feasible, Balch was not deterred by the Mrs. Grundy of public opinion, or other forms of social pressure. She knew that the Wellesley trustees would not be happy about her work for peace and in support of conscientious objectors, but she felt compelled to fulfill her duty. She was not deterred by risk, by ridicule, or by the possible drawbacks of her association with radicals. In fact, she may have felt it a special duty to act when others did fear or found the risk too great. Balch regretted that the very words *international, peace,* and *freedom* were so often seen as suspicious, questionable, unpatriotic. Lesson number two: Be unafraid.

Balch didn't get to sub-Sahara Africa, to Australia, or the Far East, but she traveled extensively in Europe. She also journeyed to the Middle East, to Haiti, and to Russia—mostly by boat or train, that is to say, slowly. She studied languages. As a young woman she studied for a year in Paris and for a second year in Berlin. She mastered Czech in preparation for her study of Austria-Hungarian immigration. She wrote about imperialism in its varieties, about "the polar regions," about China, about the world's waterways. She described her vision as "planetary." Lesson number three: Think globally.

Having reached a conclusion, Balch felt it important to get her ideas into the hands of powerful individuals. These included kings, popes, presidents, premiers, secretaries of state, and foreign ministers. Lesson number four: Think big.

Hers was a mighty and prolific pen. She wrote letters; she wrote for newsletters; she wrote for journals. When she first lost her job at Wellesley, she wrote for *The Nation.* This was all part of her mission to educate. She did another important kind of writing too. She contributed to the historical record by writing minutes, by editing proceedings, by preparing reports, by producing histories. Lesson number five: Write it down.

Many of her concepts bear repeating today. In her endorsement of the League of Nations and of the United Nations, she did not anticipate that they would bring the rule of law to the world. Indeed, she doubted that a world government would be more just or less coercive than smaller governments, but she saw as promising the wide variety of ways in which people could work together across national borders. Today's global organizations such as ILO, UNESCO, WHO, or UNIFEM would all seem to her ways to advance peace through cooperation—politics and bureaucracy notwithstanding. She saw a knowledge of economics as essential to any strategy for peace, and she recognized that reconstruction and the building of civil society was complex and difficult. She critiqued imperialism and commented specifically on "strategic imperialism," in which a nation plants military bases throughout the world. Lesson number six: Anticipate.

Yes, Balch was analytical and unmusical, but her portrait would not be complete if it did not also acknowledge her artistry and her passion. Her letters often verge on verse; in fact, she was a published poet. Her astonishing energy derived from what she called "good will" or, sometimes, "universal love." She saw this universal love as real, as powerful, as a positive force and as an effective one, unlike violence and coercion, which she saw as self-defeating. After her visit to Russia and Scandinavia she declared: "Never again must women dare to believe that they are without responsibility because they are without power. Public opinion is power; strong and reasonable feeling is power; determination which is a twin sister of faith or vision is power." In summing up her own contribution to world peace, she made this analogy: "The coral insect deposits its minute contributions far below the surface of the water, but it has done its part in building the coral island which ultimately sustains a group of living beings."[7]

Notes

1. Mercedes M. Randall's biography of Balch, *Improper Bostonian: Emily Greene Balch* (New York: Twayne, 1964), is an excellent account. This quote can be found on page 68.
2. Randall, *Improper Bostonian*, 81.
3. See Balch, *Our Slavic Fellow Citizens* (New York: Arno Press, 1969), 58.
4. Balch, *Our Slavic Fellow Citizens*, 425.
5. Randall, *Improper Bostonian*, 151.
6. Randall, *Improper Bostonian*, 245–46.
7. Randall, *Improper Bostonian*, 190, 289.

Betty Williams. Courtesy of the
Norwegian Nobel Institute

Mairead Corrigan. Courtesy of the
Norwegian Nobel Institute

Betty Williams and Mairead Corrigan: Sisterhood Created by Tragedy

Disputed Ireland

Henry VIII may have started it all when he broke with the Pope. Ireland, already unhappy with England's domination, remained Catholic. Thus political differences were reinforced by religious differences. By the seventeenth century, Protestant authority was firmly established, and the Irish in the northern part of the island had been physically displaced by English and Scottish Protestants, who were "planted" to ensure loyalty to London. Further, during England's civil war the Irish revolted, and after Oliver Cromwell had defeated the king, he turned to a ruthless subjection of Ireland. Near the end of that century, Protestant William of Orange defeated England's Catholic King James II at the Battle of the Boyne. William's Glorious Revolution ensured Protestant possession of the Westminister throne, and the Battle of the Boyne took on mythic proportion as a symbol of Protestant triumph and Catholic resistance.

During the next hundred years, practice and a variety of laws bestowed privileges on Irish Anglicans, marginalized the Presbyterians, and restricted the rights of Catholics. Irish Catholics and Presbyterians did unite in a 1798 revolt, but they were soundly defeated, and in 1801 the Act of Union integrated the Irish parliament into that of Westminster. When Britain began to enlarge its electorate in the 1800s, some reforms were carried out to benefit Irish Catholics. Nevertheless, the mostly Catholic island continued to be mostly run by Protestants.

After the Irish Potato Famine of 1845–1851, during which 1 million Irish died and another million emigrated, many who stayed home and survived began to call for Home Rule—some through politics, others through violence. Again reforms were made, but many Catholics deemed them insufficient and continued to champion Home Rule. Protestants, who were concentrated in the north in Ulster, did not want Home Rule. They feared it. As tension increased between Britain and Ireland, it also increased within Ireland between Catholics and Protestants, especially the geographically concentrated Presbyterians.

On several occasions the British parliament debated Home Rule without reaching a conclusion. That very debate alarmed Ireland's Protestants, and by 1914 they had formed an Ulster Volunteer Force (UVF) of 100,000 that vowed to fight to keep Ireland in the United Kingdom. Also, thousands of Ulster men volunteered to fight on Britain's behalf in World War I, in part to demonstrate the strength of their British patriotism.

The war temporarily diverted attention from the Irish conflict, but focus was dramatically restored by a small group of Irish nationalists. They seized the Dublin post office in the Easter Rising of 1916. Their efforts were unsuccessful, but substantial damage was done to the city and some 450 people lost their lives. However, the decision to execute fifteen of the revolt's leaders proved a mistake. Much of the Irish public now turned from moderation and support for political action with the goal of Home Rule to support for full independence. Indeed, an independence party, Sinn Féin, won the elections in 1918, and the Irish War of Independence ensued. Its outcome was a 1921 treaty that divided the island. Six of Ulster's nine counties became Northern Ireland, which formed its own parliament, the Stormont. The rest of the island became the Irish Free State, an independent member of the British Commonwealth.

The Irish Free State adopted a new constitution in 1937 that gave the Catholic Church special status. Further, the constitution's Articles 2 and 3 asserted a claim to Northern Ireland. These provisions angered and worried Ulster. More was to come. Soon after World War II began, the Irish Free State asserted its independence by choosing to remain neutral, and in 1949 it changed its name to the Irish Republic, leaving the commonwealth altogether. England's cure for its continuing Irish "headache" was to leave Northern Ireland's parliament to manage its own affairs but to show its support for Ulster by passing a bill stating that Northern Ireland would remain within the United Kingdom for as long as its parliament wished.

Unsure of the depth of England's commitment, wary of the intentions of the Irish Republic, and challenged by the (irregular) Irish Republican Army (IRA), which began skirmishes along the three-hundred-mile border between Northern Ireland and the Irish Republic, Northern Ireland's Protestants began to consider the many Catholics in their midst as potential enemies. Religious discrimination and segregation flourished.

The 1960s were a period of unrest, of demonstrations, and of calls for justice and rights in many countries. Northern Ireland was no exception. A (Catholic) civil rights movement emerged. Simultaneously, Unionists— Protestants who argued for the full merger of Northern Ireland and England— revived their paramilitary, the UVF. Moderate leaders found it increasingly difficult to enlist support for any reforms benefiting Catholics, although at least one, Prime Minister Terence O'Neill, did try.

In 1966 on the fiftieth anniversary of the Easter Rising, the UVF killed two Catholics. What would become known as "the Troubles" was about to begin. Communal rioting increased. Civil rights marches in Londonderry (Derry) and elsewhere turned bloody. Britain sent troops. The IRA split, and a segment of the party, known as "provisionals," became armed insurgents. A British soldier was killed, internment was introduced, and the conflict escalated until January 1972 when British troops killed thirteen demonstrators on what would soon become known as Bloody Sunday. Soon thereafter, Britain suspended Northern Ireland's parliament and began direct rule from Westminister. The IRA then declared a two-week cease-fire, but followed it with twenty-two bomb blasts in Belfast on "Bloody Friday." Both sides had turned to terrorism. In the thirty years of the Troubles that would follow, some 3,500 would die, or one out of every four hundred persons living in Northern Ireland. If the same proportion were killed in the United States today, there would be 600,000 deaths. Six hundred thousand!

Britain engineered what was supposed to be a solution, one that called for a power-sharing government in Northern Ireland and a vaguely defined governmental institution that was to have an all-Ireland "dimension." This was known as the Sunningdale Agreement. However, many did not accept the agreement, and it was no solution. Unionists were outraged, workers struck, irregulars turned to violence, and British troops found that practicing neutrality was difficult. The British now began to fear a two-front war. As a result, they too began to see the IRA and its Catholic supporters as a threat. In fact, Catholics became the military's enemy. This was ironic because British troops had originally been sent to Ulster to protect the Catholics.

In 1975 yet another truce was declared, and elections to a constitutional convention were held. The convention urged majority rule. This was rejected by Westminister, which believed that Catholic participation, or some kind of shared power, was essential to stability. Also at the same time, the assigning of special status to political prisoners came to an end. Britain wanted those individuals using violence to be seen by the public as criminals. Prison protests began, the truce ended, and the story of Mairead Corrigan and Betty Williams began.

Mairead Corrigan, "Angel," and Betty Williams, "Sinner"

The partnership between Mairead Corrigan and Betty Williams was an improbable one. Their lives had been quite different, although both were Catholic, and they were born only a year apart in Belfast during World War II. The northern counties of Ireland had industrialized during the nineteenth century, and Belfast had grown to a population of more than 350,000 by the time Northern Ireland was established in 1921. Although hard hit by the worldwide depression, Belfast was prosperous enough to have developed a Catholic middle class by the 1960s. At that time it was a class more interested in attaining its rights within Northern Island than in a merger with the Irish Republic, whose economy would not fully develop until after it had joined and been assisted by the European Union.

When Corrigan and Williams were five and six respectively, the Irish Republic left the commonwealth and Britain assured Northern Ireland of its continued status as a part of the United Kingdom. This meant that the Northern Ireland Catholic minority of perhaps one-third could expect to live out their lives in a community run by, and many felt, for, Protestants. Corrigan and Williams were twenty and twenty-one when the Campaign for Social Justice was organized and the Catholic civil rights movement began to take shape. They were twenty-four and twenty-five at the time of the Londonderry riots, which by convention mark the beginning of the Troubles.

Mairead Corrigan's family was large. She was the second of eight children (six girls and two boys), one of whom emigrated to New Zealand because of the civil strife. Her mother was a housewife; her father had a window-washing business. She was raised in the Falls, a Catholic ghetto that would later contribute support and young men (and some women) to the IRA provisionals. The Falls would also become a part of the battleground. Threats, riots, and death would come to the streets that Corrigan had walked in careless safety as a child.

Like other Catholic children, she had little contact with Protestants. Housing was segregated, and children of different religions rarely went to school together. Corrigan attended St. Vincent's, a Catholic primary school. When she finished, her family could not afford to pay for education beyond a one-year course at a commercial college. By the age of sixteen, Corrigan was a member of the workforce.

She continued to live at home while working as a secretary or assistant in a variety of jobs. By the age of thirty-two, she had become confidential secretary to the managing director of Arthur Guinness and Company.

Corrigan was single, but she had an active social life. Even though she lived in an atmosphere where many people claimed to hate Protestants, she was not engaged in politics. She was very involved with her family, and perhaps even more involved with her church. At age fourteen she joined the Legion of Mary, a lay missionary organization. The legion was also committed to service, and its members spent at least two hours a week doing volunteer work, in pairs, and under the guidance of a spiritual director. By age eighteen Corrigan had been put in charge of a cell of the legion. She began with only a handful of adolescent members but quickly increased the group's membership to 150. Her group's activities included opening a nursery school, obtaining funds to construct a community meeting hall, and developing programs for handicapped children.

Although she did not have an advanced degree and she lived in a ghetto, worked as a secretary, and served the poor, Corrigan's life was rich in experience. She represented the Legion of Mary at a World Council of Churches meeting held in Thailand. In fact, she traveled there with a Protestant minister from Belfast. The legion also sent her to Russia to make a film about religion in Russia. Further evidence of both her religious conviction and her sense of the larger world is shown by the fact that during the early 1970s she applied, but was not chosen, to serve as a missionary to South America.

The Legion of Mary was given permission to visit Catholics convicted of terrorism and held in the Long Kesh internment camp. Corrigan found those visits rewarding. Every Sunday for two years she visited internees, trying to understand their views and their arguments that violence was necessary, that honor required it, and that their acts were defensive and protective. In turn, she tried to persuade them to her belief that violence is not the route to peace and that a Christian is appropriately a pacifist. She recognized that paramilitary group members, both Catholic and Protestant, would have to be persuaded to accept a new society before peace could be enjoyed. Further, she realized that that society would have to be more just than the one in which she grew up, and that it would have to provide both sides with a sense of security, a sense that they could safely concentrate on building a future, and that neither their lives nor their property were in danger.

Mairead Corrigan had had early personal experience with the Troubles. An aunt had lived in a part of town where Catholic homes were burnt, and she had to be moved. A soldier threw a tear gas canister through a window and onto the altar during a Republican funeral service Corrigan was attending. She intervened when she witnessed soldiers searching some young girls, and she was beaten for doing so. Her pacifism was not naive.

The journalist who dubbed Corrigan "the angel" captured her essence: a positive, radiant personality with a strong moral compass. She has also been described as a conversationalist who enthusiastically plunges into discussions,

Mairead Corrigan. Photo by Ivan Suvanjieff. Permission granted by the PeaceJam Foundation (www.peacejam.org)

asks questions, and is keen to hear other people's views. Those who meet her invariably describe her as "smiling, always smiling." Indeed, it is hard to find her willing to be critical of anyone, even convicted terrorists. Once she watched as two IRA members threw a bomb at an armored truck and then tried to hide in her garden. Corrigan summoned them into the house to hide them and to ask why they would do such a thing—particularly why one of them, a woman who was a nurse, would want to take a life.

Corrigan has described her youthful self as happy, as lucky, as having had a "fantastic" life. She still loves mountains and swimming and books—hundreds of which she has bought and not yet read. She talks about her many friends and her habit of writing a letter a day to stay in touch with them. She is not a television watcher but does not rail about its deficiencies. Is there anything she does not like? Well, maybe money and having to manage it.

Betty Williams, born Smyth, is a very different person. She too is Catholic, but for nearly a decade she experienced disbelief. Even after returning to the faith, she has been publicly critical of Northern Ireland's church hierarchy. Indeed, her criticisms have sometimes been scathing. While the world might not condemn her as "a sinner," she has not only faulted the clergy, she has also acted contrary to church doctrine. For example, she divorced her first husband. He, like her father and his father, was a Protestant. Mixed marriages like that of the Williams were not common in Belfast.

Betty Williams's father was a butcher, one of five children. Her mother was one of twelve children, a housewife, and Catholic, with a Jewish father. When Betty was thirteen her mother had a stroke, and Betty assumed much of the responsibility for her eight-year-old sister. She also began to make most of her own decisions and to assume a certain amount of independence. Betty attended Catholic schools, and then she too took a secretarial-training course. Unlike Mairead, she married young (at age eighteen). Ralph Williams was English, and he and Betty began their married life in Ireland's antithesis— Bermuda. Like Mairead, Betty did not let her lack of higher education make her parochial.

Williams had a son, Paul, soon after her marriage. Because her husband was a merchant seaman and away for months at a time, she returned to Belfast. She had a daughter, Deborah, eight years later. With her husband so often absent, Williams, like most military wives, necessarily managed her own and her children's affairs. Also, even though her husband made a good salary, Williams worked—not just for income but because she was social and inquiring. She did most of the usual women's jobs: waitress, secretary, girl Friday. In fact, when she began her work for peace she was actually holding down two jobs. Thus even though she had the respectability of being married, she had responsibilities akin to those of a single, working mother. Such circumstances do not produce delicate personalities, and Williams is not just independent, she is outgoing, opinionated, pragmatic, colorful, challenging. Interviewers frequently refer to her as "forceful."

Williams is also tall, and her appearance in early photos is somewhat austere. Because her eyes are light-sensitive, she regularly wears dark glasses, which add to her somewhat forbidding appearance. When she became a celebrity, she became blond, and her presentation of self became almost elegant.

Betty once considered joining the IRA. She thought about getting and using a gun. One stimulus to do so was her return from a holiday with her sister and her sister's new husband to find that the young couple's home had been destroyed in their absence. While she had no desire to become a part of the Irish Republic, she was furious about the injustices being done to Catholics in Northern Ireland. Sometimes she thought only the IRA was willing to do anything about it. Ultimately Williams did not join the IRA, but she did shelter some men and smuggled others across the border in the trunk of her car.

Williams did not begin with a consistent philosophy that guided her response to terrorism. However, unlike many, she seemed fearless and was always willing to express her views. After the IRA's twenty-two bombings on Bloody Friday, she witnessed police and firemen shoveling parts of human bodies into plastic bags to clean up one of the sites. Her position then became one of condemning all violence. She even joined a Protestant minister's Witness for Peace in front of Belfast City Hall. The minister, Joseph Parker, had lost a son in one of the blasts and was calling for Catholic and Protestant churches to unite against violence. He received so little support for his ecumenical message that he soon emigrated to Canada. At the time Williams couldn't see any particular action as effective, but she did attempt and succeed in converting to nonviolence a few neighbors active in the IRA. Her argument was simple: Violence doesn't work. Even though Williams lived in a neighborhood with committed members of the IRA, she was not reticent. Others may have been intimidated into silence, but she was not. For example, one day she was window-shopping when a British soldier standing near her was shot and killed. She was horrified to realize that he really was no more than a boy, and instinctively she tried to help him. She said an Act of Contrition over his body. Some neighborhood women who witnessed this small gesture of mercy were angry that she would do even that much for a dying soldier. Also, after the peace movement had begun, she once invited two women to her home whom she knew to be supporters of the IRA. She hoped to explain to them why violence was destroying the community. They beat her, in her own home.

Her views evolved over a period of time. She recalls her aggressive attitude and language when stopped by a British patrol, and she recalls being arrested for being out late, which resulted in a frightening interrogation. This gave her more empathy for prisoners. It also made it easier for her to understand why recruiting for the IRA was successful. She also mourned the death of two cousins—both young men who had been apolitical. One was killed by Protestants, one by Catholics. Williams began to conclude that the enemy was violence itself.

Williams is a reader. The only author she doesn't like is Shakespeare. Favorites include Dickens, Tolstoy, and Taoist writings. For her the kitchen is an opportunity for creativity and relaxation.

The Community of Peace People

Between 1969 and 1976 more than 1,600 civilians were killed in Northern Ireland. On August 10, 1976, Betty Williams was walking along the sidewalk when she saw a blue Ford speeding down the street pursued by British soldiers in two jeeps. The driver of the Ford was shot; abruptly the Ford swerved onto the sidewalk where two women were walking with their children. The car

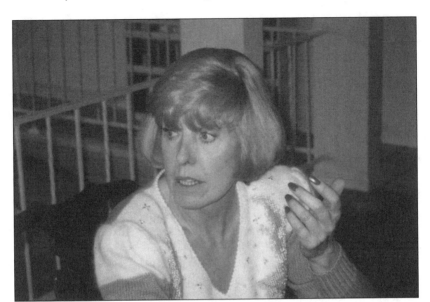

Betty Williams. Photo by Ivan Suvanjieff. Permission granted by the PeaceJam
Foundation (www.peacejam.org)

struck Anne Corrigan Maguire and her children Joanna and John, ages eight and two, and six-week-old Andrew. Joanna and Andrew were killed on the spot; John died the next day; and Anne was gravely injured. This became what sociologists call a *precipitating event*; in other words, it was the last straw. A small group of Catholic women immediately and spontaneously demonstrated against IRA violence—in an IRA neighborhood.

Anne Corrigan Maguire was Mairead Corrigan's sister. The media swarmed, and Mairead gave a tearful BBC interview in which she condemned the use of violence. It was shown several times in Northern Ireland and also in the south. It was a powerful and motivating image. One who was moved to action was Betty Williams, who had witnessed the accident. She finally had something concrete to do: prepare a petition and conduct a demonstration.

Within forty-eight hours Williams was on television displaying a petition with six thousand signatures and calling for a march the next day at the site of the deaths. She invited both Protestant and Catholic women to join her in ridding the community of IRA "bums." Williams was bold. She acknowledged fearing the IRA, but said that it was time to act. Both she and Jackie Maguire, Anne Corrigan Maguire's husband, laid the blame for the deaths at the IRA's feet. A local priest publicly agreed.

The international press covered the funeral the next day. Mairead Corrigan and Betty Williams had become acquainted by then. Corrigan told the press that demonstrations for an end to violence must continue. Williams asked reporters to announce a demonstration the following day in Andersontown and to specifically note that Protestant women had already chartered a bus so they could attend.

Ten thousand women came to that demonstration. The nonpolitical event was religious in tone but was not presided over by clergy of any kind. Prayers were said and hymns sung. Then a march was begun to the cemetery where the Maguire children had been buried. IRA supporters, mostly but not exclusively men, physically attacked the women, but none were seriously hurt.

For a movement to succeed it needs an idea, leaders, a precipitating event, and an organizational structure. Corrigan and Williams had all but the last. Often a movement is built on a preexisting organization, just as the U.S. civil rights movement was built on already organized churches. Students who are often from the upper class and therefore enjoy some impunity, and who are also at that magical time in life when they have escaped dependence and have not yet acquired dependents, can be important contributors to a movement although they sometimes lack staying power. This very spontaneous movement against the IRA was different, however, it was composed largely of adult, neighborhood women, women who did not have a preexisting base to mobilize and who had many other responsibilities.

Corrigan had some experience in organizing but Williams had little. They had no funds; they had no office; they had no staff. They began by using Williams's home telephone to confront a four-hundred-year-old conflict between vested interests that had consistently rejected reconciliation. They were also surrounded by reporters hungry for a story. It was a heady time. Catholic and Protestant women were reaching out to each other. They were praying together, and they were being attacked together. If Catholic and Protestant clergy had reacted similarly and as wholeheartedly, a miracle might have occurred. But they did not. And it did not.

One person who did sign on was Ciaran McKeown, a journalist and another Catholic. As a student of philosophy at Queens University in Belfast, McKeown, who had served as a Dominican novice for eight months, was the first Catholic to be elected president of the university's student council. His campaign was based on nonsectarian cooperation. That was in 1966. This year also marked the first time that McKeown's public statements found him in conflict with a Catholic bishop. His later criticisms of Catholic clergy would prove a problem for the peace movement. After college graduation McKeown moved from Belfast to Dublin to work with the United Students of Ireland. In 1969 he was chosen its president, thus representing all Irish students north and south. By that time he possessed a developed philosophy of nonviolence and of reconciliation, but the times were becoming unreceptive to that position. In fact, Northern Ireland's Troubles were beginning.

At the time of the Maguire tragedy McKeown, a father of four, was working as a reporter. As such he had covered, again and again, the sad stories of bombings and assassinations. When he offered his services to Corrigan and Williams, he was offering sophistication and his media, political, and organizing experience. He also brought a developed philosophy based upon the principle of nonviolence and the need for building a community from the bottom up, that is, through neighbor-to-neighbor discussion. By going to work for the Community of Peace People, the organization he, Corrigan, and Williams were to found, he not only sacrificed his job, which eventually would mean going on government support, he also sacrificed any future career as a reporter, although at the time he did not know that that would be the result.

McKeown quickly became a crucial participant in and advisor to the Community of Peace People. At first he stayed in the background, but during the first year nearly all organization decisions were made by the trio of Corrigan, Williams, and McKeown. They formed a remarkably cohesive and trusting leadership, although Williams often found action more rewarding than talking and was unsure that a consistent philosophy was more important that an effective act. Williams's impulsiveness and instinct for the dramatic sometimes seemed out of step with the patient positiveness of McKeown's philosophy, but she was a crowd pleaser. After a somber demonstration or program, she would often invite the crowd to join in singing "When Irish Eyes Are Smiling."

Within one week of their first meeting, these three people who had not previously known each other had led two demonstrations, prepared a Declaration of Peace, and laid out a plan for a series of marches. The Community of Peace People had been born. Even though most of the community's participants were women, its three leaders were clear from the beginning that this was a movement for men and women. Williams in particular wanted it to be clear that Peace People had nothing whatsoever to do with feminism. The declaration they had formed was read at every march. It said:

We have a simple message from this meeting, and from this movement for peace.
We want to live and love and build a just and peaceful society.
We want for our children, as we want for ourselves, our lives at home, at work and at play, to be lives of joy and peace.
We recognize that to build such a life demands of all of us: dedication, hard work, and courage.
We recognize that there are many problems in our society which are a source of conflict and violence.

We recognize that every bullet fired and every exploding bomb makes that work more difficult.

We reject the use of the bomb and the bullet and all the techniques of violence.

We dedicate ourselves to working with our neighbours, near and far, day in and day out, to building that peaceful society in which the tragedies we have known are a bad memory and a continuing warning.

In Northern Ireland, Protestant men's lodges have a long tradition of marching. Even though they are said to be religious processions, the marches are widely perceived as provocative and as political triumphalism, especially when they pass through Catholic neighborhoods. Women marching for peace were intended to mirror the men's marches but carry a very different message: Violence must cease—all violence. The Peace People were also clear that their movement was nonpolitical. Still, any time they took a position beyond that of simply ending violence—for example, committing themselves to the rule of law—they would be accused of being political. Also, politicians of every stripe certainly paid attention to the movement even if it refused to ally itself with any of them. Indeed, the three leaders refused even to meet with any politicians or elected officials.

Their plan was to march once a week from late August until early December. One march would be held each week in Northern Ireland, and at the same time, one would be held in Great Britain. A culminating march would be held in Great Britain in Trafalgar Square at the end of November, but the final march would be held in Ireland itself, in Drogheda, at a bridge over the River Boyne, the site of Protestant William of Orange's triumph almost three hundred years before.

The second march of the series was held in a Protestant section of Belfast. Labor unions announced their support, and so did women from a number of republican clubs. The IRA, though, accused the women and their movement of wanting peace at any price. Nevertheless, fifty thousand marchers participated in the second march. Importantly, they included thousands of working-class women whose lives until then had been almost completely segregated by religion. The only banners permitted were blue-on-white banners identifying neighborhoods. All marchers read the Declaration of Peace aloud; and this would be done at each of the demonstrations that followed.

The itinerary for the third march was from Catholic Falls Road to Protestant Shankill Road—a daring choice. People were rarely courageous or foolish enough to cross the divide between the two communities, a divide that was marked by a military checkpoint in what was essentially a wall separating the two communities. Part of the public warned of danger; part of it was awed and admiring. The labor unions again urged their members to join the march, while the lord mayor of Dublin called on the city's citizens to join in a march in Dublin on the same day. It was a breathtaking demonstration that this was an ecumenical not a Catholic movement, and that its message was to the international public and not just to those living in Northern Ireland. The march did not proceed without violence. Marchers were stoned, and Corrigan was physically attacked.

Over the next several months, Northern Ireland marches and demonstrations occurred in Londonderry, Antrim, Newry, Dungannon, Ballymena, Downpatrick, Enniskillen, Belfast (Falls Park), Craigavon, Omagh, Drogheda, and Armagh. It was Williams's English sister-in-law who energized the British marches. They were held in Liverpool, Glasgow, Birmingham, Leeds, Cardiff, Newcastle-upon-Tyne, Manchester, Edinburgh, Bristol, and London.

Londonderry was an especially important choice because it had been the scene of Bloody Sunday only four years before. The city was divided both by a river and by religion. The march was planned so that Protestant and Catholic marchers would meet at the center of a bridge. It was a great success, but as so often happens, success brought questions—some of them distinctly unfriendly—and criticism. Where was the money coming from to charter buses? Who was paying to print the pamphlets and banners? Who was pulling Corrigan's and Williams's strings? Suspicions were many. Conspiracy theorists flourished.

Internal quibbling and external criticism began to wear on Corrigan. McKeown, who was more used to others' displeasure, tried to respond with consistent patience and reason. Over and over he explained the goal of developing nonviolent communities. He tried to show how the nonviolent protests and civil disobedience of the U.S. civil rights movement, a movement that had sought to provoke a government response, was different from Peace People's goal of building a community. Thus, instead of facing down fire hoses and dogs, withdrawal could be a better tactic, and a more healing and positive choice, than willingly accepting punishment. Still, the risks of assassination were discussed. McKeown, at least, believed they should act as though the threat did not exist, and if the worst did happen, mourning should be private, and the movement should continue without interruption.

Williams for her part seemed to react to critics by disdainfully shaking them off. But stress, tension, physical attacks—none of these could be avoided. And responding to the persistent and international media provided the three leaders with many opportunities for misspeaking or accidentally creating a misunderstanding. Very early then, controversy arose and charges were made that the women were deviously political, ridiculously naive, or self-aggrandizing.

Even while he was working in the background, McKeown published a pamphlet titled "The Price of Peace." This stimulated a Norwegian newspaper to create the Norwegian People's Peace Prize as an alternative to the Nobel Peace Prize. It was awarded almost at once to the Community of Peace People and, very importantly, it included some $340,000 in prize money, a bonanza for funding the work of the organization. The international media gave Peace People participants validation, but it also opened the leaders to charges of foreign influence. Corrigan's and Williams's accepting some of the many invitations from abroad to tell the story of Peace People soon led to complaints that they were celebrities on a joy ride—that they were mere "trippers."

A second Belfast march was planned to permit Protestants to join Catholics in marching to Catholic Falls Park, a Catholic stronghold, just as Catholics had earlier marched in a Protestant stronghold. In the pouring rain the marchers were greeted with a shower of rocks at the checkpoint, and when they got to the park, the gates were closed. Just outside the gates was a group of women who launched a physical attack on the marchers. A local Catholic pastor was wounded but continued to march as the women used their umbrellas as shields. Diverted to another park, Peace People had its usual service. This time the declaration was read by Anne Corrigan Maguire.

The Trafalgar Square rally in London attracted media from Canada, the United States, and much of Europe. Joan Baez came. The Women's Association of West Germany brought a declaration of support with six million signatures. A Norwegian delegation of 150 persons attended, and the next day Corrigan, Williams, and McKeown, who had emerged from the shadows, were to fly to Norway to receive the Norwegian People's Peace Prize. The program in the square was well organized and disciplined although the speakers were regularly interrupted by hecklers crying, "Troops out!" Some of the hecklers were IRA supporters; others were committed pacifists who believed *all* violence must cease, even that exercised by lawful authorities, including British troops. The rally speakers ignored the hecklers. Then Williams, the last speaker, took the microphone. She taunted them, and when one called out an obscenity, she flashed a Churchillian V for Victory sign that was broadcast around the world on TV. She electrified the crowd, although her stance was not exactly loving and conciliatory.

Drogheda, which was to be the site of the final march, is only twenty-five miles from Dublin. This demonstration would bring Catholics to the banks of the Boyne, and the symbolism of this meeting between the northern and southern delegations, which would take place at the center of a new Peace Bridge, created great excitement. McKeown was by now energetically advocating his vision of a transformed, nonviolent community. After the program he took a Catholic cardinal aside to complain that the church had not taken a moral position on the conflict, and that it had not renounced the concept of a *just war*, as surely it must in order to be true to the Christianity of the first four centuries. The doctrine of just war has, of course, been a part of church teaching since the doctrine was first formulated by St. Augustine more than 1,500 years ago. Again, McKeown's challenges to church authorities would create tension between the movement and Catholic officials.

Phase two of the movement began in January with the distribution of a model constitution for Peace People and a pamphlet titled "Strategy for Peace." The two documents were based on the assumption that local peace committees would make decisions for themselves, that they would continue to exist and to thrive, and that they would plan and make commitments for the long term. Both documents were prepared by McKeown. Unfortunately, McKeown also wrote at this time a widely circulated editorial that was critical not only of the Catholic hierarchy but also of Protestant leaders. He named names; he also noted that during the first Peace People's march, when bystanders began stoning the marchers, two Catholic clergy who were participating in the march had run and hidden while other marchers continued the demonstration.

Disputes within the community also began. One concerned the issue of representation. Up to this point Corrigan, Williams, and McKeown had made all the decisions. They were consultative by instinct, but the movement had now become immense, and its leaders' time was consumed in travel and media appearances. A system of some sort was badly needed. Finances were a second issue. Criticisms were leveled when Williams bought a secondhand Volvo, and Corrigan moved out of her family home into a rented apartment. But the most serious division came over McKeown's publications, especially the editorial criticizing Protestant and Catholic clergy. One early and important supporter, Tom Conaty, called for financial management and for working with existing organizations, including churches. Conaty also demanded a retraction from McKeown and a commitment to not criticize religious leaders in the future. His conditions were not met, and he left the movement.

Still another issue involved "informing." Peace People took the position that whether or not to inform was a matter for the individual conscience, and that in some circumstances, informing could be better than not informing. This condoning of "touts," or informers, angered the IRA especially. A Peace People statement arguing in support of the rule of law, and therefore of the various security forces, also cost them supporters.

According to McKeown's plan, after the series of marches had been completed, the movement was to shift its attention, first to the development of more than one hundred local peace committees, and second to an April constitutional convention. Meanwhile, Corrigan was directing her attention to a campaign in the schools to teach children the practice of nonviolence. This too created controversy and criticism. Another plan considered by Peace

People involved the creation of a nonviolent paramilitary to protect neighbor-hoods. Then there was controversy over an existing organization that helped people escape to other countries, thus helping them avoid the pressure to participate in paramilitary groups. Still other Peace People activities included publication of a newspaper, *Peace by Peace*, and a program that let children have a vacation away from the Troubles. Rather grand plans were even made to build a factory to create jobs, and there was discussion about the importance of aiding people in third-world countries where suffering was both more intensive and extensive than in Northern Ireland. These plans were impressive, but while the local committees fully embraced the cause of nonviolence in the streets, the careful development of an undefined new society was less captivating.

And opposition grew. Gerry Adams of Sinn Féin laid out the IRA's position in a pamphlet, "Peace in Ireland." On the other side ultraloyalists argued that one must be for or against the IRA, and that there was no room for a position that was merely against violence. When the loyalists launched a general strike, Peace People urged people to resist by going about their normal business.

In the spring of 1977, Peace People approved a constitution that called for an assembly, composed of two delegates from each committee, that would meet twice a year. In addition, an executive committee was to meet once a month, with a liaison committee composed of one representative from every local committee. The new executive committee of twenty-one included Corrigan, Williams, and McKeown, but no representatives from the churches. Several marches were planned, and more travel was scheduled. In the United States, Irish Americans were asked to stop sending money to the IRA provisionals, or the Provos. On a visit to the United States, the three movement leaders met with Senator Edward Kennedy, UN ambassador Andrew Young, and Martin Luther King Jr.

On May 31, a demilitarization campaign was launched. Paramilitaries were asked to turn in their weapons. They were given three months to do so, and after that Peace People were not obligated to shield paramilitaries from the authorities.

The first Peace People's assembly was held in October. The constitution that was adopted provided every local group with two votes, regardless of size. This led to a very unrepresentative organization, but even more serious problems would soon arise. The day after the assembly was over, the Norwegian Nobel Committee announced that Corrigan and Williams, but not McKeown, would receive the 1976 Nobel Peace Prize that had not been awarded the year before. The ensuing exhilaration was short-lived, however. Though the prize and its money had sometimes advanced a winner's agenda, this was not to be the case in 1977.

The Nobel and After

Betty Williams's Nobel lecture suggested that women's sense of reality needed to be given "pride of place over the vainglorious adventures that lead to war." She raged at the "insane and immoral imbalance of priorities" that allowed the Pentagon and the Kremlin to enjoy gargantuan military budgets. And she acknowledged that work was still to be done to "make the lives of the Northern Irish People as beautiful as our landscape is green." She concluded by reading the Declaration of Peace.

The Nobel Peace Prize had been awarded almost as soon as Peace People came into existence. This was in sharp contrast to the years of work that preceded the awarding of the prize to, for instance, Jane Addams and Emily Balch. Indeed, Williams noted that for the Peace People leaders, the measure would be not what they had done before receiving the prize, but what they did afterward. But all three leaders also declared their intention to step down from their leadership positions in Peace People as soon as possible. Theirs (and especially McKeown's) was a philosophical position; they were opposed to personality cults. They believed in organizing from the bottom up. Ironically though, during their first year of constant activity and growth, the trio had made virtually every organizational decision. They had worked in remarkable harmony, given their different backgrounds and personalities, but now that there were the resources and an opportunity to build rather than to act and react, the differences between them became more evident.

Reporters were quick to inquire into how the prize money would be used. Williams said it would go into the Peace People account. Corrigan joked that she would buy a fur coat. McKeown prepared an agreement about the precise distribution of the money, and communicated to the executive committee the women's agreement to use the money to advance Peace People programs. He was stunned, however, when he and the other two leaders met to finalize the wording of the agreement. Williams announced, "I've changed my mind. I have a wee project of my own which I want to back with my half." The women's positions were irreconcilable. A decision then to divide the money and let each woman use it according to her best judgment seemed to be the best solution, but it was also a decision that reinforced suspicions of personal aggrandizement. The movement was further weakened when McKeown then proposed, advocated, and won Williams's and Corrigan's agreement that all three would leave the executive committee within the year.

The reception for the Nobel Peace Prize winners in Northern Ireland was lukewarm. Yet support abroad, particularly in the United States, remained strong. Indeed, the Ford Foundation made a multiyear grant of over $100,000, including a salary for McKeown, who now had five children to support. He was invited to address the UN General Assembly, but again, instead of creating support for Peace People in Ulster, this honor was ignored. And even among those committed to disarmament, McKeown's call for disarmament was not unanimously approved, for he urged abandoning efforts to pressure govern- ments on behalf of piecemeal change. He believed the group's energies should be focused on creating local, small, exemplary "disarmed communities."

In the fall of 1978, two years after their organization's founding, Peace People's leadership stepped down. Finances were now in disarray, and loans made to its local groups were rarely paid back. McKeown continued to edit *Peace by Peace*, but produced articles that the new leadership believed were detrimental to the community. An especially difficult issue was the status of prisoners who had once been considered political. Their status had now been changed to criminal. McKeown urged an emergency status for all arrested under the emergency laws, and believed strongly that without such a resolution of the prisoner issue, the whole movement and the shaky peace would fall apart. He told people so, and he also told the organization's U.S. funders. He continued to hold a position that was responsible for disbursing funds, but conflict, and accusations that he was an autocrat, increased. By spring 1979, the organization's 100 local groups had shrunk to 30, and its membership from 100,000 to 500.

McKeown then proposed that the three founders separately begin an educa- tion and noncooperation program related to the prisoner status issue. Williams chose not to participate; the distance between her and McKeown increased. It increased further when the IRA killed twenty-two people including Lord Mountbatten. Williams publicly denounced the responsible Provos, while McKeown believed a refusal to address the prisoner status issue came close to support for Ian Paisley, who staunchly opposed the cause of Irish nationalism. When Williams announced she would run again for the executive commit- tee with the new chair, Peter McLachlan, McKeown asked Corrigan to run with him, and all four were elected. After a difficult debate, McLachlan was again chosen chair. Conflict over a variety of issues, including finances and the prisoner status issue, continued.

At a February 1980 executive meeting, McKeown threw down the gauntlet: either Williams and McLachlan should resign, or he would do so. Williams stood up, announced her resignation, and left; McLachlan was then voted out by seven votes, four of which were for the removal of all four of the major players. Corrigan became the new committee chair.

By 1980 the movement had, indeed, become local. McKeown could not find work as a journalist, and he trained as a typesetter. Williams became estranged from the Peace People community. She and her husband, Ralph, who had worked hard for the community in its early days, divorced. In 1982 she remarried and moved to the United States. Corrigan, who married her sister's widower, Jackie Maguire, began a family with him but remained with the community and continues to work with it and other organizations devoted to nonviolence.

A Peacemaker's Work Is Never Done

More than twenty years after Williams and Corrigan won their Nobel Peace Prize, the 1998 Good Friday Agreement was signed, and a second Nobel Peace Prize was awarded to two citizens of Northern Ireland. This time the prize went to two men: John Hume and David Trimble, the leaders of the two opposing political parties that finally agreed to settle their differences. The settlement, brokered by an American, George Mitchell, called for an elected Northern Irish Assembly based on proportional representation with a twelve-member, power-sharing executive. It also created a consultative North/South Ministerial Council answerable to the two Irish parliaments, which was to work for cross-border cooperation in several specified areas. It created a British-Irish Intergovernmental Conference between North and South, and a British-Irish Council as well. Amendment of the provocative Articles 2 and 3 of the Irish Republic's constitution was also promised.

But once again, hopes for a sustained peace were dashed. By 2002 the government had collapsed and Westminster was again governing Northern Ireland. In 2004 Protestant marches continued; so did violent Catholic responses. In May 2005, Nobelist David Trimble resigned as head of his (moderate) Ulster Unionist Party when it was soundly defeated by the hard-line Democratic Unionist Party led by Ian Paisley. Still, in July the IRA formally renounced the use of violence and began to dismantle its formidable arsenal.

Today library shelves contain many scholarly books tracing the Irish peace process. They are lengthy and detailed. They go back to the seventeenth century. Many of them do not mention Williams, Corrigan, McKeown, or the Community of Peace People at all. Some give their movement a paragraph; one gives it a page. The broad and instant support for Peace People clearly demonstrated the community's desire for an end to killing, and the number of killings did decrease after the marches. However, a simple call to end violence can involve only what some describe as *negative peace*. They would say that without *positive peace*, a peace based on justice, conflict will recur. Corrigan, Williams, and McKeown stumbled once they began to think about how to achieve positive peace. So have the most sophisticated, experienced, and powerful politicians and diplomats among us.

Mother Teresa. Courtesy of the Norwegian Nobel Institute

CHAPTER FIVE

Mother Teresa: From Macedonia to India

A "Blessed" Prize Winner

Agnes Gonxha Bojaxhiu was born in 1910 in the city of Skopje, which is today the capital of Macedonia, a small state that was until recently a part of Yugoslavia. At the time of her birth, though, it was a part of the Ottoman Empire. Bojaxhiu's culture and language were Albanian, but while most of her fellow Albanians practiced Islam, and most of the inhabitants of Skopje were Orthodox Christian, she and her family were Roman Catholic. This made them a minority both within their ethnic community and within the community in which they lived.

She came from a part of the world, the Balkans, that saw little peace and many atrocities during the first half of the twentieth century. But the situation in her homeland was of little interest to her. In fact, she left her country at age eighteen and later relinquished her citizenship. Also, one might not expect Bojaxhiu, as a member of a minority, to have had much influence in her home community, and she did not. But for decades she did exercise influence in India, a large and complex Asian country, where her religion was practiced by an even smaller portion of the population than among Albanians. Further, while many observers saw her work for peace as caregiving, or service, she understood it quite differently. To Bojaxhiu, her work was religious, and her church has agreed. She has recently been beatified, a step in the process of being acknowledged a saint. A sketch of Bojaxhiu's political and religious environment will help to illuminate the story of her life.

As the more than four-hundred-year-old Ottoman Empire crumbled, different ethnic groups sought their independence. The Albanians first turned to arms in 1910, the year of Bojaxhiu's birth. In 1912 they declared and won their independence. Although the diplomats who set the boundaries of the new nation gave Albania the Adriatic coastline, thus blocking Serbia's access to the sea, the homeland of Bojaxhiu's parents, Kosovo, with its mostly Albanian population, was not included in the new nation, nor was the Bojaxhiu's home, Skopje. Although after World War I and as recently as the 1990s nationalists fought for Kosovo's union with Albania, Kosovo remains a part of the former Yugoslavia. And although Bojaxhiu's father did not live in either Albania or Kosovo, he was a politically active Albanian nationalist, giving money, joining organizations, and making public statements on behalf of Albanian unity. He was not Muslim.

Albania's story includes occupation during World War I, a brief postwar experience as a republic and then as a kingdom, invasion by Italy in 1939, and forty years of harsh rule by communist Enver Hoxha beginning in 1944. Hoxha shifted his sponsor from communist Yugoslavia to the Soviet Union, then to China, and then split even with China, making Albania the most isolated and least developed country in Europe. Agnes Bojaxhiu's father died in 1919. Her only brother, Lazar, became a military officer under Albania's monarch and later went into exile in Italy. During the 1930s, her mother and only sister moved to Albania where they were permanently cut off from Agnes. Even after she had become an international figure, Mother Teresa was not allowed into Albania to visit her mother and sister, nor were they allowed out.

The Bojaxhiu family's parish priest was a Croatian Jesuit. The Jesuits, or the Society of Jesus, have long been a missionary society, but Popes Pius X and Pius XI lent special support to missionary work, and a number of young priests from the Balkans left to work in Calcutta during Agnes's early teens. She and others in her parish youth group heard the missionaries' stories both from letters and from priests on visits home. Bojaxhiu had, then, an early exposure to the importance and value of missionary work and also a link to Calcutta. The Catholic Church went through a period of reform under Pope John XXIII, but the liberal changes of the Second Vatican Council (Vatican II, 1962–1965) had little effect on the work Mother Teresa was then doing in India. Popes Paul VI and John Paul II who succeeded John XXIII were more conservative. To some Catholics, their insistence on the continued barring of women from the priesthood, celibacy for priests, and abstinence from artificial birth control were unrealistic. They were not unrealistic to Mother Teresa, however. Her Catholicism remained that of her girlhood—pre–Vatican II.

Following Tradition

The Bojaxhiu family lived a comfortable, middle-class life in Skopje where Agnes's father was a merchant and contractor. He was multilingual, traveled regularly on business, and served on the town council. He died when Agnes was eight or nine. Some believed he was poisoned because of his Albanian nationalist activities. As a result of his death, the family's fortunes were diminished, and Agnes's mother, Drana, became the chief support of a family of four. Drana worked as a seamstress, did embroidery, and ultimately developed a small textile business.

Drana was devout. She demonstrated this through regular worship. This included daily attendance at church and daily, family prayer at home. She also shared her life and goods—both as the wife of a prosperous businessman and later as a far less prosperous widow. She attended the dying; she visited the old; she cared for the sick; she fed the poor even at the family table. While setting an example of love in action for her children, Drana also taught that these services and kindnesses were not for show; they were to be done unobtrusively. "When you do good," she instructed them, "do it quietly, as if you were throwing a stone into the sea."[1]

Agnes followed in her mother's footsteps, accepting the traditional role her mother played in the family and in the community. Often she accompanied her mother on her errands of mercy and enthusiastically participated in church activities. She sang in the parish choir, sometimes as a soprano soloist; she made regular pilgrimages to the chapel of Our Lady of the Black Mountain near Skopje; she participated in the Sodality of Children of Mary, a Christian organization for girls. The sodality was a society founded in 1563 and organized worldwide. The parish priest who led it challenged its members with three questions: "What have I done for Christ? What am I doing for Christ? What will I do for Christ?" That priest was Father Franjo Jambreković, whom Agnes often served as a translator, and who would serve her as a counselor when she began to consider her adult future. Agnes regularly attended Mass and taught religious classes for small children. Her brother once said that his mother and Agnes seemed to live at the church.

Agnes's first four years of schooling were in a church school where teaching was in Albanian. Later she and her siblings attended the state school where the teaching was in Serbo-Croatian. Some of her youthful interests included playing the mandolin, writing poetry, and publishing short articles.

Mother Teresa has said that she first knew that she was to lead a religious life at the age of twelve. Still, she spent much of her teens contemplating the meaning of a vocation and wondering how she could be certain that she had been called. She was told by Father Jambreković that the way to know if she had a vocation was whether or not she felt joy in contemplating it. In later life she remembered his saying: "Joy that comes from the depths of your being is like a compass by which you can tell what direction your life should follow. That is the case even when the road you must take is a difficult one."[2] By eighteen, Agnes was ready to make her declaration. Her wish was to become a nun. More specifically, she wished to join the Loreto Sisters (a common name for the Institute of the Blessed Virgin Mary) because that Irish teaching order worked in Calcutta and had been doing so since the 1840s. At first her mother refused to give her permission. When Drana did finally give it, she said that the choice was one that meant Agnes's life would now become "only, all for God."

In September 1928 Agnes's brother left to join King Zog's Albanian army, and after a farewell concert in her honor, Agnes, her sister, and her mother left for Zagreb. There they met Betika Kajnc, and Agnes and Betika bid their families goodbye. The two young women boarded a train for Paris, venturing into a whole new world—one in which they literally did not speak the language, and one that would shortly bring the two of them to a religious life in far-off India.

In Paris they were interviewed for membership in the order by the sister in charge of the Loreto Sisters there. Having won approval, they then traveled to Rathfarnham, Dublin, where the Loreto Abbey that trained sisters for service in India was located. Their training in Dublin was brief and focused almost exclusively on learning English because their training to come would be conducted in English. Within six weeks the two young women had embarked on a weeks-long voyage to India. Agnes would not leave India for more than thirty years.

Intermediate stops in Colombo and Madras introduced Agnes to the new culture in which she would live, and to poverty she could not have imagined. Steamy days, half-clad men and women, men pulling rickshaws, people living in the open air, crowded streets, a corpse by the side of the road—all these were part of her initial impressions.

After a brief stay in Calcutta, the two young women were sent to Darjeeling some 450 miles to the north, where they were to receive two years of training as novitiates. In sight of the Himalayas and at an altitude of 7,000 feet, Darjeeling enjoyed a mild climate and attracted many Europeans, especially during the summer. Because the Loreto Sisters was a teaching order, novices were prepared not only in religious subjects, but also in the subject they would teach. Agnes studied geography. She also had to learn English, Hindi, and Bengali. The young women wore traditional black habits and were cloistered during their two years of study. In 1931 Agnes was accepted into the order and took her first vows. They were the traditional vows of poverty, chastity, and obedience. By then she had formally taken the name, Teresa. This was not in honor of St. Teresa of Avila, an intellectual and the first woman doctor of the church. Rather, it was to celebrate the life of St. Thérèse Martin, whom the Pope had recently proclaimed a patron of the missions of the world.

After taking her vows, Sister Teresa taught in a convent school in Darjeeling for a short period. She also helped in a medical clinic where she witnessed physical suffering firsthand. Then she was sent to Loreto Entally, Calcutta, one of the six schools run by the Loreto Sisters in that city. Actually, there were two schools within the Entally compound. One was a boarding school where the sisters taught in English and where most of the five hundred students came from families able to pay the school's fees. The second school was St. Mary's High School, which was run by an affiliated order of Bengali women, the Daughters of Saint Anne. There the students were poorer and the teaching was in Bengali. The sisters teaching in this school wore saris, white in summer, and blue in winter. Sister Teresa taught in St. Mary's High School, and also at an elementary school outside the walls of Entally that served the most needy children and was conducted in humble surroundings with few resources.

Her teaching and influence were not confined to the classroom. She also worked with the girls in Entally's Sodality of Mary and encouraged them to visit the nearby hospital and slums even though she could not accompany them because of the order's rule of enclosure. One of her favorite texts was the story of the Good Samaritan (Luke 10:30–37), which commends those who give immediate help to those in need. Sister Teresa's description of the importance of such help was based on the "joy" it created both for the recipient and for the one who rendered assistance. Again, her emphasis was not on any benefit that resulted but on the joy experienced.

Sister Teresa's work as a teaching sister conformed to her order's expectations and practices. She was not remembered as exceptional except, perhaps, in her devotion and discipline. Her teaching was interrupted only by the annual retreat held in Darjeeling. After six years she took her final vows and became a professed nun in 1937. Her life continued unchanged, and it was lived in a most traditional way. She rose before dawn for individual prayer and study. Mass was then celebrated with the community. Every morning in the sacrament of the Eucharist, bread and wine were transformed into the body and blood of Christ, and sins were forgiven. Classes followed breakfast and were conducted in both the morning and afternoon; boarding-school students were supervised until their bedtime. A second service, Vespers and Benediction, was held every evening. There was little privacy and few amenities, for poverty did not mean just a lack of personal possessions. It also meant not using material things for the purpose of pleasure. Life was simple. Also, while it was possible for a nun to be given permission to leave the compound, she could do so only for a good reason, and in company. Thus, the sisters' isolation was not complete, but they were quite sheltered.

Sister Teresa was made sister in charge of the Bengali sisters' order, the Daughters of Saint Anne, just as life outside the convent became gravely troubled. Gandhi was leading his nationwide nonviolent campaign for independence, and at the same time England had declared war against Germany, Japan, and Italy on behalf of India. The Japanese presence in nearby Burma led to Bengal's being placed on a wartime footing. Entally and its schools were taken over for military use. Transportation was commandeered by the military, and the channels for food distribution were disrupted. Unfortunately, this occurred during a period of poor harvests and flooding. The result was the Bengal Famine of 1943, which reduced Calcutta to disorder and destitution. The famine claimed more than 2 million lives—a tragedy almost beyond comprehension.

Further, only three years later the city suffered four days of rioting between Muslims and Hindus, an outbreak called the Great Killing. Perhaps five thousand were slain and another fifteen thousand injured. The city came to a standstill. At one point during the rioting, Headmistress Sister Teresa left the convent to search for food for her three hundred students. She came face-to-face with death and destruction. Bodies lay in the gutter; the ruins of shops burned with their owners inside lined the streets; vultures hovered; smoke rose from burning funeral pyres. The suffering was immeasurable. About the same time Sister Teresa's health appeared to fail. She was ordered to take daily rests and, finally, to go to Darjeeling for recuperation. During the train ride from Calcutta, Sister Teresa received what she later described as a "call within a call." Her first call had come at age eighteen and it was to become a nun. The second call came at age thirty-six and it was to leave the Loreto convent and schools in order to work with the poor, the despised, and the forsaken by living among and like them. She experienced the call as a command because she was directed to abandon almost two decades of work as a teaching sister and to begin something wholly new. September 10, 1946, was the day she received this call, and this day is now celebrated as Inspiration Day by members of the order she would found. But first there was the matter of receiving permission to undertake her new mission. She was, after all, still bound by her vow of obedience.

The Missionaries of Charity

Sister Teresa had again embarked on the unknown. She knew only that she must leave her convent to work directly with the poor and, most importantly, to live among them. This required release from the vows she had taken as a Loreto Sister. A request was made to the Archbishop of Calcutta. He ruled that no action should be taken for a year. Then when he did give her permission to ask the Mother General of Loreto to release her, he insisted that she ask to return to lay status. Sister Teresa wanted to remain a nun; she wished to be released from enclosure but not from her religious status. The mother general gave Sister Teresa permission to request an indult of exclaustration (release from enclosure) from Rome, but the archbishop overruled this permission, insisting that Sister Teresa request secularization. She did so. Four months later she had more than her wish. She was given a year to practice her new mission, *and* she could remain a nun. It was never clear why she was given exclaustration when she had obeyed and as directed had requested secularization. Sister Teresa immediately exchanged her habit and shoes for a sari and sandals and went to a medical mission to learn something about the care that could be offered—and the importance of hygiene, rest, and nutrition if she was to work in the streets. She next spent some time with the Little Sisters of the Poor, an order that cared for the destitute but in an institutional setting. These sisters had not only taken a vow of poverty, they were committed to being wholly dependent on providence; that is, they made themselves completely dependent on continuous donations. They did not have any regular income, any savings, any endowment. They were both poor and dependent. This principle of precariousness would be central to Sister Teresa's order as well. She too would come to depend on people's continuous willingness to "do something beautiful for God."

On December 21, 1948, she packed a lunch and walked to the slum where her former students had worked. She sat down and began teaching "right on the ground." Her work began without resources, without companions, without a plan. She expected providence not only to provide but to guide.

She was given the use of a room in a house; she accepted Indian citizenship; two of her former students came to join her. By the end of the year, almost a dozen women were living together and participating in the work on the streets. The archbishop then agreed to seek formal recognition of the group as a congregation. This required a constitution and its approval by Rome.

Sister Teresa prepared the constitution, drawing heavily on that of the Loreto Sisters. The new order was to be called the Missionaries of Charity. She was to be Mother Teresa. To the vows of poverty, chastity, and obedience was added a vow "to give wholehearted and free service to the poorest of the poor." Although not a cloistered one, the sisters' regime was strictly defined, and in the years to come sisters of the order all over the world would follow a schedule almost identical to it. The sisters were to live together. They would rise at 4:40 a.m., and after individual prayers they would hear Mass and a sermon at 5:45 a.m. After breakfast and chores, they would work in different locations from 8:00 a.m. to 12:30. After lunch in their collective home and a brief unscheduled period and tea, the Adoration of the Blessed Sacrament would be celebrated from 3:15 to 4:30. Work with the poor was then resumed until 7:30. Supper, recreation, and prayers completed the day, which ended at 9:45.

The commitment of the Missionaries of Charity to "the poorest of the poor, the abandoned, the sick, the infirm, the leprosy patients, the dying, the desperate, the lost, the outcasts" is well-known. Equally important though is their commitment to their community of sisters, an intensely religious community, for as the constitution says: "We are to love each other with an intense love like Jesus loved to the very limit of love on the cross, without being concerned at all about nationality or social standing. Now that we belong to the Society this must be our true home and family."[3] Pope Pius XII granted recognition to the order in 1950, and Mother Teresa began to accept young women as novitiates the next year. The first ten were her former students. All were Indian. All were enjoined to be "cheerful."

The need in Calcutta was great, but Mother Teresa's small group of missionaries was not troubled by the impossibility of giving help to all who suffered. This was because they did not aspire to end poverty or to create a newly healthy population. Their task was simple. It was each day to offer succor to the individuals they encountered. By doing so they were rendering love to Jesus, for they perceived each suffering human as "Jesus in his distressing disguise." Their care was personal, simple, and immediate. The sisters went out in pairs each morning and afternoon to serve the poor, but they returned to their home for meals, for prayer, and to sleep. Thus they did not, for instance, engage in the kind of nursing that required continuous attendance or long-term activities. They did not invest in expensive facilities. Their service was simply a daily expression of their religion, like prayer and the celebration of the Mass.

The order's first undertaking was the creation of free schools for the children of the poor. The schools were created in the children's immediate neighborhood. The first school met under a tree; its only facilities were the chair Mother Teresa sat on. This was familiar work, and it would be greatly assisted by a government policy of erecting a school building once a school had one hundred regular students. Also, once schools were established, other governments and organizations made contributions. Within ten years the Missionaries of Charity had founded fourteen schools. The fifteenth was opened in the city's slaughterhouse area, and it was meant specifically to serve the children of lepers. It opened within a week of the time that the order had decided a school was needed. Eighty-five children appeared on the first day, many of them bearing signs of the disease.

The order's second undertaking was to provide a place for people to die in peace. The impulse behind this work was said to be Mother Teresa's finding a woman dying on the street with rats and cockroaches eating her feet and then finding that no hospital would admit her.[4] Mother Teresa quickly persuaded the Calcutta government to provide a building, an abandoned hostel near the temple of Kali. She raised the funds to equip it and successfully fought off efforts to remove her hospice because the area was sacred to Hinduism. She dedicated her home for the dying with the name Nirmal Hriday, or "Pure Heart."

Mother Teresa had agreed not to bring lepers to Nirmal Hriday, but she saw relief of their suffering as part of her call. Thus the sisters obtained a mobile clinic that brought medical attention to lepers at a series of stations. This was an extraordinary act of outreach, for lepers in Calcutta were otherwise isolated, shunned, and even feared. Later she would build a permanent dispensary for lepers, and the order's mobile clinics would continue to deliver medical care to poor neighborhoods, both Muslim and Hindu.

Finally, homes were created for orphans and for those who were destitute. But as I noted above, the Missionaries of Charity did not see their role as one of creating and staffing substantial institutions. The purpose of their order was to give care in the place that it was needed and not behind walls. Their work was in the streets, and not surprisingly, their own lives were exceedingly modest. Their poverty meant that each sister had only three saris, a spoon, a plate, an umbrella, a cross, a rosary, a bucket (for washing), and a water bottle. Although the order accepted gifts and goods to be given to or used for the poor, individual sisters accepted nothing for themselves, not even a pastry or a cup of tea. In social settings, the only thing they accepted was a glass of water—something even the poorest of the poor could offer.

For the first ten years, Mother Teresa's work was confined to Calcutta although she harbored a desire to branch out into other parts of India and was urged to do so by the young women who entered her order—young women who saw a need for the Missionaries of Charity in the areas from which they came. In 1959 the first mission house outside Calcutta was established in Ranchi, and the order rapidly expanded throughout India. The breadth of the order's work was made possible by donations from governments and agencies, by the work of numerous volunteers, and through the help of an associated group of brothers and a mostly lay group called the Co-Workers of Mother Teresa.

The Missionary Brothers of Charity was established in 1963 under the leadership of an Australian Jesuit. By church law, men could not be led by a woman, so the brothers had a separate organizatfon and constitution even though they worked in harmony with the sisters. Like the sisters they began their work with children but soon moved into parallel organizations that worked with the dying and with lepers. They also expanded their work throughout India and overseas into cities such as Saigon, Phnom Penh, and Los Angeles.

The Co-Workers were a group that began in Calcutta in 1954 when Ann Blaikie, the wife of a British businessman, went to see just what Mother Teresa and her order were doing. Blaikie and some of her friends then began working with Mother Teresa, especially in her work with lepers. Others soon joined in and contributed to a whole range of volunteer work. The volunteers included men and women, foreigners and Indians, Catholics and non-Catholics, the secular and the nonsecular. Not until 1969 did this volunteer auxiliary become a formal, papally recognized institution. Under its constitution, the organization was titled International Link, and Blaikie led it. This loosely structured organization was regularly directed *not* to raise funds for the sisters, although that was an important early function. Members were expected to pray two specific prayers each day, and at their meetings only water could be served. Simplicity in dress was prescribed. Co-Workers members also were reminded that "gifts of mind and body, advantages of birth and education—are the free gifts of God, and....No one has the right to a superfluity of wealth while others are dying of starvation and suffering from any kind of want." Voluntary poverty was expected. Another organized group, the Sick and Suffering, linked individuals with particular Missionaries of Charity, permitting them to offer their suffering as redemptive. The efforts of Co-Workers were instrumental in supporting the globalization of the missionaries, but in 1993 Mother Teresa suddenly and with little explanation closed down the organization, saying that Co-Workers should continue its work privately but without an administration, a newsletter, or bank accounts. Mother Teresa was anxious to preserve the sisters' mission of immediate and direct aid. She wished to avoid a complex and systematic administration that would divert its participants from focusing on the performance of acts of charity.

In 1960 at age fifty, Mother Teresa, who had not left India in over thirty years, received an invitation from Catholic Relief Services to attend the meeting of the National Council of Catholic Women. The meeting was to be held in Las Vegas, Nevada. This event would introduce Mother Teresa to yet another new world and would introduce that world to her and the work of her order. On this first trip abroad, she also visited Peoria, Illinois, because Catholic women there had been regularly sending funds to Calcutta. She then went on to Chicago, Washington, D.C., and to New York City where she visited the United Nations and met Dorothy Day. She visited London, Frankfurt, Aachen, and Munich, and she made visits to Dachau, Geneva, and Rome.

In Rome she made formal application for recognition of the Missionaries of Charity as a society of pontifical right. This would mean that the order would be responsible not to Calcutta but to Rome, and most importantly, that it would be allowed to take its work to other countries. While in Rome, Mother Teresa heard a Mass by Pope John XXIII and was blessed by him, but her business was conducted with the Sacred Congregation for the Propagation of the Faith. The work of the Missionaries of Charity, and its sisters' training, vows, and prayer book were carefully examined by the Sacred Congregation. The application for recognition was approved five years later. It was 1965, and a new and international era was about to begin.

European missionaries had traveled to India for centuries. Now Indian missionaries would travel west—and they would bear the tidings not of the religions of India, but the tidings of one of the West's own religions, Catholicism. Why this desire to expand beyond Calcutta and beyond India? The order's work was religious, its purpose was to testify, and that testimony was clearest and most dramatic when it was responding to the needs of the poorest. Because every community harbors the very poor, here was an opportunity to spread God's word far and wide, and that is what missionaries do. They teach, and in the case of Mother Teresa's order, that teaching is through acts of charity.

The Poor, Chaste, Obedient, International Celebrity

Mother Teresa's first expansion was to Venezuela. Here the mostly Indian sisters had to learn a new language and culture, and they faced different problems. These included a lack of family structure, and unconsecrated marriages. Also there was a shortage of priests, and the sisters found themselves conducting much of the church service and were even given permission to administer communion, although this was ordinarily forbidden. Undaunted, in the next five years the Missionaries of Charity established themselves in Australia, in Europe, in the Middle East, and in Africa. By 1970 there would be sixty centers in Calcutta and thirty in other parts of India. By the next year there would be a center in New York City. The sisters would then be on every continent except Antarctica.

Mother Teresa personally selected the sites for the work of her sisters. And she tried to stay in touch with each group, some of which were as small as half a dozen nuns. This meant that she was committed to extensive travel just to meet the needs of her order. And she was soon inundated with invitations to speak from all over the globe—invitations that would give her an opportunity to tell large and important audiences of the joy experienced in acting with compassion. These audiences were also likely to act providentially, that is, to make donations to the order's work. Thus, Mother Teresa's travels began to include both ministries to her nuns and a wide variety of public appearances.

The international media was enthralled by Mother Teresa's story. In 1968 the BBC's Malcolm Muggeridge did an interview with her. It was an unexpected hit. Even more unexpectedly, Mother Teresa was a hit with Muggeridge. He interviewed her a second time, produced a documentary about her, wrote a widely read book about her, and later, having publicly stated many times that he was opposed to organized religion, converted to Catholicism. Robert McNamara, former U.S. secretary of defense and then president of the World Bank, was another admirer. With many and important voices calling her, Mother Teresa chose to take to the podium, but she did not break her fourth vow, and when she could, she continued to directly serve "the poorest of the poor."

She began to accept awards. She won India's Padma Shri Award, and the Magsaysay Award for International Understanding from the Philippines in 1962. In 1971 she won the John XXIII Peace Prize awarded by Pope Paul VI, and in 1973 she won the Templeton Prize for Progress in Religion in a decision made by nine judges, four of them non-Christian. Her acceptance speech, though, was unrelentingly Christian.

In 1975, the twenty-fifth anniversary of the founding of the Missionaries of Charity was marked by a remarkable series of ceremonies in India and throughout the world. In Calcutta, eighteen different religious communities participated. This occurred in a country that had been split by religious riots into two countries, India and Pakistan (which had in turn split into Pakistan and Bangladesh). Jains, Moslems, Zoroastrians, and Hindus all participated in the sisters' anniversary and thanksgiving ceremonies. In an ironic way, the world media had begun to make Mother Teresa, who unhesitatingly worked with India's untouchables, into a different kind of untouchable. Because she was, or at least was described as God's "pencil," to criticize her was, for some, to criticize God himself. The media was almost adoring.

Pakistan's civil war gave birth to Bangladesh. It also resulted in a horrific number of raped Muslim women, to whom Mother Teresa offered her assistance. She promised to find homes for any unwanted children. But abortion was wrong, she asserted, no matter what the circumstances. For perhaps the first time in her public career, Mother Teresa was publicly criticized, in this case by feminist Germaine Greer.

The Nobel Peace Prize is awarded by the government of Norway. The winner is chosen by a committee appointed by the Norwegian legislature. Its deliberations are private, and the records of those deliberations are not opened until fifty years have passed. Because professors of political science, law, history, and philosophy are among those qualified to make nominations, there are a lot of eligible nominators, and they are not bound by any norm or requirement of secrecy. Indeed, some have launched what can only be called "campaigns" on behalf of particular individuals, campaigns that may extend over a number of years. Muggeridge launched just such a campaign on behalf of Mother Teresa. She was nominated as early as 1972, but in 1975 a campaign team was put together that included Robert McNamara; U.S. Senators Edward Kennedy, Pete Domenici, Hubert Humphrey, and Mark Hatfield; Canadian Maurice Strong, a former director of the UN Environmental Program; and British MP Shirley Williams. Letters were solicited from Catholic and relief organizations, and the publicity that attended the campaign led to many unsolicited letters. She did not win. Nor did she win in 1977, when Lady Barbara Ward and McNamara tried again. Mother Teresa laughed: "It will come only when Jesus thinks it is time. We have all calculated to build two hundred houses for lepers if it comes—so our people will have to do the praying." A fourth nomination in 1979 was successful.

At the December award ceremony, the Norwegian Nobel Committee chair noted that the year had been one of conflict, of extremes of inhumanity and cruelty, and of fanaticism and cynicism, and that the committee had chosen Mother Teresa because she embodied the words of a previous winner, Fridtjof Nansen, who worked with displaced persons after World War II: "Love of one's neighbor is realistic policy."

By tradition the winner gives a lecture the day after the award ceremony. Mother Teresa, who always spoke extemporaneously, began with a prayer and an extended discussion of the love of Jesus, who makes himself "the hungry one—the naked one—the homeless one—the sick one—the one in prison—the lonely one—the unwanted one" so that by loving these, one loves Jesus himself. She lamented the isolation of the old and the young's use of drugs, and then began a passionate denunciation of abortion, which she described as "the greatest destroyer of peace today . . . because it is a direct war, a direct killing, a direct murder by the mother herself." She went on to extol the virtues of adoption and of the rhythm method of birth control by saying that in Calcutta in the last six years, 61,000 fewer babies had been born because couples were using that method. She concluded by admonishing her audience to smile because even when it is difficult to smile, one must do so for it is the beginning of joy.

Although she claimed not to be political or to mix in politics, Mother Teresa knew and won the support of politicians from all over the world. They visited her in Calcutta and invited her to their countries. Pope John Paul II urged her to use the platform given to her, and for the last twenty years of her life she was a world public figure. To Mother Teresa, her stand against abortion and artificial birth control may have been only a moral— and indeed the only moral—position, but it was also a hot political issue in the many countries—including India, Japan, and the United States— where she spoke publicly about the issue, saying that "the image of God is on that unborn child." After winning the Nobel Peace Prize, she also turned more frequently to peace as a subject of her talks. In Northern Ireland she called for love and peace before a crowd that included both Protestants and Catholics. In Nagasaki she spoke against nuclear weapons. Amid shelling and bombing in Beirut she said, "Nations put too much effort and money into defending their borders. If they could only defend defenseless people with food, shelter, and clothing, I think the world would be a happier place."

Her consistent message was of the need for the protection of all human life and the relief of suffering. Her admonition to each was "You are unique, irreplaceable, and beloved." For Mother Teresa, poverty was not something that could be intellectualized. One did not come to understand it "by reading, talking, walking in the slums . . . to discover what it has of bad and good. We have to dive into it, live it, share it." Her prescription for peace was prayer, love, and compassion, not armies and arms. She could not "understand" the concept of a "just war."

She became a presence at many of the world's crises or catastrophes. After the poisonous gas leak in Bhopal, India, that killed thousands and permanently injured many more, she flew there with her New Testament message: "Forgive, forgive." In New York she opened a hospice for AIDS patients, calling it "the new leprosy of the West." She visited Ethiopia during the famine of 1985; she visited Chernobyl after its nuclear disaster; she sent nuns to work in Moscow after the Armenian earthquake. She found British prime minister Margaret Thatcher a tough sell, though, and after seeing people sleeping in cardboard "coffins" on London streets, Mother Teresa remarked, "I find poverty in a rich country more difficult to remove than poverty in a poor country." Prime ministers Thatcher and Indira Gandhi were quite happy to be associated with Mother Teresa, although both launched wars on lesser nations: Argentina and

Mother Teresa at the opening of the Muslim Bectashian Center in Tirana, Albania, 1991. Courtesy of SOVFOTO/EASTFOTO

Goa, respectively. Gandhi also supported very active birth-control programs— for women and for men—some of which bordered on coercion.

In 1994 British television broadcast *Hell's Angel,* a program presented by Christopher Hitchens. In the program Hitchens was highly critical of Mother Teresa who, he said, "has an easy way with thrones, dominions, and powers," and who, according to Hitchens, had spent millions on convents rather than on hospitals. His words, which described her as "a demagogue, an obscurationist and a servant of earthly power," were harsh. And they seemed to give permission to speak to other critics, who reported on the sisters' failure, for example, to provide the best medical care available, to separate active tuberculosis patients from other patients, to provide children with books other than religious tracts, or to provide training and long-term planning for their sisters and their missions. A Bengali doctor living in London argued that Mother Teresa's work in Calcutta was far less important than it had been described, and that other organizations and individuals were actually doing more than she in assisting the poor. Indeed, since the beginning of the 1980s, both government and private, domestic and foreign organizations working in the fields of education, health, and agriculture had proliferated in Bengal. Further, service organizations had begun to try to empower the needy and to transform their situation rather than to simply succor, or sustain. *Efficacy* rather than *joy* was their watchword.

In 1990 at age eighty, Mother Teresa offered to relinquish her leadership, but the sisters were unable to agree on a successor, and she retained her position almost until her death in 1997. Sister Nirmala, an Indian sister who had founded the first Missionaries of Charity home outside India (in Venezuela) and who was important to the founding of the contemplative branch of the order, succeeded her. At the time of Mother Teresa's death, the order had 456 houses in some 101 countries. By 2003 there were almost 4,700 sisters and novices in 710 houses in 132 countries.

Peace and Sainthood

Mother Teresa is being fast-tracked for sainthood. Pope John Paul II waived the usual waiting period, and she has already been beatified. This means that she has been judged of overwhelming virtue, that recognition of her holiness has been sustained since her death, and that after her death she has interceded with a miracle, in this case, the curing of a Hindu woman's cancer. Confirmation of a second miracle is likely to lead to a declaration of sainthood.

The choice of Mother Teresa for a Nobel Peace Prize is so unlike that of the Norwegian Nobel Committee's other choices that a review of her life and purpose is in order. She was born and came to young adulthood in an overlooked corner of Europe. She was raised by an intensely religious mother who prayed several times a day and performed regular acts of charity. Her world was a narrow one, but with the certainty that she had been called by God, she embarked into the unknown without apparent hesitation or doubt—first to leave home and join the Loreto Sisters, then to travel to India, then to work on the streets of Calcutta instead of behind the walls of a convent, and finally, to broaden her mission by bringing God's presence to every corner of the globe.

In many ways she was ordinary and unsophisticated. Her religious practices and theology remained those she had been taught in her youth. As a religious, she fulfilled the feminine roles of teaching and care and understood that she and her sisters were the "spouse of Christ crucified." She sought no expanded role for women within the church or in society. She had been trained in geography, which may have enlarged her vision and her potential for carrying her mission abroad, but she did not emphasize higher education. She encouraged at least one young woman to abandon secondary schooling to join her in her work. She did not seek university-trained sisters, and believed that there was no need to have more education than those one served. The order's homes not only lacked curtains, they did not have TV or newspapers—even in countries where such things would be present in the homes of the poor. Also, since so many of her sisters came from poor, often peasant homes in India, when these sisters went abroad, for instance to London, they were likely to be less educated than those they were to serve.

Mother Teresa was consistently obedient to her church superiors, and once she became the leader of her own order, she expected similar obedience. Consultation and delegation were not characteristic of the missionaries under Mother Teresa's leadership. This was driven both by her certainty that she was fulfilling God's wishes, and by her sense of immediacy. Once she decided to do something, Mother Teresa acted almost at once. A decision to begin a school could mean that classes would open the next week. This immediacy was underpinned by her certainty that God would provide—and that he would continue to provide. Providence, in other words, was proof that God willed the work. This helps to explain Mother Teresa's aversion to institution building, planning, and investment. This extended even to a story that she reproved of sisters who canned tomatoes that could neither be eaten nor given away—they were not to expend energy on providing for the future.

Still, Mother Teresa has been described as democratic because of her interaction and consideration for the poorest and her equally direct interaction with the mightiest, who sometimes described her as certain, and at other times as determined, persistent, persevering, ruthless, uncompromising, even ferocious and aggressive when she was seeking resources.

But her life was a religious one. The sisters lived together, and prayed together in regularly scheduled communal prayer—something that was abandoned by many orders after Vatican II. As she said in her Nobel acceptance speech, "[we] may be doing social work in the eyes of the people but we are really contemplatives in the heart of the world." Her recurring themes were the story of the Good Samaritan mentioned above and the Gospel of St. Matthew, "I was hungry and ye gave me to eat. . . . Inasmuch as ye did it unto one of these my brethren. . . . Ye did it unto me" (Matthew 25:35–40). Another favorite theme referred to Christ's suffering on the cross and his cry "I thirst" (John 19:28). These words appear with the crucifix in every Missionaries of Charity chapel. Christ's cry was understood to mean he thirsted for souls, but Mother Teresa also used the metaphor to refer to man's search for God.

Bertha von Suttner could not have been more worldly or more different from Mother Teresa. Von Suttner may not have been formally educated, but her power came from the printed word; also, she believed she needed to live in style if she was to be persuasive with those who wielded power. Both Jane Addams and Emily Balch were exceptionally well-educated and specifically committed to social work. Both were guided by strong moral rather than conventional religious conviction. Von Suttner, Addams, and Balch championed women's right to vote. All were opposed to war and endured strong criticism for their pacifist convictions. Each sought to make a better world here on earth, and each seemed to have precisely fulfilled Nobel's intentions when he created the prize for peace. They shared little with Mother Teresa except, perhaps, their beginning work for peace only in middle age.

Betty Williams and Mairead Corrigan, who won the prize three years before Mother Teresa, were ordinary citizens, but they were like Mother Teresa in that they took immediate and direct action in response to suffering, which one of them, Williams, witnessed and the other, Corrigan, experienced through the death of four in her family. Their reaction was not to an international war but to a national insurgency that was killing hundreds. Their method was not example but a mobilization of the public. Their local focus and spontaneity were different from that of von Suttner, Addams, and Balch. And their efforts to mobilize collective pressure were different from those of Mother Teresa. They were, though, forerunners of the recipients of other Nobel Peace Prizes, which would be given to people working to end domestic violence through nonviolent means.

Did Mother Teresa advance peace? Given the premise that peace is not just an absence of fighting but requires some semblance of justice and well-being, it is hard to argue that Mother Teresa saw it as her purpose. After winning the Nobel Peace Prize, she did speak for peace and against war more often, but they were never her primary concern. Indeed, the public policy concerns she gave most attention to were birth control and abortion. She was, though, indefatigable in urging individuals to take immediate and direct action to help or comfort those most in need. Perhaps her greatest contribution was her demonstration that absolutely everyone has the capacity to do this. Absolutely everyone can give consolation to another, and this will bring joy to both.

Notes

1. Kathryn Spink, *Mother Teresa: A Complete Authorized Biography* (New York: HarperSanFrancisco, 1997), 7.

2. Anne Sebba, *Mother Teresa: Beyond the Image* (New York: Doubleday, 1997), 19.

3. Eileen Egan, *Such a Vision of the Street: Mother Teresa—the Spirit and the Work* (Garden City, N.Y.: Doubleday, 1985), 111.

4. Sebba, *Mother Teresa*, 57.

Alva Myrdal. Courtesy of the Norwegian Nobel Institute

❧

CHAPTER SIX

Alva Myrdal: World Diplomat

Witness to a Century of War

Alva Myrdal was born in Sweden in 1902 and died there in 1986 although during her lifetime she lived in several different countries and traveled to many more. Sweden had once been a warrior nation. The seafaring Vikings of Scandinavia chilled the hearts of the inhabitants of coastal cities within range of their warships. In the ninth century the Danes and Norwegians conquered London and Normandy, and ranged as far as Spain. People from what is now Sweden moved into part of what is now Russia and reached into the Middle East and the Mediterranean. Sometimes the motive was trade, sometimes simply pillage.

After a long period of continuous warfare, the monarchies of Sweden, Norway, and Denmark formed a unified kingdom dominated by the Danes in 1397. This lasted until 1520, when Sweden's Gustavus I established an independent Swedish monarchy with a centralized government and a state church (Lutheran). In the following centuries, Sweden became a major European power and participated in many of its wars.

However at the beginning of the nineteenth century, Sweden lost Finland to Russia, and partly as a result, a new Swedish constitution was adopted that preserved the monarchy but strengthened the parliament. That constitution remained in place until 1974.

The last time Sweden participated in any war was when it fought against Napoleon almost two hundred years ago. At that war's conclusion, Sweden was united with Norway under the monarchy, although Norway had a separate

*Gunnar and Alva Myrdal with their children—Kaj, Jan, and Sissela—going
to the United States in 1938. Courtesy of the Labour Movement Archives and
Library, Stockholm*

constitution. About one hundred years later Norway received full independence by agreement. There was no war of liberation, just difficult negotiations.

Sweden's democracy developed gradually but always placed an emphasis on
society's welfare. Among its nineteenth-century reforms were an Elementary
Education Act and an act of 1870 that granted girls the right to graduate from
upper-secondary school. Women did not get the right to vote in national
elections in Sweden until 1921, although Sweden adopted universal male
suffrage in 1907.

When Alva Myrdal was a young teen, most of Europe went to war. Bertha
von Suttner had tried to avert this shocking conflagration by urging that
institutions for arbitration be put in place and that arms limitation agreements
be signed. When the war began, women like Jane Addams and Emily Balch
tried to persuade the heads of both participating and neutral states to stop
the fighting and let mediators craft a peace. The women's peace movement

failed in its efforts, the war continued, and at its end the world order had been changed. The German, Turkish, Austrian, and Russian Empires had collapsed, and a small step toward world government was taken with the formation of the League of Nations. Myrdal's family was politically active, and she was therefore well aware of these developments. But Sweden had remained neutral. Her citizens, Myrdal among them, witnessed, but did not have to participate in the Great War.

Sweden did participate in the Great Depression, however. Its Social Democratic government placed emphasis on the creation of jobs and on cooperation between trade unions and corporations. It did not create defense industry jobs, however. In fact, it cut the size of its military and reduced military spending.

When World War II began, Sweden maintained its historical position of neutrality. It did so even though Germany invaded her neighbors, Norway and Denmark, and Russia attacked Finland. With its small military, Sweden could not have defended itself, but Sweden's neighbors tended to think that its interpretation of neutrality was biased in favor of Germany. For instance, Germany was allowed to move troops through Sweden, and Swedish steel and ball bearings were exported to Germany. As the tide turned against the Germans, adjustments were made. For example, use of Sweden as a German transit zone ceased. For a second time, the Swedes were close witnesses to an international calamity in which they did not participate, although at least one of their diplomats, Raoul Wallenberg, played a role in saving many Jews from German concentration camps.

Postwar Sweden adopted a position of armed neutrality in which it was committed to defend its neutrality by military means, if necessary. Neutrality was chosen in the face of the cold war soon begun between the United States and the Soviet Union. Thus Sweden was one of the few Western European nations that stayed out of the North Atlantic Treaty Organization (NATO). It strongly supported the idea of collective security and the United Nations, however. Indeed, a Swede, Dag Hammerskjöld, served as the UN's secretary-general from 1953 to 1961.

Swedish armed neutrality requires every Swedish male to register with the government at age eighteen, and at age twenty to serve on active duty for a period of seven and a half to fifteen months, depending on his specialty. Today in practice, all Swedish males are not required to serve. However, all conscripts serve as enlisted personnel. Those who stay in the military may become officers, but all officers must first serve in the enlisted ranks. This is different from the United States. In general in the United States, if you have a high-school diploma, you are in the enlisted ranks. If you have a college degree, you are an officer. This results in a class structure within the military. Also as a result, young officers are, in fact, often dependent on experienced enlisted men and women to tell them how to fulfill their duties.

In time Myrdal would become disenchanted with both sides of the cold war. Sadly, she died only a few years before its unanticipated end.

Early Life

Alva Myrdal's daughter, philosopher Sissela Bok, has written *Alva Myrdal: A Daughter's Memoir*, which provides a thoughtful account of Myrdal's life. Alva was an intellectual and an activist who sought to develop and implement just public policies and to establish a secure place for women both at home and in public life. As Bok notes, Myrdal found this a challenge even in her own life.

Alva Myrdal's parents were part of the first Swedish generation to leave the farm, going first to a small town, later to Uppsala and Stockholm, and then back to the farm of her mother's childhood. Her mother had apprenticed as a seamstress but devoted herself to her family. Her mostly self-educated father was a committed participant in the temperance, labor, and cooperative movements, the "people's movements" that helped to transform Sweden into a prosperous and democratic nation in the early part of the twentieth century. He was also an atheist and an active Social Democrat whose principled refusal to exploit others economically led to an unsteady income and an anxious wife.

Alva was close to her younger sister, Rut, for her whole life, but both understood that their younger brother, Folke, whom they called "the gold dumpling," was more important than they because he was a boy. Another sister, Maj, was delicate and died young. A still younger brother, Stig, became the responsibility of Alva and Rut when their mother became a semi-invalid after his birth. Even as a girl Alva saw the misery her mother experienced because of her economic dependence and her fear of further pregnancies, and Alva vowed not to repeat the pattern. To her, her childhood had been "hellish." The family moved constantly, and their return to the farm was not the idyll her father had imagined.

Education was the obvious route to a different life, but the town's gymnasium, or secondary school, was only for boys, and neither of her parents saw any need for Alva to have more education. If seven years was enough schooling for 95 percent of the Swedish population, it was enough for Alva. She took a commercial class therefore and began office work at fifteen. Her salary permitted the purchase of a good number of books, and she also surreptitiously worked her way through the local library—surreptitiously because her mother, who had lost two siblings to tuberculosis, forbade use of the library's books, fearing them to be a likely source of infection. Alva pursued her self-education with energy, exploring religion and even deciding to be confirmed before backing away, although she continued to see the world as an arena in which good struggled against evil. Among her favorite authors were Jean Jacques Rousseau and John Stuart Mill—almost as antithetical themselves as good and evil.

At sixteen she was admitted to a boarding school and she arranged a loan through a friend of the family. But parental permission was required and was not given. In fact, Alva's mother angrily tore up the application. Eventually Alva's father arranged for her and nine other girls to study privately with the local school board's blessing. The girls had to pay ten times what boys paid for the same education. Alva's father lent but did not give her the money for tuition, and she worked during the summer to repay him. She completed the four-year course in three years and passed her official oral examinations in Stockholm with high honors. The university was next.

Alva was still focused on independence and avoiding the role of housewife. As a teenager she had had an extended personal correspondence with a young, former teacher and another with a Norwegian pen pal she never met. But in the summer of 1919 she met the confident and charismatic Gunnar Myrdal, who promised her love and a life of activity and of the intellect. She saw the possibility of a marriage in which each partner's creativity and energy would be fully utilized. She made a commitment, although they did not marry for five years, waiting until both had completed advanced degrees.

At the university she read widely and took courses in literature, the Nordic languages, and the history of religion. Gunnar's degrees were more focused and technical: one in law and then one in economics. For both Alva and Gunnar, the period was one of almost giddy intellectual discussion, debate, and exploration. Both were fully committed to the Enlightenment belief in progress through reason. They debated the positions of traditional thinkers like Hobbes, Ricardo, and Mill, and those of the newer ones like the neo-Darwinists and Democratic Socialists. They had a special affinity for the work of Sidney and Beatrice Webb, who worked as an intellectual team.

Alva was committed to marriage and to a family, but was determined to avoid the situation both of her mother, who had taken to bed, and of her mother-in-law, who had taken to complaining. Clearly, what was required was control of reproduction. That meant using contraceptives, which were illegal. Breaking the law did not trouble her, but Alva found that she had not escaped Gunnar's and her own expectations of a wife and the wife's role, and that breaking the tradition of wifely service and of the support that Jessie Bernard refers to as "stroking" was difficult. Gunnar may have admired and respected Alva's intellect, he may have encouraged her career, but he was wholly engrossed in his dreams and assumed that she would facilitate them. He had an Olympian view of himself and his future contributions and had no time for domestic concerns. Alva therefore was to assume those responsibilities. He seemed not to notice that this left her less freedom and less time to give to her own growth and dreams. Still, she did not reject the role of Gunnar's muse and assistant. She typed manuscripts, looked up library references, and read drafts. She did so willingly because she believed he was a genius.

Having first suffered a miscarriage, Alva gave birth to a son, Jan, in 1927. Alva was still devoting her attention to Gunnar and his work, but she was also studying for an advanced degree in psychology. For the first time she came face-to-face with a reality that many a later feminist would have to confront: there are not enough hours in the day to be a model wife, a model mother, and an outstanding professional. Sometimes affluent women can purchase time by hiring cooks, maids, nannies, research assistants, and typists, but this option was not available to Alva and Gunnar. Neither of their families were wealthy; indeed, Alva's in-laws were struggling to avoid bankruptcy. Nor was her young academic husband able to support such a lifestyle.

Travel is often illuminating. One not only encounters quite different ways of life and assumptions about life, one also has a chance to see one's own beliefs and assumptions more clearly. Sometimes travel just means going from the countryside to the capital; sometimes, as for John Stuart Mill, it means merely crossing a body of water, in his case, the English Channel. The young Myrdals made their first trip to England in the spring after their marriage, and acquainted though they were through study with its language and culture, they found there was much more to learn. For example, from Indian students, one of whom was a nephew of the poet Rabindranath Tagore (long admired by Alva), they learned about racial discrimination. They also traveled throughout Sweden and to Weimar Germany, but their first great adventure would involve crossing the Atlantic Ocean.

Both Myrdals had applied to the Rockefeller Foundation for fellowships, and both were successful. In 1929 that was a rare event. Each was to have a stipend of $750, and each was to study social-science methodology, she in social psychology, he in economics. But Jan was under two. Should he make the trip to the United States or should he stay behind? Both sets of grandparents urged the young couple to leave Jan in Sweden. Their pediatrician agreed.

Gunnar was sure this was the right thing to do, and Alva concurred. Jan would live on a farm surrounded by two sets of grandparents, an uncle and aunt with a child his age, and two additional uncles. There was never any doubt that the fellowships would be taken up, and extended families in Sweden often helped with child rearing. The choice was obviously right. Still, Alva described herself as being "punished" for not being with her son, and her mother suggested that perhaps Alva should not have had a child since she cared so much about her education. Gunnar experienced neither guilt nor regret.

Before embarking for the United States, the young couple went to London for three months of intense work. Gunnar was working on what would become a classic, *The Political Element in the Development of Economic Theory*. Alva was working on a dissertation about Freud's theory of dreams. She was also interested in child development and education, and she prepared a literature review titled "Emotional Factors in Education."

The Myrdals arrived in the United States just in time for the stock market crash of October 1929. While it may have made their stipends go further, and may have been an interesting time for an economist, it was a tragedy for hundreds of thousands. The system collapsed; people lost their possessions and their hope; and the government offered only platitudes, its officials firmly committed to a policy of laissez-faire, minimal government, and waiting it out. Even though Alva came from a family of Social Democrats, the situation in the United States made a powerful impact on her. Both she and Gunnar were radicalized. They saw no excuse for the failure to provide for the general welfare, or for the failure to use government to help its citizens. They saw no excuse for over-consumption by the wealthy in the face of widespread poverty. They saw no excuse for racial injustice. And both would begin thinking about practical social policies that could alleviate suffering and increase justice. They became what are now known as "policy wonks."

Alva's U.S. sponsor was Robert Lynd, half of a husband-and-wife research team that had authored *Middletown*, a sociological study of Muncie, Indiana. He provided help and encouragement beyond any Alva had experienced before. Also, for the first time she worked with a woman professor, Charlotte Bühler, a child psychologist, and with another academic couple, Dorothy Swaine Thomas and William I. Thomas, who had recently published together *The Child in America: Behavior Problems and Programs*. William I. Thomas's other recent works were *Sex and Society*, and *The Unadjusted Girl*.

The American academic world proved welcoming and stimulating. After a stint at Columbia University, Gunnar and Alva traveled for six months. Alva was particularly interested in the nursery schools and kindergartens associated with universities where new scholarship about learning and development was being applied in actual classrooms. She enthusiastically prepared a list of some fifteen possible research topics ranging across the disciplines but focused on education, psychology, the status of women, and most importantly, child development and psychology. Clearly, the left-behind Jan was always on her mind.

Swedish academia was not so welcoming when they returned. While Alva was in America, she had worked on her thesis about Freud's theory of dreams. Unfortunately, her sponsoring professor had died, and his successor saw no merit in Freud or even in critiquing him. Her work was for naught. She proposed another topic: work on a scale for measuring the abilities of preschoolers based on work done in Minnesota. Her new supervisor was interested only in a scale he had himself developed for older children. Myrdal was not prepared to fit herself to the Procrustean bed that would have won her a *licentiat*, the equivalent of a doctorate. Once again her education was truncated, this time just short of its goal.

The good news was that the family had been reunited, and that Gunnar had been invited to teach in Geneva. With Gunnar's younger sister and Jan in tow, they set off for a year in Geneva. It was a year not to be remembered for Alva. She suffered a miscarriage, a resistant infection, surgery for a tumor, and was told that she needed a second procedure that would preclude her bearing more children. She refused the operation. Children were important.

Life as an Activist

When they returned to Sweden, both Myrdals joined the Social Democrats. This was in line with Alva's beliefs and those of her father. As did her father, Alva believed all privilege should be abolished and attention given to those left out of society. Her views were wholly in accord with those of the new social democratic prime minister, Per Albin Hansson, who called for a country where every citizen would feel "at home" and be provided with all basic necessities.

Gunnar returned to the faculty at the University of Stockholm, Alva to a part-time job in a clinic for psychiatry and law at a jail. By now she had become engaged with issues concerning the status of women, parenting, children's education, and the population problem. That problem was one of low birth rates. In 1934 she and Gunnar collaborated on a book, *Crisis in the Population Question*. The book focused on what it would take to make people want to have more children. It especially took into account why women did not want to have more children, and its recommendations included free medical care, access to contraceptives, sex education in the schools, subsidized housing, education loans, pregnancy leaves, free school lunches, and government allowances for children.

The Myrdals expected that the public would warmly receive these obviously reasonable proposals. The public did not. In fact, the book was a scandal. Gunnar was publicly denounced by his mentor. One of his colleague's forbade his wife to speak to Alva, and Alva was especially criticized because she accepted speaking engagements related to the book, which took time away from her new daughter. The book presented a pro-family argument, but one calling for carrots not sticks, for innovation not tradition, and it was one that analyzed and supported women's need for a full and creative life. It also critiqued an individualism that was heedless of society's needs and that thought the general welfare would magically emerge from individuals' pursuit of pleasure.

A second daughter was soon born, but Alva now had the income needed to hire the help that gave her freedom to work, and enough money, also, to create what she believed would be an ideal environment for her children's development: a new home in a Stockholm suburb.

But Alva was under the worst kind of pressure. It was difficult enough to be at the same time a wife, mother, and excelling professional. Alva, though, had made her challenge even greater by having chosen as the area of her expertise families and children. Just as a dentist's children must have beautiful teeth, and a pastor's children, perfect behavior, Alva, the child development specialist, was expected to produce happy, well-adjusted, and high-performing children. Two of her children would later write books about the family. One would be sympathetic but analytical, the second highly critical.

Alva took an active role in speaking about and promoting the proposals from *Crisis in the Population Question*. Her certainty and enthusiasm carried her through public attack and criticism. The coauthored book resulted in invitations to Gunnar to chair a housing commission, to become a member of a population commission, to run for parliament, and to chair the National Parents' Association. Alva was invited to be a consultant to a commission.

The project that Alva undertook on her own was the founding of the Seminar for Social Pedagogy, a school for training preschool teachers. She had two purposes. One was to provide a good education for children. The other was to develop creative and professional teachers. Men as well as women were sought as students, and teachers were expected to have a social life, to marry, and to continue in their profession. Spinsterhood was not to be a precondition for teaching; nor was marriage to be a reason to abandon the classroom.

The school had only been open for two years when Gunnar was invited to do the research for what would become *An American Dilemma: The Negro Problem and Modern Democracy*. The family packed their bags. Alva, meanwhile, worked on *Nation and Family: The Swedish Experiment in Democratic Family and Population Policy*, which reviewed Sweden's social progress, but concluded that the female sex was "itself a social problem." The book also argued that racial discrimination was a difficulty for many and violated democracy's basic tenets. Similarly, Alva saw women's role as a worldwide problem, but one that most people did not see as a concern or as violating tenets about justice and equality. Even though Alva could not see a resolution for this problem, she worked for amelioration, for example, by proposing giving women equal pay for equal work and requiring leaves for pregnancy.

When Germany invaded Norway and Denmark in April 1940, the Myrdals decided to return to Sweden with their children. But the war did not come to Sweden, and they had no jobs there, so they collaborated on a second book, *Contact with America*. Its purpose was to urge their fellow Swedes not to give up their democratic principles in the face of threat. The book also held up America's public schools and American society's openness and idealism as a contrast to Sweden's tracking and formality.

Gunnar soon decided to return to the United States, and he urged Alva to follow and to leave the children, then age fourteen, six, and four, behind. Although she would later regret it, Alva felt she had no choice but to join him, and she undertook a lengthy trip, flying to England, Lisbon, the Azores, Bermuda, and finally, the United States. A year and a half later they returned. Europe was still at war, and a mini-war soon erupted between Gunnar and a rebellious, fifteen-year-old Jan. Jan left home soon thereafter to work as a journalist, choosing not to go to the university. Having a perfect family proved difficult even for an expert.

Alva began writing newspaper columns that were characteristic of her entire career. They would begin with discussion of a grave wrong described with great realism and supported by data, then with an unfeigned optimism would urge specific action. For the rest of the war she worked with Gunnar on postwar planning and on support for and integration of refugees. When the war ended, she was invited to serve on the Swedish School Commission, which was charged to reform the education system. Indeed, she was mentioned as a possible minister of education. However, she knew that Gunnar might be (and he was) offered the post of minister of commerce, and that the prime minister could not appoint both of them to the cabinet. She withdrew her name from consideration.

Gunnar was not the success in government that he was in academia. In government his passionate advocacy of new ideas and his willingness to try to rouse the public when officials were slow to take his advice made his colleagues unhappy. In particular, he was roundly criticized when food rationing was reinstated in 1947. Now the Myrdals experienced severe and also personal criticism, a criticism that wounded Alva as she had never been wounded by criticism of her ideas. She was accused of hoarding by the press, which discovered that the day before rationing was reimposed she had bought a large supply of coffee. Ultimately she made a full public accounting of her purchases and the contents of the family's food storeroom, explained her long-standing practice of buying in bulk, and noted her husband's complete inattentiveness to all things domestic, including her grocery purchases.

Both now began to consider an international life. UN Secretary-General Trygve Lie offered Gunnar the position of directorate of social affairs for the UN. He turned it down, saying his expertise was economics. The same position was then offered to Alva, who also turned it down; working in New York would be too hard on her family. Alva was then offered the job of assistant director of UNESCO, which was headquartered in Paris. This was her own offer and made to order for her interests and expertise. She turned it down too; Gunnar did not want to move to Paris. But he was then offered and took the chairmanship of the United Nations Economic Commission for Europe (EEC), located in Geneva. He had actually had Alva insert notice of his interest in this job in the letter she sent turning down the job offered to her in New York.

When Alva read Simone de Beauvoir's *Memoirs of a Dutiful Daughter*, she identified completely with the description in it of de Beauvoir's youth. Later when she read *The Prime of Life*, in which de Beauvoir describes her willing decision to completely give her life over to Jean-Paul Sartre, not to marry, and not to have children, Alva found such choices beyond comprehension. Nevertheless, in her midforties she found herself refusing wonderful opportunities, giving up work she cared about, and disrupting her children's lives to follow her husband as he undertook a new assignment after his unsuccessful stint in the Swedish cabinet. The task he undertook was to develop and integrate East and West European economies, hoping to avert a split between the two. Other forces would prove too powerful, however, and the cold war would, instead, force a separation between the two Europes.

Alva's role was now suddenly diminished. Gunnar was fully involved with the EEC, but as a foreigner Alva could not work in Switzerland except for the UN, and she could not work there because of nepotism rules. At age forty-five, the peak for many a male career, she had little meaningful work to do. This is reflected in the title of an invited lecture she gave at the UN, "The Surplus Energy of Married Women," and also in the title of a book she had begun to formulate and would later coauthor with Viola Klein, *Women's Two Roles: Home and Work*. That volume would suggest that women first devote themselves to home, and when their children reached a certain age, perhaps age nine, that they then embark on a career. Instead of both being done at the same time, the roles could be done sequentially. There was also a very mild reference in this book to the possibility that fathers assume a domestic role as well.

A year later Alva was again invited to head the UN's Department of Social Affairs. This time, for the first time since she had met Gunnar at age seventeen, she put her own work first. In early 1949 she left him and her two daughters in Geneva. At age forty-seven she began her career. She did so in New York City and as the highest-ranking woman in the UN Secretariat. Not long after, Gunnar would be involved in a serious auto accident, and his health would begin to deteriorate. Just as she began her international career, his would begin to decline.

International Diplomat

Alva's view of the world had never been narrow, but her serious work had until then focused on the United States and Europe. At the UN, Alva would soon adopt an international perspective. She would also adopt an individual perspective. For the first time, she would experience the freedom to manage her own time and social life, to choose her friends, to explore and enjoy the arts. Never before had she enjoyed such freedom, and it was a freedom coupled with a capacity to use that freedom. She was economically independent, and her family was provided for in her absence. She wrote to Gunnar's sister, "I have never had this same chance to do what I can and be what I am; it is an 'unfolding' that almost astonishes me myself."

Her next position was with UNESCO in Paris as head of its Division of Social Sciences. This brought her physically closer to her husband and teenage daughters—but only physically. Here the issue that she worked hardest on was access to contraception for women. She had few allies in support of such a program, however. Among others, the communist bloc and the Catholic Church were firmly opposed.

A trip to India reawakened her interest in its culture and, in particular, in Gandhi's philosophy of nonviolence, a means to change that she publicly suggested might be used to resolve tensions over Kashmir and between North and South Korea. This led to her personal and long-lasting friendship with independent India's first prime minister, Jawaharlal Nehru. India had become the leader of a group of countries determined to be neutral in the cold war between the United States and the Soviet Union. Alva's experience with neutrality found that position quite reasonable. Not everyone found neutrality reasonable, though, and a funny incident occurred when she went to New York to address the UN's Commission on the Status of Women. Even though she had both a diplomatic passport and a visa issued by the U.S. embassy in Bern, she was refused entry, and no reason was given. Eventually she was allowed in when she signed a "temporary release on parole." Later, Secretary of State John Foster Dulles declared her persona grata. Still, no explanation was ever given for her mistreatment, although her son, Jan, was then helping organize a youth festival in communist Hungary.

The senior Myrdals would be reunited in New Delhi. He would begin work on *Asian Drama: An Inquiry into the Poverty of Nations*, and she would become Sweden's first woman ambassador to India. Nehru, who was trying to maintain India's independence and neutrality in spite of pressure from England and the United States, and the Soviet Union and China, renewed his friendship with Alva. Her views shifted from the pro-American position she had held through World War II to one of active neutrality similar to Nehru's. Five years as an ambassador had given her great insight into the problems of combining democracy and economic development. Her sympathies were clearly more with problem-wracked India than with any of the UN Security Council members who tried to influence her.

At age fifty-nine she was back in Sweden and needing something to capture her "complete enthusiasm." After returning, she had written and given lectures on world poverty and the responsibility that countries like Sweden had to help other countries out of their misery. But what was to become her enthusiasm for the next several decades was something with which she had had virtually no experience—disarmament. The stimulus was a request from the Swedish foreign minister. He was soon to take his leave from the UN General Assembly and wished to offer a set of proposals on disarmament in his farewell address. The year was 1961. John F. Kennedy had run for president with a promise to close the "missile gap," and the Bay of Pigs invasion had heightened tensions between the Soviets and the Americans. The Soviets erected the Berlin Wall. First the Soviet Union and then the United States announced that it would resume nuclear weapons testing. The arms race had been restarted; the "Spirit of Camp David" was no more.

Alva's proposal for a "non-atom club" was set before the UN by Sweden's representative. The rationale was that all nations were endangered by the nuclear arms race and therefore those without nuclear weapons, the "lesser

Alva Myrdal and Nehru. Courtesy of the Labour Movement Archives and Library, Stockholm

powers," should be a part of the debate over their testing and control. In addition, "non-atom club" members should not only not produce nuclear weapons, they should not let them into their countries. It was also proposed that nuclear-weapons-free-zones be created, for instance, in Latin America.

In 1962 Alva Myrdal was elected to the national parliament and appointed to lead the Swedish delegation to the Geneva Disarmament Committee. Thus she began what would become twelve years of labor in the cause of disarmament. She undertook the task with relish, and found she was a good politician and a good speaker. Her physical attractiveness and impeccable dress may have eased her way in diplomatic circles, but she was always meticulous about having clear and well-documented positions when she participated in debate or discussion.

When she began her work there were five hundred intercontinental ballistic missiles (ICBMs) in the world. Within a decade there would be more than five times that number. The eighteen-member Disarmament Committee included nuclear and nonnuclear nations, and eight of the eighteen were nonaligned nations.[1] Still, both the United States and the Soviet Union seemed to be concerned only about their own interests. They did not see disarmament as a general, a global concern. For them it was a matter of one outdoing the other.

Myrdal's first goal was to try to reach agreement on a test ban treaty. A small first step was achieved in 1963 when the United States and the Soviet Union, acting bilaterally, agreed to end tests in the atmosphere. Underground testing and the kind and number of inspections needed to monitor possible cheating were more complicated issues, and remained unresolved.

Her next step was to persuade the Swedish government to establish the Stockholm International Peace Research Institute (SIPRI). Its purpose was to provide data that would be accepted as sound because it was produced in a country that was not a part of the competing international blocs. She was its founding chair. After she joined the Swedish cabinet in a newly created position, Minister for Disarmament, Gunnar became the chair.

In her new positions, Myrdal argued that disarmament would make the world safer and also that the savings from reductions in the Swedish defense budget should go to economic and social development programs both at home and abroad. She was important to Sweden's 1968 decision to renounce nuclear weapons unilaterally and later chemical and biological ones as well. About this time she headed a study, "Towards Equality." This would again put her in the center of controversy, a place she had just escaped after developing a plan for disestablishing the Lutheran Church in Sweden, then attended by only 5 percent of the Swedish population. "Towards Equality" called for larger family allowances, paid parental leave, nine years of compulsory schooling, and raising the income of those with the lowest salaries. But when the government raised the salaries of primary-school teachers, secondary-school and university teachers, military officers, civil servants, and others went on strike. They were not to lose anything, but they did not want the gap narrowed.

On the international front, Swedish opposition to the Vietnam War and its acceptance of American draft evaders and deserters led to a break in diplomatic relations with the United States. Disarmament floundered, and when Myrdal stepped down in 1973, her parting words to the Committee on Disarmament were "When is some action for disarmament to start in earnest?"

Being retired from public life did not mean that Alva did not pursue her goal of reducing the threat of a nuclear Armageddon. She set to work on *The Game of Disarmament*. Gunnar planned an update of *An American Dilemma*, but in a continued role reversal, he assisted Alva with *The Game*. The next year Gunnar won a Nobel Prize in Economics, a joy diminished by having to share it with conservative Friedrich von Hayek of Austria.

The focus of *The Game* was on the great world powers' reluctance or refusal to come to an agreement about reducing nuclear arms, but it also criticized their militarization of the economic and national life of so many other countries by enlisting them in alliances, arming them, and by selling weapons for profit. In this book Alva consistently made the link between ever-increasing military budgets and the loss of the resources and talent needed for social programs to eliminate poverty—again, at home and abroad.

But nuclear weapons were not her only concern. She argued that the proliferation of chemical and biological weapons must be addressed, as must the proliferation of what we now call weapons of mass destruction, a destruction that particularly means the killing of innocents, of civilians. Myrdal also pointed out that while the "great powers" might be comfortable with a "limited" war, what they meant by that was a war in Europe in countries that had no control whatsoever over decisions that could utterly devastate them. In her usual way, once she had written a powerful and emotion-provoking critique, Alva then provided a set of concrete steps designed to curb the expensive, dangerous, and, she argued, irrational buildup of arms.

She was unheeded. The Soviet Union invaded Afghanistan and deployed SS-20 missiles in Eastern Europe. In turn, NATO decided to deploy Pershing II and cruise missiles in Western Europe. Ronald Reagan was elected president. In the face of such belligerence, Myrdal turned her efforts from national leaders and parliaments to the public and peace movements. She helped found the Peace Forum in Sweden and Women for Peace, which mobilized women throughout Europe. She was not, though, a pacifist. Nor did she believe that women had any special, any maternal instinct that made them more peaceful than men. Surely *all* rational beings opposed the spiraling arms race. Surely sober reason could lead to only one conclusion: the use of nuclear weapons was unacceptable. Surely reason required nuclear nations to commit to no first use, and to freeze all production—at a minimum and as only a preliminary.

In 1982 Alva Myrdal was awarded the Norwegian People's Peace Prize. This prize was created especially for her when she was passed over for the Nobel Peace Prize, having been nominated for it several times, and even though members of the Norwegian Parliament had publicly spoken on her behalf.

Just at the moment of celebration, though, word came of her son Jan's new book *Childhood.* Although he had completely broken with his parents long before, his devastating portrait of Alva describes her as so cold one shuddered at her touch. If anything, he was even harder on Gunnar. The media provided endless accounts of Jan's disaffection, and Gunnar launched an ugly and public attack on Jan, much to the rest of the family's dismay.

That fall Alva learned that she would, indeed, receive a Nobel Peace Prize. She was to share it with her UN colleague, Alfonso García Robles of Mexico. By then her health was frail, but she managed to prepare and give the traditional address. In it she deplored what she called "a culture of violence" that she saw as enveloping Western culture. Still, she proclaimed her hope that popular movements and the common sense and will of the people would cause politicians to step back from using violence to achieve political ends. Acting against Gunnar's wishes, she divided her share of the prize money between two projects. One project was intended to make the oceans free of nuclear weapons. The second was to support a study of the culture of violence and of those participating in and profiting from it. She also wished to explore the potential of "antiviolence," that is, nonviolent ways of resisting violence and its culture, which featured so prominently even in Sweden's media.

The Appendix and the Battleship

In later years, Alva described her life as unplanned and as never constituting a career. In wondering at the more than two decades of her "ludicrous" compliance with Gunnar's wishes and plans, she referred to herself as having been an "appendix." Although Gunnar gave her verbal encouragement, society did not expect her to succeed, so she was not mentored; and she diverted much of her energy to the roles of wife and mother. When she did begin full-time professional work at age forty-seven, she began to employ a new metaphor, that of she and Gunnar as consort battleships with coordinated but separate missions in an insecure world.

Myrdal is the only woman to win a Nobel Peace Prize by following a path well-worn by men: that of successful national politician and international diplomat. She was also the first to try to "have it all," that is, to have a lifelong partnership, children, a beautiful home filled with interesting guests, and a career. And although she and Gunnar became members of Sweden's intellectual elite, both of them came from families of modest means. Neither wealth nor servants cushioned her early life.

Just as von Suttner used her title to gain access to the public sphere, Myrdal benefited from her husband's illustrious career. But she was also like Addams and Balch, who gained access through higher education, something that was largely unavailable to the women of their day. Like other prize winners too, she found her work was controversial. She quickly learned that public acclaim is often matched by public criticism. But like other winners, she persevered. Mrs. Grundy did not deter her or them.

Further, as Addams, Balch, and Mother Teresa did, Myrdal identified poverty as a social ill that demanded action. Unlike Mother Teresa, the other three sought to eliminate poverty, not just to relieve it, and they did not hesitate to call for government intervention of various kinds. Like Addams, Balch, and Mother Teresa, Myrdal's concern for society's welfare was lifelong even if her work related to peace was begun only in middle age. And, as did Betty Williams and Mairead Corrigan, she called for action by "the people." Like them too, Myrdal won the Norwegian People's Peace Prize before she won the Nobel Peace Prize.

It is clear now that Sweden's twentieth-century efforts to advance women's equality were quite successful, and that Myrdal was very much a participant in those efforts. When it came to peace and disarmament, though, she judged her work as having been largely futile. In both cases, she proceeded on the assumption that reason and evidence would suffice—that if a certain course of action was the wise thing to do, it would be done. That is why, for instance, she thought a research institute like SIPRI could make a difference. In the case of women's equality, reason was, for the most part, up to the task. In the case of peace and disarmament, it was not.

In *The Game of Disarmament*, Myrdal took both the United States and the Soviet Union to task. She argued that "unreason" reigned, that the Soviets' profound attachment to secrecy made reaching an agreement almost impossible, as did Americans' support for elected leaders who argued the need for U.S. supremacy in all things, and whose defense budgets provided a living for large numbers of military personnel, defense contractors, union workers in defense plants, university researchers, and more, all of them voters. Myrdal provided a detailed account of "lost opportunities," and following her pattern, she then offered an agenda, an "urgent" agenda, for stemming the production and distribution of conventional weapons, for checking the proliferation of nuclear weapons, for eliminating biological and chemical warfare, and for effective verification—all this at the height of the cold war. She placed the UN at the center of disarmament efforts. Although she set forth the limited Soviet, American, and European points of view on disarmament, she argued for an international, a nonaligned or nonpartisan, point of view. She assumed that serving mankind as a whole would also serve the best interests of individual nations—at least in the long run.

To Alva Myrdal, following the dictates of reason implied a moral result. She believed disarmament would eventually lead to peace, the rule of law, and progress for all people. Her world and ours may not have reached that goal, but her commitment was firm: "Despite all frustrating experiences, I feel we cannot give up." Her goals may have been idealistic, but the concrete steps she proposed to them were always realistic.

Note

1. In 1970 the UN Disarmament Committee would expand to twenty-six members, and its name would be changed to the Conference of the Committee on Disarmament. By 1976 when Myrdal was writing *The Game of Disarmament*, its membership had expanded to thirty-one.

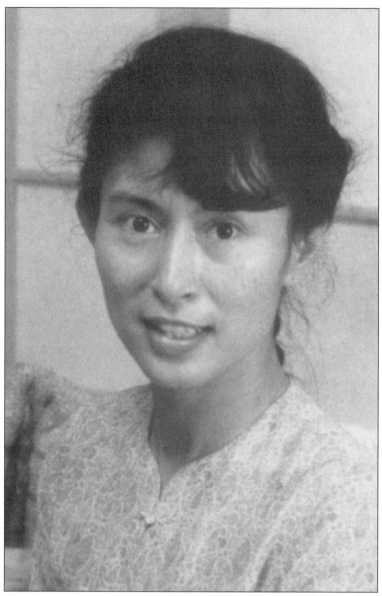

Aung San Suu Kyi. Courtesy of the Norwegian Nobel Institute

❧

CHAPTER SEVEN

Aung San Suu Kyi: Resisting by Staying Home

The Back Story

Burma, now known as Myanmar, has had a brief, troubled existence. No one should be surprised. The region now within Myanmar's boundaries has always been multiethnic. While the reach of Burman kings ebbed and flowed, neighboring tribes at different times submitted to rule, fought for independence, or enjoyed autonomy. This Texas-size land has a population of some 50 million, perhaps two-thirds of which is Burman and 85 percent of which is Buddhist.

Myanmar's geographic boundaries today were drawn by the British, who gained control over the region in a series of nineteenth-century Anglo-Burmese Wars ending in 1826, 1852, and 1885. In the last war, the British captured the Burman capital, Mandalay, and installed a government that administered what is now central and southern Burma, known as "Burma Proper," and the northern and northeastern regions, known as "the Excluded Areas." As is often the case, control in these areas was exercised through local tribal leaders. Also, minorities were selectively recruited to serve in the police and the military. A further wedge was driven between individual groups by Christian missionaries' successful conversion of many Karens, Chins, and Kachins. Further, foreigners, especially Indians, came to Burma where they became prominent in commercial life. The Burmans, long dominant although never fully in control of the region, found themselves displaced. Downward mobility is a sure recipe for discontent, and it took only twenty years for the seeds of a nationalist movement to emerge.

The movement began as the Young Men's Buddhist Association, an organization rooted in the country's dominant religion, but obviously influenced by the evangelizing Young Men's Christian Association (YMCA). After World War I, the Burmese were angered by the fact that the British stated that India would be granted self-government at some time in the future, while no such promise was made to Burma. After protests involving students, Buddhist monks, and a host of political parties, Burma was given its own governor and allowed to elect an assembly (with little real power) in 1923. By the 1930s, Indian and Chinese businessmen became the targets of protest, and race riots became a part of the landscape in which the Dobama Asiayone (We Burmans Association) rallied its members. These members addressed each other as *thakin*, which means "master," and which is what the Burmese were then expected to call British officials. Among the Dobama's student leaders were U Nu and Aung San.

In the midthirties a new government increased the responsibilities of the Burmese elected assembly. Even though minorities had reserved seats in this parliament, not all of them were pleased with the possibility of future home rule for Burma. To the minorities, independence and democracy suggested control by the Burmans.

Several political parties organized militias. Aung San was a founding member of one of these, the Communist Party of Burma. In 1940, what came to be known as the "Thirty Comrades," including Aung San, formed the Burmese Independence Army (BIA) with Japanese help. It accompanied the conquering Japanese into Burma, and Aung San soon became minister of defense of an "independent" Burma. But when it became obvious that the Japanese did not plan real independence for Burma and were also losing the war, Aung San and his army switched to the side of the British.

After the war, the British Labor Party made plans for Burma's independence. One step involved integrating the country's various ethnic militias into a single national army. Aung San, however, kept a private force of some 3,500 and began agitating for immediate independence. He left the Communist Party, and in 1947 won an agreement for independence from Britain. Questions about federalism and the degree of autonomy to be enjoyed by the various Burmese ethnic communities were discussed but not resolved. Aung San did not live to see Burma achieve sovereignty. He and six other officials were murdered by Burman rivals, and six months later, his long-time comrade, Nu, was installed as the first Burmese head of state.

Within two months, civil war had been initiated by the communists, who were soon joined by a collection of ethnic parties led by the Karens and supported by defecting army units. Order was only restored when London and

Delhi reinforced the central government. From then until now the Burmese government has made national unity a priority. But it and its citizens have paid a high price for that unity.

In practice, unity meant putting Burmans in all important positions and reserving opportunities for them. It meant granting privileges to Buddhist monks. It meant offering power temporarily to General Ne Win. It meant fighting as many as thirteen ethnic groups at the same time. It also meant a 1962 coup by Ne Win and the army. The government put in place by that coup continues in power four decades later.

The principles of government Ne Win proclaimed were unity, Buddhism, socialism, and Burmese culture. A new constitution in 1974 formally reduced minority rights. Sadly, preserving unity has therefore meant nearly continuous conflict and repression. Official Buddhism distressed Christians, Muslims, and animists, but did not necessarily make Buddhists happy. Socialism led to an ever-reduced standard of living. Burmese cultural imperialism kindled resistance. And two other factors bear mention. One is the country's flourishing trade in opium, which began as support for China's Kuomintang, which later funded civil warfare, and which today supports drug lords and almost certainly some government and military officials as well. A second is the fact that the Burmese military has long been involved in profit-making businesses. A military that is funded by profits is quite different from one that is funded by taxes.

In September 1987, a demonetization sparked riots. Demonstrations grew. After a quarter century of harsh rule, Ne Win retired in July 1988 as the government response to demonstrations turned bloody. And, in a surprising turn of events, Aung San's daughter, Aung San Suu Kyi, emerged as a national leader in Burma's "second war for independence."

Aung San Suu Kyi's Prepolitical Life

Exactly what is this Nobel Peace Prize winner's name? Suu is her personal name. It is the name her husband used in writing about her. Kyi was her mother's name, and it is appropriately used. Aung San was her father's name, and it also is properly used, although Suu Kyi's government foes *never* use that name. When they are not calling her "axehandle," "puppet princess," or other sobriquets, their preference is for "Mrs. Aris" because it suggests that she is a mere wife and a foreigner to boot. Her supporters frequently refer to her as "the Lady." She will be referred to here as Suu Kyi.

Suu Kyi was born in 1945, two years before her father Aung San's assassination. Her mother, who had been Aung San's nurse during his recovery from war wounds, was honored by the new regime as the widow of a national hero. Suu Kyi had two brothers, one of whom drowned as a child. Photos of the family show Suu Kyi's mother wearing native dress, a tubular skirt called a *longyi*, and Suu Kyi and her brother wearing Western clothes. As part of the new ruling elite, the family was well provided for, and Suu Kyi received a sound education. Suu Kyi has described herself as a bookworm who carried a book everywhere, reading in the car whenever it came to a stop—but unable to read while it was in motion. She describes her mother as strict and as a perfectionist.

Although the family's private life was comfortable, the country was troubled and its socialist economy floundered. When Suu Kyi was fifteen, the government honored her mother by appointing her ambassador to neighboring India. This was shortly before Ne Win's 1962 coup. In spite of the change of government following the coup, Suu Kyi's mother remained in this position until she retired in 1967. Suu Kyi accompanied her mother to India. Except for family visits, she would not return to Burma for twenty-six years. When she did return, she would herself be a wife and mother.

The schooling her mother arranged for Suu Kyi in New Delhi included standard academic subjects but also flower arranging, riding lessons, and Buddhism. At her mother's diplomatic residence and in her school, Suu Kyi met India's rulers and their children. Her mother was particularly close to Jawaharlal Nehru, and Suu Kyi eagerly studied recent Indian history. Specifically, she became well-versed in the philosophy of Mahatma Gandhi. Her life was not, however, cloistered. At one point she spent a summer in newly independent Algeria, helping to build houses for widows.

She completed her secondary studies at about the same time that Ne Win seized power in Burma. Instead of returning to Rangoon for higher education, she stayed with her mother in New Delhi where she studied political science for two years. She then went to Oxford where she studied politics, philosophy, and economics at a women's college, St. Hugh's College. A classmate has reported that Suu Kyi's closest friends at the college were Indian or African, although she did make friends with a young English man named Michael Aris. She usually wore native dress and had a flower in her ponytail, but she did have to wear a pair of pants when she decided to learn how to ride a bicycle. Although intellectually curious, Kyi was also said to be extremely proper, especially about alcohol (tried once for the sake of information) and sex (not tried).[1]

After graduation, Suu Kyi planned to do graduate work at New York University, but Manhattan logistics proved daunting, and instead she took a position at the UN where U Thant of Burma had become secretary-general. She worked there for three years, the last two as staff to the Advisory Committee on Administrative and Budgetary Questions, which oversaw the programs and budgets of the UN and also of its specialized agencies. These three years provided her with an excellent overview of the UN organization, its ideals, its bureaucracy, and its politics. Also, she was a part of U Thant's social circle and of that of the Burmese ambassador's as well. Thus she maintained her Burmese identity at the same time that she acquired a thoroughly international viewpoint. She continued her tradition of service by working as a volunteer at Bellevue Hospital on First Avenue in New York, a large, public hospital that largely serves the poor. Her acts of service, therefore, included direct service on behalf of those who were needy. They were not limited to the impersonal raising of funds or to activities providing enrichment for children already privileged.

In 1971 she traveled to Bhutan to visit her friend from Oxford, Michael Aris, who had become a Tibetan specialist. In Bhutan, Aris was tutoring the royal children and doing fieldwork. A photo of Suu Kyi there shows her riding a donkey while wearing native dress and with a flower in her usual high ponytail. Suu Kyi obtained a position with Bhutan's foreign minister, and she and Aris decided to marry, a ceremony that was performed in London the next year. Suu Kyi then began the life of an English academic's wife. She also became the mother of two sons, Alexander and Kim. She has been described as ever-gracious, egalitarian, and kind and generous, but also as reserved and ethically strong. She expects much of herself and much of others.

Even before marrying, Suu Kyi had told Aris that at sometime she might be called to serve her country and that if this should happen, she would have to answer Burma's call. Aris has quoted a letter she wrote in 1971:

> I only ask one thing, that should my people need me, you would help me to do my duty by them. . . . Sometimes I am beset by fears that circumstances and national considerations might tear us apart just when we are so happy in each other that separation would be a torment. And yet such fears are so futile and inconsequential: if we love and cherish each other as much as we can while we can, I am sure love and compassion will triumph in the end.[2]

From the beginning then, Aris knew of Suu Kyi's deep patriotism, her sense of responsibility, her belief that she might possess a destiny.

Suu Kyi's commitment to her country was manifested by her continued study and writing about Burmese history and literature. She even mastered Japanese in order to better research her father's relationship with the Japanese government during World War II. In fact, she spent a year as a scholar at

Aung San Suu Kyi arrives at the mausoleum of her father and Burma's national hero, late General Aung San, for a wreath-laying ceremony in Rangoon July 19, 1996. Courtesy of Reuters

Kyoto University (1985–1986); later she worked at the Indian Institute of Advanced Studies in New Delhi.

One of her first published works was a biography of her father. In a 1984 article, she detailed his rise from country boy and student demonstrator to Communist Party officer, military leader, and finally the diplomat who secured his country's independence from Great Britain. Described as Burma's George Washington, Aung San had been murdered before he could become its first prime minister, but Suu Kyi's scholarly essay reinforced the fact that her father had become a Burmese icon standing for Burma's independence and also for its unity.

Suu Kyi also published "My Country and People," emphasizing the different times at which Burma had been unified—1486, 1752, and since 1883. She described the different cultures of three of the main Burmese ethnic groups, the

Mons, Burmans, and Shans, and noted that seven of Burma's ethnic groups, including the Mons and Shans, were associated with geographic administrative units. She described traditional village governance in Burma as a basis for democracy and suggested that ordinary people have the burden of upholding "justice and decency." Her essays are informative, didactic, even-handed, and, most importantly, accessible to English speakers who tend to have but hazy knowledge of this country snuggled in between Bangladesh, India, China, Laos, and Thailand.

A significant part of Suu Kyi's description of Burmese culture addresses the influence of Buddhism. Her own commitment to this faith is shown by Suu Kyi's having her sons initiated as novice monks. This is not unusual, for Buddhist males often become monks for parts of their lives: briefly as adolescents, again as young men, and once again in maturity.

Because Buddhism is fundamental to Suu Kyi's thinking and to Burmese culture, a brief description of it is appropriate. Buddhism holds that this life is but one in a cycle of births and rebirths. According to Buddhism, our place in this life is determined by karma, which makes our conduct in our previous life the basis for our place in society in this life. Further, this world is one of suffering, suffering that is caused by craving or desire. Thus, we can only eliminate suffering by eliminating desire. The way to do this is by following what is known as the Middle Way or the Noble Eightfold Path, which requires

Right Understanding
Right Resolve
Right Speech
Right Action
Right Livelihood
Right Effort
Right Mindfulness
Right Concentration

The goal is to eliminate all desire and thus achieve release from the cycle of births and rebirths. We are then said to have achieved nirvana.

There are also Buddhism's Five Precepts, which are to be taken as a first step, and which should guide the Buddhist's everyday life. These are

Do not kill.
Do not steal.
Do not commit adultery.
Do not lie.
Do not drink intoxicating drinks.

Buddhism also calls for positive, virtuous action. This includes generosity, loving kindness or *metta*, and meditation, which leads to both tranquility and insight.

Buddhism tends to accept tribulation. But it can also create a community that values ethical behavior. It is understandable, then, that the leaders of the new nation of Burma made it the state religion. It is also understandable that the Burmese military government granted it privileges and sought its support. The Buddhist community of monks and nuns, the Sangha, does not command wealth and secular power, but any regime benefits from its support.

Buddhism, unlike the Hinduism of India, is not hierarchical. While there are certainly elites in the society, the system is not rigid, nor is it based on birth. This means equality is an important value. Also, while women cannot become Buddhas from this life, Suu Kyi and others describe women as equal to men in Burmese culture. Still, women are not military leaders, and since the military has ruled Burma for over forty years, women have not been part of the political scene. Education is highly valued, but years of a dismal economy and university closures because of student activism has greatly reduced access to it.

In 1985 Suu Kyi traveled to Japan to advance her research. She left her adolescent sons with their father in England. Both she and her husband regularly traveled internationally. Sometimes one or both of the boys accompanied their parents; sometimes the boys remained in England. Both boys certainly made a number of trips to Burma. Indeed, they were there with Suu Kyi when she was first arrested in 1988.

The previous spring Suu Kyi had returned to Burma to nurse her dying mother. This was precisely when antigovernment riots began to shake the Burmese military government. One casualty was Ne Win, who resigned after decades of often harsh rule. Destiny, indeed, was about to catch up with Suu Kyi. In her midforties she would emerge as the best-known leader of the National League for Democracy, which would provide a serious challenge to the military's long rule in Burma.

To the Prize

The Burmese had up to this point endured years of control by a military government, years of an ever-declining socialist economy, years of rebellion by communists and the numerous Burmese ethnic groups, and years that oversaw the development of a profitable illegal-drug trade. But in the fall of 1987, demonetization ruined the small part of the population that was still affluent. This led to student riots, and by March 1988, rioting in Rangoon became so widespread and destructive that the army decided to use tanks and tear gas to disperse the crowds. Particularly outrageous were the deaths by suffocation of forty-two students who had been arrested. On March 31, Suu Kyi received a telephone call from Rangoon reporting that her mother had had a stroke. She left for Burma the next day.

During the next several months, Suu Kyi cared for her mother while students and others continued their demonstrations, demonstrations that included much destruction of property. By midsummer, some in the army had begun to doubt the wisdom and effectiveness of using force on their fellow citizens. In July General Ne Win, who had held power for more than a quarter century, abruptly resigned. This did not lead to a more moderate policy. His replacement was the commander of police, Sein Lwin, known to many as "the Butcher."

The demonstrations continued. In their anger, groups that had not previously agreed on much of anything began to coalesce around a commitment to democracy. Strikes spread throughout the country and violence increased. The army's response was more repression. By August 8, the whole country was involved in demonstrations. The military killed and arrested thousands. Although the number of casualties was far higher than those that would occur the next year in China's Tiananmen Square, the international community responded slowly. "The Butcher" resigned. The next leader tried a different tactic. He lifted martial law and promised a referendum that would permit the people to decide whether the nation should remain a one-party state or become a multiparty state.

Even though she was still nursing her desperately ill mother, Suu Kyi was drafted into the leadership of the pro-democracy movement. Her heritage made her an obvious rallying point for a wide range of discontents. In fact, on August 2 over 500,000 people attended her first major public address at Shwedagon Temple. She urged discipline, unity, nonviolence, restoration of human rights, and multiparty democracy. Eleven of the Thirty Comrades who forty years before had joined her father, Aung San, in his effort to overthrow the English were still alive. Nine of them gave their support to the demonstrators. Elections and change were in the air. Then on September 18, 1988, a group of generals seized power. They abolished the constitution, massacred more students, and established the State Law and Order Restoration Council (SLORC). In turn, Suu Kyi and her colleagues formed the National League for Democracy (NLD).[3]

Suu Kyi became the party's secretary-general. An important item on SLORC's agenda was economic reform; in particular, it encouraged entrepreneurship. But as things would work out, most of the new opportunities went either to members of the military and their families or to foreign investors. Another item was elections. In preparation, parties were allowed to register, and 234 did so; elections were then scheduled for May 1990. But at the same time the military began to increase in size, growing from about 200,000 to 400,000 or more. New and top-of-the-line weapons were purchased. Museums were built to commemorate the military's role in creating and preserving the nation. Many schools and all the universities were closed. Burma was renamed Myanmar, and other place names were also changed from the English to the Burmese name.

Suu Kyi's mother died in late December, permitting Suu Kyi to focus her energies on the NLD. After the funeral she began touring the country, sometimes speaking two or even three times in a day. Merely by speaking to crowds of five or more, she was violating a government edict. Often she spoke to large crowds and in the presence of armed soldiers; still she was personally challenged only once.

In July 1989 she publicly declared her belief that the army was still under the influence of Ne Win and that it had no intention of turning the government over to civilians no matter what the outcome of the scheduled election. The regime then moved to isolate her. She was prevented from leading a march to honor her father, and then was placed under what would become six years of house arrest. At the time she was arrested her husband, Michael Aris, was in Scotland attending his father's funeral; her sons, age twelve and sixteen, were with her in Rangoon. Aris was allowed to visit Suu Kyi shortly after her arrest. SLORC clearly hoped that he would persuade her to leave with him and her sons, but this was not to be. Forced to choose between her family and her country, Suu Kyi saw herself as having no choice. She refused to become an exile.

Many of Suu Kyi's followers were imprisoned when she was arrested. Suu Kyi then began a hunger strike on their behalf. She ended it twelve days later only when SLORC promised that the prisoners would not be tortured and that legal due process would be followed—a promise that was almost certainly not fully kept.

SLORC next began a series of activities designed to ensure victory in the coming election. In particular, it disqualified and vilified Suu Kyi. It began a campaign to portray her as a dupe of the Communist Party and also of the CIA. It charged her with being anti-Buddhist and sexually deviant. It also disenfranchised many voters, relocated others, limited TV access, and censored party presentations. It even prohibited any campaign references to Ne Win, SLORC, the economy, or the army. With confidence, SLORC held the election.

But it was in shock that SLORC counted the ballots. The NLD had won 392 of the 485 seats, and 60 percent of the vote. SLORC had won 10 seats.

SLORC then explained that the vote was not, after all, for seats in a parliament that would exercise governmental authority, but only for an assembly that would prepare a new constitution. However, even that assembly would not be allowed to begin its work until a variety of steps had been completed, and the army's approval had been given. It is sixteen years later. There is no new constitution, and while SLORC has changed its name—it is now the State Peace and Development Council (SPDC)—it has not stepped aside.

SLORC next began efforts to increase its popularity by building new Buddhist pagodas and by negotiating cease-fires with some of the Burmese ethnic groups. But the election and SLORC's failure to transfer power to the winners had caught the attention of the international community. Outside pressure began. The United States and the European Union tried to get other nations to embargo the country newly named Myanmar. Myanmar's neighbors in the Association of Southeast Asian Nations (ASEAN), however, argued for "constructive engagement."

House arrest was not pleasant, but Suu Kyi knew her imprisoned friends and colleagues were suffering far more. She also knew some would not leave prison alive. She read Gandhi, Martin Luther King Jr., and Nelson Mandela; she meditated; she listened to the BBC; she refused to accept anything from SLORC, but was permitted packages from Aris. However, once the government made this "privilege" public, she refused his packages and letters too. She survived by selling her furniture to SLORC, which then provided supplies. Her initial sentence of one year of arrest was extended to three more years. Her sentence was then extended a second time. She would not be released until 1995.

The NLD's election victory and the arrest of many of its members, including many of those who had been elected, was followed by demonstrations by monks in August and by government raids on 130 monasteries in October. In December a provisional opposition government was created by some of the elected NLD members who had escaped to a border area occupied by the Karens. There they joined with other dissidents who had also sought refuge there. One leader of these dissidents was Sein Win, a cousin of Suu Kyi. The refugees called their new government the National Coalition Government for the Union of Burma (NCGUB). It is now in exile in Washington, D.C.

In 1991 while under house arrest, Suu Kyi was awarded the Nobel Peace Prize. Her teenage son, Alexander, gave the Oslo acceptance speech on her behalf. He emphasized that the Burmese military's oppression violated the principles of Burma's Buddhist heritage, and that its oppressive policies were not unanimously supported within the military itself. As evidence, he pointed to NLD electoral victories in constituencies that were almost entirely composed of military personnel and their families. He noted too that his mother's quest was a spiritual one—that it rested on an inner strength derived from the belief that what she was doing was right even if there were no immediate and concrete results.

The international publicity accompanying the awarding of the Nobel Peace Prize may have made Suu Kyi physically safer, but it also made it harder for her to compromise her position or to return to private life. She was now always in the spotlight. Any misstep or weakness would be known to the world. That same year, her husband published a collection of her letters and essays titled *Freedom from Fear*. It merits attention.

Suu Kyi's early essays include a biography of her father, a descriptive essay about Burma, another about intellectual life during colonialism, and one on Burmese literature and its link to nationalism. The letters and essays written during the early days of her arrest are political. In one essay, "In Quest of Democracy," she seeks to reconcile human rights with Buddhist principles. These principles include the value of each individual, and the guarantee of justice to even the weakest. She particularly explains how Buddhism's Ten Duties of Kings, which include morality, self-sacrifice, austerity, and non-opposition (to the will of the people), are applicable to modern government.

Perhaps her best-known essay in the West is "Freedom from Fear," which was written for a 1990 ceremony, which she could not attend, at which she was awarded the European Parliament's Sakharov Prize for Freedom of Thought. She memorably wrote that "It is not power that corrupts but fear. Fear of losing power corrupts those who wield it and fear of the scourge of power corrupts those who are subject to it." Fear, then, is the most potent source of corruption, but according to Burmese tradition, she noted, there are three other sources too: desire, spite, and ignorance. Suu Kyi called on victims of oppression to display the courage to claim their rights. Freedom from fear was to be both the means and the end. This would require "a revolution of the spirit," a turn to the courage of her father, Aung San, and to that of Gandhi, who had taught the Indian masses to be brave and to endure. "Concepts such as truth, justice and compassion cannot be dismissed as trite when these are often the only bulwarks which stand against ruthless power," she concluded.

In Myanmar, her best-known speech may be her first major address, that given at the Shwedagon Pagoda in August 1988. It begins, "Reverend monks and people!" and its theme is the importance of unity and discipline in the pursuit of human rights and multiparty democracy, and in "the second struggle for national independence." Suu Kyi emphasizes that the struggle must be nonviolent, and that the nation must reconcile the people and the army—the institution that secured the country's independence and has maintained its unity. Any resolution must also encompass the older generation and student groups, including those that choose violent rebellion. It must include Burma's many ethnic groups. And, most importantly, the strong must not be vengeful toward the weak. If government is to change, supporters of the previous government must not be oppressed. Those now in power must not fear what will happen to them if they relinquish power.

Suu Kyi, who had worked at the UN, appealed to its Commission on Human Rights and also to Amnesty International. She well understood the culture of international organizations and the value of their support. Her education and flawless English helped her articulate her country's suffering and its hopes. However, she was also deeply imbued with Burmese culture. She understood only too well the centrifugal forces generated by its many ethnic groups, and in talk after talk she described the unity of Myanmar's many peoples as they sought independence. She urged the Burmese to re-create that unity as they struggled for democracy—and to be certain to maintain it once democracy was achieved. However, she provided few specifics about just how the minority areas, so often administered separately, should be related to the central government. She was quite clear, though, that any new government would have a difficult time. Reality would not meet aspirations, and freedom would be abused. Prosperity would be slow to arrive. Disunity would threaten. Self-discipline would be crucial.

The Struggle Today

Suu Kyi won the Nobel Peace Prize more than a decade ago, but neither her commitment to democracy nor her government's repression has ended. The prize did make the international community more attentive. Indeed, while the UN General Assembly continues to recognize the government of Myanmar, it has regularly condemned its abuse of human rights and has called for it to seat those elected in 1990.

In 1993 while Suu Kyi was still under house arrest, SLORC did begin a discussion with dissidents about the country's future. This has periodically recurred but with little progress. About the same time, SLORC created the Union Solidarity and Development Association, a government-sponsored citizen's group of some 8 million, presumably to be the basis for a government-friendly political party if elections are held. In addition, it sponsored a military-dominated national convention to begin design of a new constitution. SLORC's proposal included the provision for a strong president, and a requirement that 25 percent of all legislative seats be allocated to the military. There was little room for discussion, and all convention speeches had to be preapproved by SLORC. The NDL boycotted the convention. Eight Nobel Peace Prize winners tried to pay a personal visit to Suu Kyi, but they were not allowed into the country. The military apparently believed it could move ahead without the NDL's participation, but no constitution emerged.

Meanwhile, the government's campaign to gain control of areas occupied by ethnic minorities has continued. One tactic has been to try to drive wedges between the ethnic groups and also to split particular groups. In 1995 a small number of troops composed of Karen Buddhist monks defected from the Peace and Democratic Front and joined the SPDC. This enabled the government to score a major psychological victory over the Karen, the best organized and most resistant ethnic group. Meanwhile, the government began to sign bilateral cease-fire agreements with other groups. Even though many countries were critical of the regime, its relations with neighboring Thailand and more especially China improved, and in 1995 outside pressure, plus the army's increased confidence, led to the release of Suu Kyi. She promptly began weekly meetings outside her home. Mere attendance at these meetings was made a crime. Nevertheless, the meetings continued—and with substantial crowds.

In 1996 the army proclaimed victory over the country's most visible drug lord, Khun Sa. He moved to Rangoon and began a trucking company. The drug trade has not diminished. Also, the army extended its "protection" to fifty thousand Shans, and relocated twenty thousand Karennis. Suu Kyi, who was still free, continued her work. The NDL called a party conference. Soon thereafter, hundreds of NDL supporters were arrested, and there was an attack on a caravan in which Suu Kyi was riding. A variety of international agencies began to discuss economic and other sanctions against Myanmar. As a poor country, Myanmar could be hurt by sanctions. However, Myanmar had been isolated from the world for so long that the world's severing of relations with it would not have the impact that it would have on a country that was integrated into the global system.

Fourteen ethnic groups held a Nationalities Seminar in 1997 near the Thai border to call for peace and the restoration of democracy to Myanmar. This resulted in the Maetharawhta Agreement, which spelled out a commitment to cooperation and to resolving Myanmar's political problems by political means. It also specified support for Suu Kyi's push for democracy and human rights. A coalition was formed, the Ethnic Nationalities Council (ENC), which continues its work today.

The government, however, continued its campaigns, focusing especially on the Karens and Shans, who were outnumbered and whose forces lacked the equipment and logistics of the national military. In spite of its repressive actions and in spite of the thousands of refugees seeking shelter in Thailand and

Martin County Library System
Cummings Library
(772)288-2551
Press 2 for phone renewals

Items that you checked out

Title: Champions for peace : women winners
of the Nobel Peace Prize
ID: 50547102420733
Due: Tuesday, July 06, 2021

Total items: 1
Account balance: $0.00
Tuesday, June 22, 2021 3:11 PM
Checked out: 2
Overdue: 0
Hold requests: 0
Ready for pickup: 0

Thank you for using the 3M™ SelfCheck
System.

Stay connected with us online at
www.library.martin.fl

Bangladesh, Myanmar was admitted to ASEAN that year. ASEAN did urge the government to meet with Suu Kyi and the NDL to find a peaceful solution to the conflict. By this time the government's position was that a constitution was so important that it must be arrived at not by a mere democratic process, which could mean winners and losers, but by consensus, as is done in many UN negotiations. Meanwhile, NDL supporters were being arrested in droves, and Suu Kyi was still virtually under house arrest.

Outside pressure intensified. Boycotts of consumer goods were declared; IMF, World Bank, and Asian Development Bank loans were suspended; the United States banned all new investment in Myanmar; officials were denied visas; the International Labor Organization (ILO) called for a trade boycott, charging the use of forced labor.[4] In spite of this, Myanmar was not isolated. China continued to give it support, and other Asian nations did not support coercive economic measures. SLORC by this time had reorganized and become the SPDC, at the same time giving its twelve regional military commanders more prominence. The SPDC continues to rule.

Ten years after the uprising of 1988, Myanmar began pumping gas to Thailand through a new pipeline constructed by Unocal Corporation. It also invaded Karen refugee camps in Thailand. The NDL chose to take positive—though unilateral—action by asking the government to call a meeting within ninety days of the legislators elected in 1990. When the government did not do so, the NDL formed the Committee Representing the People's Parliament (CRPP). This group of ten had collected 251 proxies from the individuals elected eight years before. Now it began to act as a government, and it started by repealing a number of the government's edicts. One thousand of its members were promptly arrested, and forty-three of its offices were closed. At the same time, the ILO issued a scathing report about the plight of workers, especially those providing "free service." Also, the UN Human Rights Commission asked a rapporteur to prepare a formal report on the status of human rights in Myanmar. The military government was still in control, but it enjoyed little respite. Internal resistance and external pressure continued.

The next year was a particularly sad one for Suu Kyi. Her husband became ill and died without her. He was not permitted to come to Myanmar, and she knew that if she went to England she would not be allowed to return. He died and she mourned alone.

Tension increased in 2000, the tenth anniversary of the elections. Although a UN special envoy was permitted to visit the country that fall, Suu Kyi was arrested for the second time. She had been isolated during most of her first arrest, but this time, at the government's discretion, she was able to consult with government representatives, NDL colleagues, and even with selected foreigners. She remained under arrest until May 2002. A new dialogue between the NDL and the government did begin. Suu Kyi even expressed some optimism, but there were no concrete results. With the death of Ne Win in December 2002, some began to hope that an agreement could finally be reached, but hopes were dashed the next year, when a scorched-earth policy was pursued against the Karens.

In May 2003 after a brutal attack on her caravan, Suu Kyi was arrested for a third time; the pretext was that it was for her "protection." Although she has since been offered her freedom, she refuses to accept it unless the thirty-five NDL members arrested at the same time are also released. She remains at home today. In fall 2003 a new prime minister, General Khin Nyunt, announced plans to restart the constitutional convention by offering a Seven Point Plan toward democracy. The plan was poorly received, however, especially by the ethnic groups. In 2004 the UN human rights envoy was told he could again visit, and the ILO was promised an opportunity to "freely check" complaints about forced labor. The junta appeared to be making accommodations, but in late fall General Khin Nyunt, who had proposed a "road map" to democracy, was arrested, as were his two sons and a large number of his subordinates. The government's grip remained firm.

The international community continues to watch and to exert pressure. To the average citizen of Myanmar, though, things do not appear very different today than they did when the campaign for democracy began in 1988. Suu Kyi has been consistent and persistent in her message. She has been under formal house arrest about half the time, but she has never failed to speak publicly when given the opportunity. Her message is simple and clear: democracy and human rights, nonviolence, unity, and discipline. Economic development should follow, not precede democracy.

The Karen resistance has been sustained, but even they are talking with the government. Over the last decade, most of the other armed ethnic groups have agreed to cease-fires under which they are permitted to keep control of their geographic areas. They have also kept their weapons. Meanwhile, Burmans continue to control the central government, the economy, and the military. The military continues to insist that the unity of the nation is its top priority and that democracy will naturally follow economic prosperity.

The Burmese military is over 400,000 strong. It is equipped with modern weapons, transportation, and communication facilities. It faces no external threat. Its concerns are domestic. Also, its concerns focus on its own well-being. We must assume that the generals worry about what would happen were they to give up power. Letting go of a tiger's tail is dangerous. Suu Kyi, at least, has been consistent in arguing that the army must be reconciled—that there must be no revenge taken against it—and that any transfer of power must not mean persecution of the formerly powerful.

Recently the Internet has become a voice for all sides of the conflict. The government has a web page published by the Ministry of Defense. It features "the Truth." The Free Burma Coalition website, created by a student at the University of Wisconsin in 1995, conveys information and strategic recommendations—mostly to people outside the country. The National Coalition Government for the Union of Burma is on the web; so is the Democratic Voice of Burma. If Myanmar's citizens gain access to the web, the struggle will acquire yet another dimension.

But the drug trade continues; AIDS spreads; the army directs; and the struggle goes on. A strategy that goes beyond economic sanctions, censure, and the installation of persons who won an election fifteen years ago is needed. It has not yet emerged.

Voice as Power

In *The Voice of Hope*, a book based on interviews conducted soon after her release from her six-year arrest, Suu Kyi expresses a philosophy rooted in both democracy and Buddhism. Her religion, her desire to achieve "purity of mind," she says, has enabled her to escape both hatred and fear—even when she walked alone toward guns aimed directly at her. While she urges *metta*, loving compassion, and advocates nonviolent action, she expresses strong affection and respect for the army and believes it has a role as the nation's "protector." To some these views may seem contradictory, but Suu Kyi has voiced them again and again. Indeed, she emphasizes the importance of not being dogmatic. She stresses flexibility. She makes no threats and is even reluctant to say, "If this, then that." "Keep all options open," is her constant refrain.

She sees her strength, and so do others, as being a "trier," one who never gives up. She also sees herself as having been given a priceless opportunity—that of working for something truly worth working for: democracy. Her democracy though is not necessarily a capitalist one. To her, democracy must be based on the people's will and it must provide a daily life free from fear and from want. She has said her greatest fear is letting down those who have put their faith in her, but she is confident that democracy will come, and that she will be there to see it.

Von Suttner aroused her public's passion through the printed word. Addams and Balch used their education and organizing skills to argue for peace in government's most hallowed halls—even before women were allowed to vote.

Suu Kyi's words are not passionate. They are always measured, and her printed pieces are short and few. She has written no books, but she has brought Burma and Myanmar's story to the international community through speeches and interviews. Similarly, she takes the message of democracy and human rights to her fellow Burmese in speeches throughout the country, when free, and from her doorstep when under arrest. Although she was the most visible leader of the NLD, she was not engaged in the kind of nuts-and-bolts organizing so natural to Addams and Balch.

Like Myrdal, Suu Kyi has worked with the UN to give visibility and legitimacy to her cause, and like Myrdal, her opportunity to work for peace came only in middle age and because she was already a public figure, a figure who inherited a public place from her father. This was also true for women like Indira Gandhi and Benazir Bhutto.

In some ways, Suu Kyi's role is most like that of Mairead Corrigan and Betty Williams. All three were "on the ground" when arrests and the deaths of innocents had become a part of daily life. By speaking up, all three helped to create a spontaneous mass movement opposed to the killing in their communities. All three became heroines to the international press. Although the movement created by Corrigan and Williams did not endure, Suu Kyi's has. It has done so partly because Suu Kyi is an icon for a happier past. Even more importantly though, her movement has widespread legitimacy because it so overwhelmingly won an election that should have resulted in a transfer of power.

Like Mother Teresa, Suu Kyi's spirituality has given her direction and strength. But Buddhism is very different from Mother Teresa's Catholicism. There is little structure or ritual in Buddhism and more meditation than prayer. Suu Kyi's certainty comes from self-discipline rather than from doctrine, revelation, or higher authority. But religion was clearly important to both these women. It enabled Mother Teresa to work day after day with the most forsaken, and it has enabled Suu Kyi to endure years of isolation, house arrest, and public vilification. It helped her withstand separation from her husband and sons. It has helped her persevere while her NDL colleagues, her other "family," suffered in prison. It has kept her steadfast even though she never, ever, knew what would happen next. Always she has been at the mercy of men who have often been merciless. Her story continues.

Notes

1. Aung San Suu Kyi, *Freedom from Fear*, ed. Michael Aris (London: Penguin, 1991). In chapters 22 and 23, two contemporaries give their recollections of Aung San Suu Kyi as a young woman.

2. Aung San Suu Kyi, *Freedom from Fear*, xvii.

3. Student riots are often the trigger for social change. The government is reluctant to be too oppressive because the rioters are largely the children of the privileged. Also, as young people, the students are more likely to act on their ideals because they have not yet been forced to make a series of "realistic" compromises, if only because they are at that brief time in life when one is emerging from dependency (on one's parents) and has not yet acquired dependents (a spouse and children).

4. The Myanmar government's answer was that unpaid work teams were a part of traditional Buddhist community service and that no one objected when they were used under British rule.

Rigoberta Menchú Tum. Courtesy of the Norwegian Nobel Institute

CHAPTER EIGHT

Rigoberta Menchú Tum: A Story That Broke the World's Heart

When Should the Story Begin?

More than a thousand years ago, Mayan Indians inhabited much of Central America and what is now southern Mexico. During its late classic period, from AD 600 to 900, Mayan culture developed a sophisticated knowledge of science and astronomy. Mayans predicted eclipses, constructed a highly accurate calendar, and created a hieroglyphic script. Their cities featured elaborate stelae, pyramids, and temples that were decorated with mosaics, murals, and carvings. Around the same time, Europeans were in a dark period and Islam was sweeping the Middle East and North Africa.

About AD 500, the Guatemalan city of Tikla was begun. It would become the greatest Mayan city, with a population estimated at ten thousand. But it and some of the other Mayan sites would be abandoned by AD 900, and the Mayan population would gradually disperse and return to subsistence agriculture. Today, Tikla is a wildlife preserve and an archaeological site favored by foreign tourists.

Around AD 1500, the Spanish began their exploration and conquest of Mexico and Central America. Perhaps 2 million Mayans and most of the elite were killed during the conquest and the next fifty years. Guatemalan Mayans were subdued by Pedro de Alvarado between 1523 and 1524. The last of the major Mayan city states, though, did not lose its independence until 1697. That did not bring peace. There have been intermittent insurrections ever since—the most recent in Chiapas, Mexico, in 1994. The Spanish were finally forced from Mexico and Central America in 1821, and by midcentury

Guatemala emerged as a separate but not a happy country. For the next century it was plagued by a series of dictators, insurrections, and coups.

In 1951 a civilian, Jacobo Arbenz, was elected president of Guatemala, and this is when many would say the story should begin. It is less than a decade before the birth of Rigoberta Menchú Tum. Let us look at some facts about Guatemala before turning to her story.

Guatemala lies between the Caribbean Sea and the Pacific Ocean and is bordered by Mexico, Belize, Honduras, and El Salvador. It has a population of between 12 million and 14 million and is about the size of the state of Tennessee. It is mountainous and forested. It has exotic orchids and colorful bird life. Mother Nature is also represented by volcanic eruptions and devastating hurricanes.

Mayans comprise half of Guatemala's population, and most of the rest of the population is of mixed race. Traditional crafts are well-developed, and the beauty of Guatemala's indigenous textiles is evident in the multi- and brightly colored *huipil* (blouse) and *corte* (skirt) that Menchú always wears in public. *Ladino* is the name given Guatemalans of any ethnicity or social class who do not follow Mayan culture. Some twenty indigenous languages are spoken in this small country; perhaps 60 percent of the population speaks Spanish. Literacy is relatively high, at 60 to 70 percent. So is longevity, at sixty-six years.

About half the population is involved in agriculture. Many are subsistence farmers in the mountains, but there are also large coffee, sugar, and banana plantations. Much of the population is poor. The gross domestic product (GDP) per person is just over $2,000. The Catholic Church is dominant, but 40 percent of the population describes itself as Protestant, and a small number practice traditional Mayan religion or a syncretic religion. What may be most distinctive about Guatemala, however, is its last half century of bloodshed.

As noted above, Arbenz was elected to the presidency in 1951. In Guatemala's over one hundred years of independence, he was one of only a handful of democratically elected presidents. He ran as a reformer for a multiparty coalition that included the Communist Party. This unsettled some Guatemalans, but even more controversial was his program of land reform. This included expropriating (while paying an appraised price for) land that was not being cultivated, including land belonging to the United Fruit Company. A U.S. corporation with millions invested in Guatemala, United Fruit owned or controlled most of the country's communications facilities, its rail lines, and Guatemala's Caribbean port. The United States became alarmed. President Dwight D. Eisenhower publicly warned that Guatemala might become a communist "outpost," and in 1954 the United States supported an invasion by Guatemalan exiles through Honduras. Indeed, Americans paid by the CIA bombed the Guatemalan capital from the air.

After Guatemala's 1954 "liberation," the United States provided some $80 million in aid, and promised to make Guatemala a "showplace" for democracy. Within three years, however, the new president had been assassinated, and the country was again thrown into disarray. Another president was elected, who then provided a base for the CIA to train Cuban exiles to invade Cuba just as the CIA had trained Guatemalans to invade Guatemala only a few years before. Outraged, a significant portion of the military staged a coup in 1961. This was put down with the assistance of the United States. A number of officers then left for the countryside and the mountains. They were determined to continue their resistance against a government that they believed had become a pawn of the United States. The United States under John F. Kennedy sent planes and special forces to Guatemala, and the insurgency was repressed, but political conflict continued. In fact, the remaining military then staged yet another coup, and yet another president was elected. Again the United States sent its Green Berets to Guatemala. And again the insurgents were suppressed. This cycle, or something like it, would continue for more than thirty years. A peace accord was not signed until 1996. Before that, and in particular at the end of the 1970s and at the beginning of the 1980s when hostilities were at their worst, Guatemala suffered more than 150,000 deaths and hundreds of Indian villages were destroyed.

Rigoberta's Story

Rigoberta Menchú Tum told her story at the age of twenty-three by dictating it in Paris to anthropologist Elisabeth Burgos-Debray over the period of a week. There are two quite different themes in *I, Rigoberta Menchú: An Indian Woman in Guatemala*. One is Menchú's personal account of her life and of the effect on it of Guatemala's political conflict. The other is her description of Indian village culture.

We will first follow Menchú's account of her life from her birth in 1959 in the mountain village of Chimel to the day she found herself speaking into a microphone in Paris. Next, we will explore her description of Indian village culture and, in particular, the role of women in that culture. This is important because Menchú's sense of mission evolved from one of resisting violence with violence to one of preserving and honoring Mayan culture. Finally, we will examine how she won the Nobel Peace Prize, the attacks on her that followed, and the role she now plays. Life after winning such an honor is difficult. How can one live up to oneself? It may be best to get such a prize in old age as did Addams, Balch, and Myrdal.

Menchú's father, Vicente Menchú Pérez, was an orphan. He was raised by his grandmother, who gave him away at age five because she could not support him and his two younger brothers in her job as a servant. At fourteen Vicente left his unpaid work for a family to work on a plantation. He then brought his grandmother and brothers there as well. Vicente was particularly happy to be able to support his grandmother because she had been forced to become her employer's mistress. Soon he was drafted, and when he was released by the army, he found his grandmother was dying. After her funeral, the brothers split up. Vicente then met Juana Tum K'otoja'. They married and moved to an uninhabited part of the mountains, cleared the land, and founded a village, Chimel, that was accessible only by foot or horseback. The land was beautiful but so unproductive that the family had to work on coastal plantations for part of the year. The family was large; Rigoberta was the sixth of nine children.

Menchú describes the misery of the trip to the coast in a covered truck, the swarms of mosquitoes, the exploitive labor contractor, and the plantation owner's canteen where too many workers drank away their wages. She describes her first view of the plantation's owner. He was wearing something called a "watch," very fat, surrounded by fifteen armed soldiers, and he was directing the workers to mark a piece of paper called a "vote." At age eight Rigoberta stopped helping her mother, Juana, and began to earn wages herself by picking coffee, bean by bean.

Plantation work was grueling and the living conditions wretched. As many as four hundred migrant workers lived in sheds in close contact, but because they came from different villages they could not communicate with each other, more or less with their Spanish-speaking overseer. Two of Rigoberta's brothers died young, one apparently from pesticide poisoning, the other from malnutrition. Because Juana missed a day of work arranging for the second boy's burial, she and Rigoberta were ordered off the plantation, and were not given any wages or any transportation back to the *altiplano*. The rest of the family was working on other plantations and knew nothing of their ordeal until they were reunited in the village. Menchú describes this as one of her earliest experiences and one that created hatred—great hatred.

Work in the mountains was hard but communal. Land had to be cleared, crops planted, and water fetched from two and a half miles away. Rigoberta Menchú's tenth birthday was also her formal introduction to adulthood. Her responsibilities were explained, and she was committed to the service of the community. By twelve she had been chosen by a Catholic priest to become a catechist, a teacher of religious texts. She undertook the task willingly, seeing no conflict between Christianity and her traditional religion, as both were ways to express one's faith. She acknowledged, though, that while Catholicism was "very important," she didn't understand it. Because she could not read, she memorized the texts and taught them from memory.

Determined not to lead her mother's hard life and wanting an education, at nineteen she went to the capital to work as a maid, against her father's wishes and in spite of her older sister's experience as a maid that had led the sister to conclude "rich people are bad." There Menchú began her education in Spanish, in the ways of the city, and in the ways of an upper class that had toilets, ironed their clothes, and fed their dogs better than their servants. The maid she worked with also taught her passive and active resistance. Among other things, this maid refused to initiate the family's three sons into sex even though she was offered money if she would do so. At Christmas the same maid was dismissed after a row in which mistress and servant each threatened to shoot the other. Menchú then did the work of two for several days. After making two hundred tamales for the Christmas feast, however, she was not allowed to eat even one. She left for home.

The news there was bad. Her father Vicente, the village founder and its elected leader, was in prison. A rich family had arrived and had begun "measuring" the land that the villagers had cleared, cultivated, and brought to productivity. There ensued a legal and bureaucratic struggle involving the landowners, the villagers, government officials, and a multitude of lawyers. The struggle included bribery, the signing of documents that could not be read, and the eviction of the villagers. Some of the villagers' possessions disappeared in their forcible removal. Other belongings, like their cooking pots, were deliberately destroyed. Many of their animals, even their dogs, were killed. Menchú's hatred grew.

After forty days the villagers returned to their homes determined to stay even if it meant death. They were told they could stay if they agreed to work as laborers, not as landowners. They refused, and were thrown off the land again. By then Vicente had been released from jail and had begun to travel seeking help. Villagers began to reoccupy their houses; they trained their dogs to attack strangers; children were enlisted as sentinels. At length a government official came and asked the villagers, including the children, to sign a document giving them title to the land. They did so and resumed their village life.

Two and a half years later the rich family arrived again, this time with a "title" saying that the document the villagers had signed said that they would live in the village for only two more years and that then they would leave. Vicente sought help from the unions and was arrested for "compromising the sovereignty of the state." The lawyers the villagers paid worked through an interpreter who had been bribed to say that the villagers agreed that they were not the owners of the land. About this time Vicente was again imprisoned, for more than a year. When he was released, he redoubled his efforts on the part of the villagers and within months was kidnapped. A son who was with him at the time escaped, rallied the villagers, and all went in pursuit with machetes, hoes, and knives. Vicente was found so wounded and tortured he could not walk, and he spent almost a year recovering; fortunately, he was provided with funds by nuns and priests and some Europeans who had previously worked with the villagers as agronomists. Menchú's hatred now encompassed all *ladinos*, not just landowners and officials. The importance of learning Spanish and of acting collectively was becoming apparent to her.

In 1977 Vicente was again arrested. He was said to be a communist and given a life sentence, but was released after fifteen days of protest by the village, by unions, and by nuns and priests. However, he was warned not to continue his work or he or one of his children was likely to die. From then on Vicente worked in secret. His imprisonment had convinced him that the peasants must unite, and so he helped to form the Committee for Peasant Unity (CUC). The issue was now understood to be one of landowners against those who worked the land. The issue was exploitation. The issue was the rich against the poor. Preparation for violent resistance was made.

Peasants, Menchú has often said, do not have to read a book. Their experiences, their sufferings are their political education. Menchú too began clandestine political organizing. By now she had begun to doubt the acceptance and forgiveness taught by the Catholic Church. Soon she would reject entirely its view that it was a sin to kill, for she was watching the regular killing of her family members and neighbors.

After a two-week occupation of Chimel by the army, the villagers planned a systematic defense including drills, an emergency camp, traps, and emergency exits—to be used first by the men because they were most at risk. Hot water and lime (thrown in the eyes) were identified as weapons, and Old Testament characters like Moses for the men, Judith for the women, and David for the children were used as inspiration. The Bible was even described as a weapon because it taught that one should not accept exploitation, discrimination, hunger.

When the army came to Chimel again, the villagers were prepared. Menchú describes an ambush in which she, three other women (one a girl age fourteen), and a man kidnapped a soldier and seized his weapons. After urging him to carry a message back to his commander that Indians should not kill Indians, and also that the village was prepared to resist any future visits, he was released. The army shot him as an informer and deserter. In another village, a soldier was captured and persuaded to desert.

After a massacre in Panzós in 1978, the CUC began a public campaign for a fair wage and Indian rights. This was followed by even more repression. It was in 1979 that Menchú definitively cast her lot with the CUC. She traveled in the mountains as an organizer but also spent time in a convent where she learned Spanish and to read and write. The year proved to be one of great change and horror.

Menchú, her parents, and her older brothers had left Chimel to support the resistance in 1978 or 1979. Her sixteen-year-old brother, Patrocinio, stayed behind to manage the family's affairs and serve as the village secretary. In September he was arrested and endured grisly and long-continued torture. Finally, Indians from a number of villages were summoned for a public punishment. This included a lengthy lecture about communists, Cubans, and subversives, while a group of mutilated prisoners stood naked before them. One of these was Menchú's brother. The public punishment culminated with each of the prisoners being doused with petrol and set afire.

A few months later, Vicente participated in a march demanding the withdrawal of the army from the mountains. In an effort to capture international attention, the marchers occupied the Spanish embassy. The government burned the embassy to the ground. All inside, including Menchú's father, Vicente, were killed.

In February 1980, a two-week strike of perhaps eighty thousand peasants and workers paralyzed the Guatemalan economy. Repression became even more severe—villages were destroyed, crops were burned, napalm was dropped, and young men drafted. A United Front was formed, and the resisters armed themselves with "people's weapons": work slowdowns, sabotage, boycotts, demonstrations, and phone threats.

A few months later Menchú's mother, Juana, who had been organizing women in a number of villages, was kidnapped, raped, and tortured for days. She was then left to die in public. After she died, her body was left to rot while guards stood by to prevent her being buried.[1]

By then the Catholic Church was divided between a hierarchy urging forgiveness and acceptance and its clerics who supported the peasants and workers. At the same time, a government campaign against dissident clergy and nuns had begun. Menchú was now a hunted person, but with the assistance of nuns from two convents, and disguised as a *ladina*, she was able to fly to Mexico. From there she went to Chiapas, where the religious community "brought her back to life." She regained her faith and learned more about her Mayan identity and also how to serve as a health worker.

Menchú's two younger sisters were briefly reunited with her in Chiapas, and all three decided to return to Guatemala. Her sisters, then ten and thirteen, went to the mountains to join the guerrillas, but Menchú chose to work as an urban organizer for the CUC, teaching "Clear Head, Caring Heart, Fighting Fist of Rural Workers." Soon the repression and massacres increased, and she had to leave the country again. Thus in 1981 she assumed a new role, that of an international representative of Guatemala's indigenous population. For the next decade she would be on a pilgrimage, one through which she told her story and that of her people to the world. Moving from country to country virtually every month, and with her possessions in a single suitcase, she called for justice—a call that "wasn't born out of something good, it was born out of wretchedness and bitterness. . . . [My people have] been radicalized by the poverty . . . and by the exploitation and discrimination which I have felt in my flesh."[2] That decade would also find her personal position evolving from one of support for the guerrillas to one of support for human rights.

In her second exile, Menchú was associated with the Guatemalan Committee for Patriotic Unity. She was one of only two indigenous members of the group of sixty. There the issue of diversity and multiculturalism was constantly debated. With a Dutch priest and a Guatemalan labor leader, Menchú was sent on a ten-country European tour to tell the story of Guatemala. At the tour's end in Paris, she told her story yet again—this time to Elisabeth Burgos-Debray's tape recorder.

Indian Village Culture and Women's Roles

The culture of Menchú's Mayan village was one based on family, community, and ancestors; one marked by daily and age-linked rituals and prayers; and one closely tied to nature, the earth, and maize. Menchú is proud of this culture and wants both to preserve it and to have it honored and respected in multicultural Guatemala. While she describes many customs and beliefs in her narration, Menchú is clear about the fact that other details remain the community's secret. It is also important to remember that hers is an oral culture. The traditions of this culture are told, heard, and repeated; they are not recorded and read.

According to Menchú, each village has an elected representative. He and his wife are like a father and mother to the whole community. (The Menchús were the leaders of their village, Chimel.) On the first day that a woman knows of her pregnancy, she goes to these representatives to announce the fact. This is because the child will belong not just to the parents but to the whole community, which must give the child support and direction. During the pregnancy, the child is instructed in the hard life it will lead, and at seven months in the womb it is introduced to nature by the mother.

The birth is attended by the father, the village representatives, and the parents of both the husband and wife. For the next eight days the mother and child are kept separate from the other mothers and children. Villagers bring gifts and take care of all the family's expenses for this period. The child's hands and feet are bound to show they are sacred and only to be used rightly. At the end of the eight days there is a candle-lit feast introducing the child to the "universe," and the child is told of the suffering and sorrows it must be prepared to endure and also of its responsibility to the community, whose rules it must obey. After forty days the child is baptized. The community accepts the child as a member, and the parents pledge to teach the child the community's customs, culture, and secrets. Ancestors are remembered, and the child is told it will "eat maize."

At age ten children are again instructed by the community about their culture and their now adult responsibilities. They are taught that they too will become parents, and that their life will be one of work, poverty, and suffering, but that through it all they must maintain their dignity. The children are told that the Spanish colonizers dishonored their ancestors, and that it is the children's responsibility to maintain their culture and keep its secrets. Special respect is owed, they are told, to the elderly and to pregnant women. The earth and its life-giving maize are to be honored as the core of the culture. A public promise is made to serve the community.

Before marriage a young woman is instructed in her duties to her ancestors and in the importance of marrying and having children. Birth control is considered unnatural, and great sympathy is given to childless couples. Young men too are instructed in their duty to raise children. The courtship lasts a long time.

The first step is a visit by the young man and his parents to the village representative to announce his wish to marry a particular young woman. A request is then made of the girl's parents, who inevitably refuse one, two, three times. If the door is "opened," then the young people can meet (with adults present) to get to know each other. If the girl finally accepts, a fiesta like that held at a child's birth is prepared. The grandmother gives her granddaughter a gift, and the groom-to-be's parents bring seventy-five large tamales, and a cooked and a live lamb. An elaborate ceremony with ample *guaro* (a homemade liquor) is performed, which begins with the grandparents' stories of their lives. A pledge to the Indian race is made, and reference is made to the "sinners and murderers" of the Spanish conquest. A whole day is spent in eating and talking—much of it about the evils brought by "the White Men." The ceremony in which the couple exchanges vows can come months later.

The vows are given before the elders and involve a promise to maintain Indian ways, to endure the suffering both husband and wife will experience, and to ensure that the next generation does the same. A small fiesta is then held for the immediate family. Only after all this does the actual marriage, a farewell ceremony, take place. It is a grand party, first in the young woman's village and then in the young man's. In each, elders instruct them in their responsibility to each other, the community, and their ancestors. Again, it is important to remember this is an oral culture. All its history, traditions, and secrets must be told and retold so that they will survive from generation to generation.

Within this culture, each person is said to have a protective spirit known as a *nahual* or *nawaal*, which is determined by the day of one's birth. However, one does not learn one's *nahual* until one is ten or twelve years old, that is, as an adult, and one often keeps it secret even after learning it. The *nahual* is a living thing, often an animal, and this emphasizes the fact that humans, like the sun, water, and earth are part of the natural world.

Death is considered natural, and it is prepared for. The coffin is built ahead of time. Shortly before death, the dying tells his story and offers his counsel. As in the other ceremonies, there is wide community participation and extended teaching. After a death, the whole night is then spent talking about the dead person's life. The next day his most treasured possessions are buried with him. Like birth ceremonies, death ceremonies are paid for by the community. But because proper ceremonies were difficult to conduct for those fighting in the mountains during the civil war, in Menchú's village a ceremony was sometimes held before their departure. Those who were going told their stories and gave their "recommendations."

The villager's relationship with the earth is of paramount importance, as are the community's sowing and harvesting ceremonies. The earth's permission is sought to sow, and she is thanked at harvest time. Incense, candles, prayer, and promises are features of both ceremonies. Planting is communal and organized by the village's woman representative. Girls' work, like that of women, is never done, but weaving, fetching water, and other chores are done in company. The work is social. Girls are always together or with an adult. Menchú learned a woman's role and tasks, but she was exceptional for the amount of time she also worked with and learned from her father.

Part of the reason Indians objected to young Indian men's being drafted was that it separated them from their community—it changed them. That was also the reason many did not want their children to pursue an education. For example, Menchú wanted an education, but her father feared she would forget her community if she went away to school. Still, when working on the plantations she saw the life of the educated and well-off; she was also able to compare the life of her village to that described by workers from other villages. She saw that the villages shared problems, and in this way she developed a concept of herself as Indian first, then a woman, then a peasant, and last a Christian. Yes, the many village fiestas in Guatemala celebrated Christian saints—but these saints had been integrated into Indian history. Their stories might not have been recognized in Rome. And Guatemalan independence was not celebrated in Indian communities—resistance to the Spanish conquest was.

When Menchú's father left the village, Chimel, in order not to endanger it because he was working in resistance to the government, he gave the young women of the village their freedom, saying that he hoped they would use it for the good of the people.[3]

The challenge for the villagers was to maintain what was central to their culture while adapting to change. Thus at age nineteen, Rigoberta, who was committed to preserving her culture and to following her father's rule to "Do it for our ancestors," understood that to preserve that culture, she would have to change. At a minimum she would have to learn Spanish and to read and write.

Rigoberta's mother, Juana, was one of Rigoberta's most important teachers, but she taught by telling Rigoberta about her own mother (Rigoberta's grandmother) and her experiences, her pregnancy, for example, not her own. And she taught by contrasting the life of an Indian woman to that of a *ladina*. Juana emphasized the importance of wearing the full Indian costume including shawl and apron and of not cutting one's hair. She taught Rigoberta about natural medicines. She taught the crafts as well: weaving, basketry, pottery. Juana taught her daughter that one must always offer hospitality; she taught the care of cooking pots and other belongings. Washing was especially important. Men's and boy's clothes were washed separately and first because men and women were different and because men needed to be "encouraged." For the same reason men were given more food, but it was the women who managed the family money.

Because Juana was a healer and midwife, she was frequently away from home. Rigoberta's mother also organized women politically in other villages, thus exercising more freedom than was typical of Indian women. Still, she did not lose the respect of others because of her relative independence.

Even though she believed that men and women had distinctive roles, Juana believed that women had to participate in the struggle against the government. Although she herself did not join a specific organization, Juana told Rigoberta that her struggle must be equal to that of her brothers. Further, she was to do "important" work; she was not to be a mere follower. Again, strong in her belief in women's special role and duties, Juana saw women as powerful, valuable, and responsible—even for political activity. This was so, even if some men did not accept women as *compañeras*, or were made uncomfortable by women's participation. Those men were to be reproved. Women must contribute. They must not be dependent.

Rigoberta saw machismo as a part of the culture, the fault of neither men nor women. She believed, though, that any separate organization for women would be feeding the sickness known as machismo. *Compañeros*, she believed, needed to learn about women from women. The sex barrier needed to be lowered. Other barriers that needed to be dissolved were those between Indians and *ladinos*, between intellectuals and the illiterate, and those between the many language groups.

During the struggle, Rigoberta made a decision not to marry.[4] She thought it would not be possible to raise a family in such a dangerous world and that her duty was to her people, not to her own happiness. As a revolutionary, though, she saw women's motivation as different from men's. Women may have filled every role in the revolution, and may have experienced every danger and every torture, but they did not do so because they sought power. Their motivation was service, and dedication to the next generation. And so women willingly engaged in a *just war*, a war against exploitation and terrorism, but they did not seek to become the next rulers.

In exile, and anguished at leaving her home and by the horrible deaths of her parents and brother, Rigoberta thus began to tell her story and the story of other Guatemalans to international audiences. Her younger sisters fought from the mountains. One of them had joined the guerrillas at age eight. Rigoberta's choice was different. She too was ready to offer her life for justice in a world she saw as evil and bloodthirsty. In her fight, however, words would be the weapon.

The Nobel Peace Prize and Its Aftermath

Ten years elapsed between the time Menchú told the story that would become *I, Rigoberta Menchú: An Indian Woman in Guatemala* and when she won the Nobel Peace Prize. Except for brief visits and an attempt to return home in 1988—when she was arrested, an event that created a good deal of local publicity for her cause—Menchú spent this ten-year period in exile. Not until 1996 would a final peace accord be signed in Guatemala. In 1998 she would continue her story in a book titled *Crossing Borders*.

In this later account, Menchú's narrative is more emotional, sometimes even mystical. Nature, signs, and dreams play a larger part in her narrative. She also reveals the names of the people and groups who gave her shelter and assistance, now that they are no longer endangered. She especially pays tribute to her mother, who she says continues to teach her—as her conscience. She displays the anguish of the survivor and identifies both with indigenous peoples and with women, two groups that experience particular discrimination. In addition, she notes that her father's family had been landless for 150 years and moved about like "gypsies," which made them (and young Rigoberta) an object of discrimination even among other Indians. Nevertheless, she always wears her readily identifiable red and black clothing.

While Catholic liberationists recognized economic injustice and repression in Guatemala, Menchú does not credit them with understanding indigenous life. She is even less charitable, actually she is critical, about development experts, anthropologists, and the government's land agency, which finally began giving land titles to Indians—but titles good only for their lifetime. This meant there was no provision for the next generation, no provision for cultural continuity.

It was not until Menchú went into exile in Chiapas that she learned something of the history of the Mayans and then grasped it as part of her own identity. It was not until 1982, after she had visited with members of the American Indian Movement (AIM) in the United States, where "our indigenous souls united"—even though the Americans were huge and wore braids—that she began to grasp the shared grief of indigenous peoples, and to appreciate how different was the position of those in Guatemala, where they were a majority, from those in the United States, where they were but a tiny minority.

In 1982 she was invited to a meeting at the UN in Geneva by the International Indian Treaty Council. She arrived with a few hundred dollars and found no one to meet her at the airport and no one there who spoke Spanish. The only resource she could think of was the Nicaraguan embassy. Happily, a taxi driver was able to understand her request, and she was given a room with a woman whose daughter had been killed in Nicaragua while working as a doctor. The community supporting indigenous peoples at the UN was thrilled to have a K'iche Mayan among them, but at first their lobbying activities were a total mystery to Menchú. Still she was a quick learner, and would be in and out of Geneva for the next ten years.

She and four others became the Unitary Representation of the Guatemalan Opposition (Representacao Unitaria de Oposicao Guatemalteca; RUOG). Even without consultative status as a nongovernmental organization (NGO), they found they had opportunities to speak in different UN forums.[5] Tirelessly, they told the story of Guatemala's human rights violations. Just telling the story was painful; but finding diplomats and bureaucrats who feigned interest and then did not listen attentively was worse—it was "humiliating."

Even Menchú was surprised when a resolution on human rights in Guatemala was passed. Her joy was tempered, though, by the lack of resolutions for Chile, Argentina, El Salvador, and others, and by the pressure the United States was exerting to destabilize the Sandanistas' Nicaragua and Castro's Cuba. A decade of lobbying gave Menchú a good understanding of how the UN works and doesn't work. She especially noted that tyrants in one part of the world will shamelessly defend victims in another part of the world. Still, it was clear to her that the UN was a crucial, or perhaps the only, forum for the world's victims—those who "have no choice."

In addition, she found that governments with indigenous populations often participated in the Office of the UN High Commissioner for Human Rights (OHCHR) Working Group on Indigenous Peoples with representatives from those populations, and that the representatives' distance from home and low visibility sometimes led to fruitful dialogue and negotiation. Menchú saw her goal, a Universal Declaration on the Rights of Indigenous Peoples, as within reach if the international conscience could be stimulated by the unified effort of indigenous peoples. But complications arose with the end of the cold war. Many new groups joined in lobbying the UN. Debate over the meaning of *indigenous* versus *ethnic* versus *minority* became heated. All claimed rights; the three overlapped, still, they were distinct.

In different places, different terms were used—*indigenous, original,* or *founding*—but in the Caribbean and Central and South America, the definition of *indigenous* was clear. It meant the people who were there when Christopher Columbus arrived. To Menchú, what distinguished them from other exploited ethnic and minority groups was their "cosmovision," a philosophy of life rooted in a shared history with governing laws and norms, and a spiritual connection with Mother Earth. Her evaluation of ecologists and their Earth Summit in Rio in 1992 was, however, a mixed one. She found that while participants' convictions seemed genuine, they borrowed from indigenous culture without attribution, and that there was a danger that for some, the environment would be but a passing fancy. For the indigenous, it is their "life."

Spain planned a 1992 quincentenary celebration of the European discovery of the New World, but a counter-celebration of resistance was organized in Colombia in 1989, and a celebration titled "Indigenous, Black, and Popular Resistance" was held in Guatemala in 1991. There a resolution was put forward nominating Menchú for the Nobel Peace Prize. After dissent and debate, including dissent by Guatemalans, the motion was passed. A third conference titled "Self Discovery" was held in October 1992 in Nicaragua. Shortly after this conference, Menchú returned to Guatemala to learn she had, indeed, won the prize. The civil war was still very much in progress, however, and

Jody Williams (l) with Rigoberta Menchú Tum (r). Photo by Ivan Suvanjieff. Permission granted by the PeaceJam Foundation (www.peacejam.org)

while she wished to invite representatives of the resistance, the army, and the government to her celebration, this proved impossible. (The president of Guatemala developed an "ear infection," but his wife did attend.) The political context had been dramatically altered. The majority Mayans had now become a part of the political discussion. When the president instigated a "self-coup," Menchú played a role in forcing his resignation.

In 1994 Menchú returned to Guatemala with the foundation she had created with her prize money (the Menchú Foundation). Its emphasis was on a get-out-the-vote campaign focused on women and Mayans. The war continued, but the government and the Guatemalan National Revolutionary Unity (Unidad Revolucionaria Nacional Guatemalteca; URNG) signed a human rights agreement that created the Historical Clarification Commission. They also signed an agreement on resettlement, and one on indigenous rights in 1995. This was a first step in the direction of peace. In October of the next year, though, there was a massacre at Xamán, a community that had recently been reestablished by exiles and that was partly supported by the Menchú Foundation. Menchú accepted the village leaders' request that she act as a co-plaintiff in a civil case on behalf of the community. This was remarkable because it challenged the Guatemalan judicial system to provide a remedy for a military massacre. Later Menchú would succeed in having a Spanish court indict former president Efraín Ríos Montt for war crimes. Menchú was now subscribing to the use of legal instruments in the pursuit of justice.

A peace accord was finally brokered in 1996 with the assistance of the UN and leaders from several other nations. It was a remarkable document that provided for disarming of the guerrillas and their reorganization as a political party, reduction of the army by a third, disbanding of the civil patrols, land reform, and tax reform, and more.

Soon after the signing of the peace agreement, which was actually a whole set of separately negotiated documents, three publications disturbed the peace. The first was the 1998 Catholic Church's report "Recovery of Historical Memory." Next was a UN-sponsored report of the Historical Clarification Commission. Both documented numerous and horrendous killings, mostly by the military. At almost the same time an American anthropologist, David Stoll, published *Rigoberta Menchú and the Story of All Poor Guatemalans*. While conceding that the Nobel Peace Prize may have been a good idea, and acknowledging that Menchú was an appropriate icon for indigenous peoples, and even that her general account of the atrocities committed was true, Stoll challenged the accuracy of some parts of her story. A media furor ensued. But Stoll did not consider the details of Menchú's story to be the central issue. For him there were two more important issues, neither of which commanded much public attention.

One was the interpretation of the thirty-six year conflict. Did it involve a peasant and indigenous uprising? Was it a popular movement? Or was it merely a conflict between Left and Right elites in which indigenous peoples were the principal victims? Stoll opted for the last explanation, deploring the romanticism of resistance by international leftists. Irregular war, he argued, always results in brutality toward civilians.[6]

Stoll was even more passionate in his critique of his fellow anthropologists for not caring about the truth, and for ignoring the costs associated with simply accepting a symbol and her narrative as truth. Symbols, he noted, always subsume contradictions. Anthropologists have a responsibility to understand this, and to be analytical about them.

The factual points at issue involved, first, whether or not Rigoberta personally witnessed her brother Patrocinio's death. She later said that her mother did so, and that she had repeated her mother's story. A second question involved the amount and formality of her schooling. This schooling was, in any event, limited to primary school, completed at age nineteen, and she may or may not have been a regular student. A third issue involved the nature of the land title disputes in Rigoberta's village of Chimel. Most, says Stoll, were between Mayans not between Mayans and *ladinos*. Menchú's prize was tarnished for some. To others she remained a heroine.

The Meaning of Her Story

The books by Rigoberta Menchú and Bertha von Suttner moved thousands. The first of these authors was an Indian woman from a mountain village in a small, impoverished country. The second was born a countess and lived in a dazzling imperial capital. The first, like Mairead Corrigan and Betty Williams, knew personally the cost of decades of civil conflict. The second feared the clash of empires. One was a young woman who spoke with the voice of oral tradition in a language she knew imperfectly. The second was a mature and already successful writer.

Neither limited her efforts to narrative, however, and those efforts had quite different results. Both spent years lobbying internationally. Von Suttner lobbied for mediation and arbitration as the way to settle international disputes, and she died just before World War I made peace advocacy irrelevant and also, to many, unpatriotic—as Jane Addams and Emily Balch found out. Menchú's story was told and published at the height of the Guatemalan resistance and of the killing, kidnapping, jailing, repression, displacement, or forced exile of tens of thousands of Guatemalans. Her account brought international attention to the suffering of her people and both private and official support. Ironically, by the time Menchú was awarded the Nobel Peace Prize, this repression had been largely effective. In fact, the awarding of the prize resuscitated efforts to create a formal peace with outside guarantors, a peace that would realize some of the defeated left-wing guerrillas' goals. Thus the resistance may have lost in the mountains, but internationally it did win hearts and minds. Ironic also was the fact that by the time of the prize, Menchú's concern had shifted from a focus on resistance by and justice for villagers, to an emphasis on human rights, in particular, the rights of indigenous peoples throughout the globe, and on the use of law to win those rights. In fact, indigenous rights were the basis for her prize.

It is hard to be an icon. An icon stands for many and contradictory things. At a distance and in times of stress, contradictions can be overlooked. Before the peace treaty was signed in Guatemala, differences between the goals of the Left and those of the Pan-Mayan movement were papered over. In the passions unleashed by the celebration of five hundred years of resistance to colonization, the differences could be ignored. But after the peace, the Left (which had supported and vetted Menchú's 1982 book) thought she had deserted them, while many Pan-Mayans were suspicious of her political sympathies. A Nobelist who has been selected for "representing" rather than for "doing" is subject to a wide variety of unanswerable questions about who and what and how she represents. Also, Menchú had left the country as a young and unknown refugee and then had worked on the international scene for

Rigoberta Menchú Tum holds a child as she attends a rally in a small community in the Ixcan province of Guatemala in late 1996, in support of the December 29, 1996, signing of the peace treaty between the Guatemalan government and the URNG rebels which ended the civil war. Courtesy of Scott Sady Photography, photographersdirect.com

the next ten years. She was little-known at home, and considered an enemy by many in power there. Coming home was not easy. Today her foundation focuses on human rights and on the founding of a Mayan university.

Her efforts are those of a single human being and have not been sufficient to transform her country into one enjoying either peace or prosperity. In the elections of 1999, the party that incorporated the URNG resistance won only 12 percent of the vote. The party of Montt, who had been president during the worst years of the repression, won 48 percent, and he became the president of the congress. That same year the leader of the left-wing party was assassinated, and a referendum that included indigenous rights and a designation of Guatemala as a multiethnic state was soundly defeated although both Menchú and the government campaigned for it. Street and organized crime became rampant. The peace accords were ignored. Prospects seemed dim.

However, in 2003 Montt ran for president and came in third. Apparently Guatemalans were now not quite as desperate for order and hoped for more law. Menchú too sees the law as a route to change. She has supported the Spanish judge who issued an arrest warrant for the Guatemalan interior minister who presided over the attack on the Spanish embassy where her father died. She also won a suit against five political activists for racist comments about her in 2005. Further, the new president of Guatemala, Oscar Berger, has done something remarkable. He has signed an agreement that gives a UN-appointed commission responsibility for investigating and prosecuting the country's clandestine security services and those accused of actions against rights activists, journalists, and judges. Berger also appointed a well-known human rights attorney to direct an office on human rights, and invited Menchú to oversee his new government's implementation of the almost two-decades-old peace accords.

Notes

1. Rigoberta Menchú's three sisters and a brother, Nicholás Menchú Tum, survived the civil war; Patrocinio, another brother, Victor Menchú Tum, and the latter's wife lost their lives.

2. This is the conclusion of *I Rigoberta Menchú: An Indian Woman in Guatemala*, ed. Elisabeth Burgos-Debray, trans. Ann Wright (London: Verso, 1984).

3. It is not unusual for rules about sex roles to be suspended when a society is in crisis. When peace comes, traditions are often reasserted.

4. In 1995 she married Angel Francisco Canil.

5. Menchú was also serving as an international spokesperson for the CUC.

6. He is certainly correct. But so does regular war, and so does repression. And what is the responsibility of the Right, which did most of the killing, and of the United States, which contributed substantial support to the Right?

Jody Williams. Courtesy of the Norwegian Nobel Institute

CHAPTER NINE

Jody Williams: Internet Activist

A New Era and an Old Weapon

For almost fifty years after World War II, the international scene was dominated by the rivalry between the United States and the Soviet Union. Particular concern was focused on both countries' nuclear arsenals. These had the potential for devastating the northern hemisphere, and citizens of every nation felt vulnerable. Many national and international peace movements sought the dismantling of both the weapons and their delivery systems. Nobel Peace Prize winner Alva Myrdal, in particular, worked for years to forge a disarmament agreement that would eliminate or at least reduce nuclear stockpiles. However, neither the United States nor the Soviet Union were prepared to reduce their capacity, redundant as most of it was.

The United States obtained the monstrous weapons first and was shocked when the Soviet Union produced them only a few years later. Some believe that that was fortunate—that if the United States had been able to maintain its monopoly, it would have used nuclear weapons in Korea, Vietnam, or elsewhere. However, once the Soviets broke the U.S. monopoly, a stalemate was created and the world was spared the possibly routine use of nuclear weapons. In short, proliferation deterred. And even today some experts argue that further proliferation could increase deterrence. As an example, they cite the balance achieved between Pakistan and India now that both have nuclear weapons. Nevertheless, current U.S. policy is one of counterproliferation— of taking the action necessary to prevent more nations from acquiring or developing such weapons.

But even if "mutual assured destruction" deterred nations at the time from using nuclear weapons, it did not mean that the world enjoyed peace. Indeed, both the Soviet Union and the United States supported a variety of proxy wars designed to prevent the other from gaining any advantage. Major conflicts like those in Korea and Vietnam are well-known and well-understood, but there were a number of smaller conflicts in which outside support of a civil war led to terrible consequences for the local population. Angola is an example, and there were other conflicts that were defined in such a way that the United States thought it urgent to support one side in a largely internal conflict. This was especially true in Central America.

With the disintegration of the Soviet Union, it was no longer necessary to interpret all world events through the lens of the struggle between two global superpowers. It became possible to see local conflicts as local. Thus, after years of slaughter, El Salvador, Guatemala, and Nicaragua found some respite. Nobel Peace Prize winner Rigoberta Menchú was able to return to her homeland. Peace treaties, human rights investigations, and truth commissions were designed to create a positive peace, that is to say, one based on justice.

It also became possible to focus energy and attention on recovery from armed conflict. Nongovernmental organizations (NGOs) brought workers from many countries to the war-torn countries to assist in such things as delivering humanitarian relief, stimulating economic development, holding elections, and aiding refugees. The requirements for a sustainable peace were much debated, as was the nature and importance of civil society. While the United States expressed reluctance to engage in nation-building, other countries considered it essential.

The feelings of combat veterans about their former enemies can be complex. For instance, U.S. Air Force Captain Pete Peterson was shot down over Vietnam and imprisoned for six years in "the Hanoi Hilton," a former French prison complete with guillotine. Now a museum, the former prison has his flight suit on display.[1] Thirty-one years later, Peterson eagerly accepted appointment as the first U.S. ambassador to the now communist Democratic Republic of Vietnam. Other American veterans also returned to Vietnam to work in various capacities. One group of veterans applied its efforts to assisting landmine victims, especially those needing prostheses.

Landmines are an old weapon. They were first used regularly and in large numbers in World War I as a defense against tanks. During World War II, antipersonnel (AP) mines were developed. At first they were used in conjunction with antitank mines to prevent removal of the larger mines. However, they were soon used more generally, especially to protect perimeters from infantry or guerrilla attacks.

A major advance in landmine technology was made in the 1960s. Mines were developed that could be delivered from the air. This made it possible to deploy large numbers of mines, although their precise location would not be known. (Mines planted by hand were, at least sometimes, mapped.) It also meant mines could be used for offensive purposes, not just for defensive reasons. The United States used AP mines in large numbers in Vietnam, and the Soviet Union used them extensively in Afghanistan. Landmines also became a weapon of choice in many low-intensity conflicts in Asia and Africa.

Landmines share two important characteristics with nuclear weapons. First, they are indiscriminate, often killing more civilians, including children, than soldiers. Second, they can damage or kill long after they are first put into play.

Jody Williams, the tenth woman to win a Nobel Peace Prize, tackled the old problem of AP mines. She did so in the new, post-Soviet era, and she worked with the Vietnam Veterans of America Foundation, while using the most up-to-date technology.

Preparation

Born in 1950, Williams grew up in Putney, Vermont. While not an isolated or unsophisticated community, Putney was so small that students had to go to Brattleboro to attend a public high school. Like Jane Addams, Williams was raised in a comfortable, small-town environment where her parents, one a judge and the other a housing supervisor, were respected members of the community. Both were also attentive to local and state political events, and Williams, also like Addams, was taught that the principles of democracy were to be taken seriously. These included the belief that government should be based on the informed consent of the governed, and that citizens have a responsibility to participate in improving their community.

Williams has described the Vermont of her childhood as full of white people and cows. Indeed, she claims never to have spoken to an African American until she was in her twenties. Homogeneous though her community may have been, Williams's views about freedom, equality, and democracy were views shared both by the independent-minded Vermonters of many generations and newer immigrants from urban areas. It was only after leaving Putney that Williams would grasp the size of the gap between the values she had been taught and life as it is lived. Her values required her to try to close that gap. Also, her commitment was so strong that she did not believe her actions should be confined to Vermont, or even to the United States. Her vision was international.

Williams attended the University of Vermont in Burlington. With a population of over 38,000, Burlington is the largest city in the state. The era was that of the civil rights movement, which had as its goal the extension of rights to all citizens. But it was also the era of Vietnam, where a war was being waged by the U.S. government, an undeclared war to which Williams and many others had not given informed consent. While troubled, Williams did not yet have a plan of action. After completing her bachelor of arts in 1972, she worked for and received a master's degree in Spanish and in English as a Second Language (ESL) in 1976.

She taught in Mexico, in the United Kingdom, and in Washington, D.C., and then decided to work for a second master's degree, this time at Johns Hopkins School of Advanced International Studies in Washington, D.C. Many of her fellow graduates saw this prestigious degree as an entrée into the diplomatic corps, other government service, or international business. None of those prospects appealed to Williams.

The year of her graduation was 1984. Williams had long been concerned about U.S. policy in Central America, and was especially concerned about human rights. While Guatemala, El Salvador, and Nicaragua were all being torn by civil strife, it was Nicaragua that was then in the headlines. This was because rebels there had won. A revolution was being made.

Nicaragua's history as an independent nation had not been one of good government and prosperity. Most of its numerous regimes had been repressive, and in 1972 an earthquake had destroyed the economy and Managua, the country's capital. The economy did not recover, and when the editor of an antiregime newspaper was assassinated, the Sandinista National Liberation Front (Frente Sandinista de Liberación Nacional; FSLN) took up arms. That was in 1978. By 1980, the Sandinistas were in control. They established a team of five members to govern. That team included Daniel Ortega Saavedra, and the widow of the assassinated editor, Violeta Barrios de Chamorro. At first the United States supported the new regime, but soon it began funding anti-Sandinista guerrillas known as Contras. When the FSLN signed an aid pact with the Soviet Union in 1982, the fat was in the fire.

Two events important to Nicaragua took place in 1984. First, elections were held, which Ortega won easily. However, his popularity would decline after he declared a state of emergency and began a radical economic program that included confiscations and land redistribution. Second, the U.S. Congress passed the Boland Amendment, prohibiting U.S. support for the Contras.[2]

Also, two individuals took actions important to Nicaragua then and in the next several years. One individual was Oliver North. As a staff member for the National Security Council, North engineered a deal by which U.S. weapons were sold to Iran (an illegal act), and the profits were then sent to the Contras (also illegal). Apparently the sale was also part of a deal (which was against public policy) to gain release of a U.S. hostage in Lebanon. North's actions resulted in the Iran-Contra scandal. The second individual was Jody Williams. Her activity took place through her role as coordinator of the Nicaragua-Honduras Education Project.

No, this was not a project to build classrooms or train teachers for rural Central America. The education was for adult Americans. It consisted of bringing groups of individuals to visit Nicaragua and Honduras, which was then being used as a base for Contra activities. The delegations were from all over the United States. The project's purpose was to influence public opinion by letting community leaders see for themselves what was happening in the two countries. Churches often sent delegations, and Jimmy Carter and Julian Bond were among those encouraging the effort. Thus Williams began what would become a career as a political activist, an activist who has often been at loggerheads with the U.S. government. Her two years as coordinator taught Williams valuable organizing skills. They further enhanced her ability to work across cultures and to persist when funds were low and criticism strong. Unlike von Suttner, Addams, and Myrdal, Williams did not direct her energies toward persuading the already powerful. Her target was those who bestowed power in a democracy—the voters and opinion leaders.

In 1986 Williams accepted a new position: Deputy Director of Medical Aid for El Salvador, a country that was then at the midpoint of a twelve-year civil war. She would remain in that post until the end of that war, that is, for six more years.

Williams's work in Nicaragua had been an extension of her training as an educator. In her job in El Salvador, she assumed a different kind of responsibility—organizing humanitarian relief. Relief per se was nothing new. What was new in El Salvador, and in the post–Cold War period generally, was the fact that relief workers were starting to insert themselves into conflict situations. Even if the workers believed their work to be dispassionate and neutral, opposing forces were almost sure to conclude that their presence was, in fact, an advantage to one side or the other. Thus, relief workers and their supplies would sometimes become targets. In the 1980s, though, even if relief work was difficult, it was not as perilous as it would become in the future.

The name Medical Aid for El Salvador accurately reflects this group's work. It consisted of soliciting donations from hospitals in the United States, getting supplies to El Salvador, and distributing them where they were most needed. This required advocacy skills, sound logistical management, and the ability to shift roles and cultures as required. While academic degrees may provide an intellectual understanding of the complexity of a situation, the most crucial skills for NGO workers are learned on the ground and from experience. In some ways, NGO workers like Williams were the antithesis of the military culture that played so prominent a role in El Salvador's affairs. These workers tended to be foreign, young, educated, idealistic, and committed to democratic principles. They had an instinctual aversion to hierarchy, a certain amount of distrust for governments as well as militaries, and trusted the judgment of those in the field over those at home. Their success required skills in fund-raising, public relations, and negotiation.

El Salvador's story was not so different from that of Guatemala or Nicaragua. It had also experienced repressive governments, periodic revolutions, and military rule. A reform slate was defeated in a fraudulent 1972 election, and reformers and leftists began to consider insurrection. By 1979 a civil war had erupted. Guerrillas and the army were soon joined in the fray by paramilitaries. Death squads carried out attacks on noncombatants. One victim was the country's archbishop, Oscar Romero, whose crime, apparently, was to have publicly urged the United States not to give aid to the El Salvadoran military. Other victims were four U.S. nuns who were raped and murdered. In 1981, a massacre at El Mozote killed close to one thousand civilians. The world now began to pay attention to El Salvador's plight. The United States, in particular, chose sides and began financing the war against the guerrillas. In ten years it contributed about $3 billion in economic aid and $1 billion in military aid to the government.

While civil war raged and paramilitaries continued their terrorist activities, a new legislature was elected in 1982, and a new constitution was written in 1983. The Farabundo Marti National Liberation Front (Frente Farabundo Martí para la Liberación Nacional; FMLN), composed of five separate guerrilla organizations, rejected the election results and other reforms as nominal. Still, in the presidential election of 1984, the rightist candidate was defeated. However, in the 1989 election, which was boycotted by the FMLN, the rightist candidate won. The FMLN then responded with a major offensive. About the same time, six Jesuit priests, their housekeeper, and her daughter were murdered in San Salvador. Although the FMLN offensive was not able to seize power, its strength and the shock of the brutal murder of the priests led both sides, and the U.S. government, to conclude that there would have to be a negotiated settlement—a victory by either side was impossible.

Finally, more outsiders intervened, but not on behalf of one side or the other. The intervention was on behalf of peace. Specifically, Central American presidents asked the UN to step in, and in the fall of 1991 under the sponsorship of Secretary-General Javier Pérez de Cuéllar, the two sides signed the New

York City Accord, which established the Committee for the Consolidation of the Peace (COPAZ). The committee included government, FMLN, and political party representatives, as well as observers from the Catholic Church and the UN. This was followed by a series of further agreements, a cease-fire, the demobilization of the FMLN, and its reincarnation as a political party. In December 1992, a ceremony marked the official end of the conflict.

There was jubilation. Great and international efforts had been made to make the peace just and sustained. Even though a gap has since developed between what was promised and what has happened, the El Salvador settlement remains a model for what a positive settlement might look like. (See the suggested reading for details of the agreement and its implementation.)

Williams was ready for her next challenge, and it came almost at once. Her next employer would be the Vietnam Veterans of America Foundation.

The International Campaign to Ban Landmines

In September 1991 the Asia branch of the U.S. NGO Human Rights Watch and another U.S. NGO, Physicians for Human Rights, issued a report titled "The Coward's War: Landmines in Cambodia," which documented the horrific consequences of the extensive use of landmines there. The report concluded with a call for a total ban on AP landmines. Separately, in November the Vietnam Veterans of America Foundation and a German NGO, Medico International, decided to organize a campaign for that very purpose. Within a year the four groups were joined by two others, Handicap International (UK), and the Mines Advisory Group (UK). A conference on landmines was planned for 1993 in London, and Jody Williams was hired to coordinate the efforts of the newly formed International Campaign to Ban Landmines (ICBL).

Early and important small steps included getting the United States to impose a one-year moratorium on the export of landmines. The success of this measure was due to the efforts of Vermont's senator Patrick Leahy. Also, the European parliament passed a resolution deploring the use of landmines. Although Europe was mostly a producer of landmines, it was also affected: the former Yugoslavia was awash with mines.

Another step was France's request that the UN hold a review conference on the 1980 Landmine Protocol to the Convention on Certain Conventional Weapons (CCW). This put into motion an effort to use the existing international disarmament machinery to create a ban. No treaty or convention would emerge from a series of CCW conferences, but they were, nevertheless, of great importance. One reason was that they showed that the established way of doing things under the auspices of the UN didn't work. Equally important, the ICBL held shadow conferences at the same time and in the same place as the CCW meetings. This gave ICBL representatives access to the media covering the official meetings. In this way, ICBL's messages and data reached the public. Further, by haunting the corridors outside the formal sessions, ICBL representatives had an opportunity to learn what was and what wasn't happening inside, and to develop personal relationships with many of the official conference delegates, some of whom were frustrated by the official meeting's lack of progress.

The first ICBL conference was held in London in 1993. Forty NGOs sent representatives. One ongoing strength of the ICBL has been the number and breadth of the groups that have participated. In addition to groups formed specifically to work against landmines, its participants have included medical and relief groups, children's and women's groups, religious and human rights groups, and disarmament, development, and antiwar groups. Each believes it has a stake. Ultimately more than a 1,200 NGOs from eighty countries would become part of the ICBL network.

At the 1993 London conference, the founding six NGOs were named a steering committee, and the Vietnam Veterans of America Foundation was given responsibility for coordination. That was its only task—coordination. No authority was vested in the leadership. There was no bureaucracy. There was no constitution, no executive, no assembly—just a coordinator and a provision for regular meetings where information would be exchanged and plans of action developed. Groups were responsible for organizing themselves and taking whatever action they believed appropriate to their circumstances. In fact, when the ICBL office was called to be informed that the organization was to share the Nobel Peace Prize with its coordinator, Jody Williams, Bobby Muller, who answered the phone, said, "We've got a problem. There's no there, there. The ICBL is just a name given to the collective action of a lot of organizations. All we do is collect and pass on information." (In the end the ICBL did figure out how to receive and cash the Nobel check.)

Another secret of the ICBL's success was its rapid exchange of information. This had a technological basis. The fax had just come into common use when the ICBL was founded. The snail-like pace of surface mail and the chanciness of getting a phone answered became unimportant. Information turnaround could be accomplished in hours instead of days or even weeks. Then, when the organization began to work regularly with countries of the south where phones and faxes were less available, the ICBL's work was advanced by yet another technological marvel—the Internet. Yet even though the ICBL used the Internet extensively for communication, it did not create a website until

1998. Revised in 2004, its website (www.icbl.org) is an excellent window into the campaign's history and its continuing work.

A variety of actions followed in the wake of the first conference. UNESCO made landmines a priority. Its assistance in conference funding was of great importance. Also, the UN General Assembly called for a moratorium on the export of mines. Sweden (Alva Myrdal's homeland) announced an end to both the export and the production of landmines. So did Italy, which was the third-largest manufacturer of landmines in the world. In the United States, President Bill Clinton called for the "eventual" elimination of mines. In short, success seemed to breed success. Williams called this "the lemming effect." Countries vied to show leadership.

The next year, the ICBL conference was attended by representatives of almost twice as many NGOs—seventy-five. That year Holland announced a plan to destroy more than 400,000 stockpiled landmines. Also, the International Committee of the Red Cross (ICRC) abandoned its usual policy of nonadvocacy to support a ban. The ICRC also made another crucial contribution. It sponsored a series of seminars on landmines in Zimbabwe, Ethiopia, Kenya, and Mozambique. The seminars were well-received. The Middle East, though, was slow to get on board.

Although the campaign's early efforts had been focused on landmine-producing countries, which tended to be northern, affluent, and unmined, it quickly reached out to affected countries, which were mostly southern and poor. This was a remarkable endeavor because NGOs from countries with dramatically different conventional measures of power were equals within the campaign. Further, the campaign was not dependent on any of the world's superpowers for either funds or leadership.

Belgium was the first country to announce a total ban on production, use, procurement, sale, and transfer of landmines (1995).[3] Canada and Switzerland joined the chorus soon thereafter. The Organization of African Unity, the Islamic Conference, and Pope John II called for a ban. The campaign continued to expand. The third ICBL conference included four hundred people from forty-two countries.

This groundswell calling for action did not affect the CCW Review Conference. A crippling fact of UN life is that most matters have to be decided by consensus, that is, unanimously. When the 1996 CCW conference again resulted in no progress, those attending ICBL's parallel meeting decided the time had come to develop their own proposal, in short, to do the conference's work for it.

ICBL members were well-qualified to do so. They had firsthand experience, and they had also become technology and data-collection experts. In fact, Williams's graduate research skills had enabled her to coauthor a more than five-hundred-page study on landmines in four countries titled *After the Guns Fall Silent: The Enduring Legacy of Landmines*. The study took more than two years to complete, but by the time it was published, the ICBL had probably become the single, most authoritative source for information related to landmines. Countries and even delegates at the CCW asked the ICBL for its data.

Meanwhile, individual states and regional associations continued to act. Belgium and Holland began destroying their stockpiles. The Congo, Honduras, and Jamaica registered their support. Germany and Australia (which had changed its position), Austria, Norway, and Denmark called for a ban. The Organization of American States (OAS) called for a hemisphere free of mines. The six Central American countries declared a ban. So did the Caribbean countries. In the United States, fifteen high-ranking retired officers, including Norman Schwarzkopf, called for a ban. However, President Clinton's position was equivocal. He said that by 1999 the United States would stop using "dumb" landmines, except in Korea, and that it would continue to use "smart" landmines until an international agreement was reached.[4] He could hardly have anticipated that an international agreement was, in fact, imminent.

Laws are made by states not by NGOs. Thus, at some point the ICBL had to form a partnership with a state or states. Or, it could relinquish leadership altogether. Canada was the nation that made the ICBL's dreams come true. It did so by inviting the supporters of a landmine ban to Ottawa in 1996 to plan for a treaty. This was a remarkable event for three reasons. First, only countries that were interested in a positive outcome were invited. Those who were opposed were not welcome. Fifty countries came to Ottawa, having already pledged to a complete ban; twenty-five, including the United States, signified interest and were permitted to attend, but only as observers. Second, while observers did not sit at the table, the ICBL did. The NGOs and nations worked, as the military would say, jointly, as equal partners. And the ICBL was prepared. It had a well-thought-out, evidence-based proposal. Third, instead of giving every nation a veto, that is to say, instead of working by consensus, in Ottawa democracy was practiced. Votes were taken. No single country could stall, derail, or veto the work of the conference.

In the end, the ICBL's mantra, "No exceptions, no reservations, no loopholes," was adhered to, and the Ottawa conference's final declaration called for an immediate and complete ban on landmines. Further, the conference agreed upon an Agenda for Action, which outlined the sequence of steps that would have to be accomplished before a treaty would be ready for signing.

Mutual and self-congratulations were just beginning, however, when Canada's foreign minister, Lloyd Axworthy, stood to close the meeting. He did so in an extraordinary way—by inviting all present to return in one year to sign a treaty! Twelve months? The NGOs were exhilarated; the diplomats were stunned. Prepare a multinational treaty in one year? It was a dramatic moment. Axworthy went on to say that a treaty *would* be signed next year—even if Canada were the only signatory. A new international norm was needed, and needed at once.

There were many doubters, but a core group of middle-size countries decided to try to meet the challenge. Canada, Norway, Austria, Germany, South Africa, Belgium, and the Philippines worked together to see that each of the steps outlined in the Agenda for Action was taken in the proper order and speedily. Specifically, the countries arranged for a set of conferences to decide all outstanding issues. They were determined to have a treaty-signing within the year.

The bandwagon rolled on. The first preparatory meeting was held in Austria in February 1997. In all, 111 countries attended. The ICBL meeting in Maputo the same month attracted 450 participants from 60 countries. The second Ottawa-generated conference was held in Germany in April. It addressed technical problems, and 120 countries attended. At Belgium's meeting in June, 106 countries signed a declaration saying they would sign a treaty. In September in Norway, the final wording for a comprehensive ban was agreed upon. At a parallel meeting of NGOs an Action Plan for obtaining the necessary ratifications was adopted.[5] Then in December 1997, 122 governments came to Ottawa to sign the Mine Ban Treaty. The NGOs set the year 2000 as their goal for the treaty's becoming law. They would accomplish that goal by 1999.[6]

What does the treaty say? It provides that states that sign will not use or "develop, produce, otherwise acquire, stockpile, retain or transfer" AP landmines. They are also required to destroy all stockpiles within four years of the treaty becoming law.[7] Within ten years, countries are to have cleared landmines in their own country or to have supported the removal of landmines in other countries. Landmine-affected countries are charged to educate their population about landmines and to care for and rehabilitate landmine survivors.

No exceptions are permitted and states that join the treaty may not withdraw from it.

Landmines designed to injure individuals are covered, but so are antivehicle landmines with antihandling devices or sensitive fuses.

A small number of landmines may be kept for training purposes.
Landmines may be transferred for purposes of destruction.
Some items that are not covered are unexploded ordnance, landmines triggered by a combatant, and antivehicle landmines.
Nonstate actors cannot join the treaty, but they are considered to have a responsibility to abide by international humanitarian law. By 2004, more than forty such groups had specifically renounced the use of landmines, and the ICBL had made it a priority to get others to make and implement similar declarations.
States are required to send an annual report on implementation to the UN Secretary-General. They are also required to meet annually for the first five years and at intervals thereafter to review the progress on implementation.

The first five-year review was held in November 2004 in Nairobi.

The Prize; the Treaty Becomes Law; Implementation

The Norwegian Nobel Committee didn't wait for the treaty-signing. Almost as soon as the treaty's wording was agreed upon, the committee announced that Jody Williams and the ICBL would share the 1997 Nobel Peace Prize. The *New York Times* photo of Williams on the day of the announcement shows her as she frequently appeared: barefoot, in jeans, and with a little skin on display at the midriff. Pretension is not a part of her persona, nor is reverence. Indeed, she had some harsh words to say about the U.S. failure to sign the treaty, a failure she attributed to President Clinton's cowardice. Nor has President George W. Bush been spared. She has described his administration as "drunk with power" and wanting to "make the rich richer." She is not diplomatic and says she doesn't know how to be different. In an interview about her Nobel medal she said, "Sometimes I wake up and feel like I'm proud. But what am I supposed to be, a pompous fool because I got a medal? . . . What makes you important is who you are and what you do, not what you have. . . . I can't just live without taking any action."

The ceremony in Oslo that fall exalted the Mine Ban Treaty. Both the presentation and the acceptance speeches also celebrated a possible new model for diplomacy, a model in which civil society and small and middle-size and even poor countries could play a central role. After all, a collection of grassroots organizations from all over the globe had stimulated a group of such countries to create a treaty that the UN could not. They had succeeded by working together. NGOs had cooperated with other NGOs; NGOs had cooperated with governments; and governments with a commitment had cooperated with each other. A good idea, good communication, leadership, and expertise had prevailed.

In 1998 the ICBL Steering Committee was expanded to sixteen members (later reduced to thirteen) and renamed the Coordination Committee. The original six members were joined by the representatives of Afghanistan, Cambodia, Kenya, South Africa, and Columbia, and by representatives of five NGOs: Japan's Association to Aid Refugees, the Inter-African Union of Human Rights, the Landmine Survivor's Network, the Lutheran World Federation, and Norwegian People's Aid. The office is now in Ottawa and a staff of six is led by Liz Bernstein. Little has been made of the fact, but it should be noted that ICBL and affiliated NGO leadership positions have been filled by many, if not a majority of, women.

Typically for the ICBL, its initial success was a stimulus to work harder, not a signal to relax. Two new plans were developed. One was for obtaining the ratifications necessary to make the treaty law. As we saw above, this turned out to be easier and more quickly accomplished than even the campaign had hoped. The second plan was for the implementation of the treaty. That would require time, money, and persistence.

But implementation also meant that more education was necessary, and 1998 marked conferences in, among other places, Amman, Baku, Khartoum, Kampala, Johannesburg, Ouagadougou, Kathmandu, Phnom Penh, Peshawar, Tuzla, Budapest, Kiev, Belgrade, and Moscow.[8] Arab countries and former Soviet republics now began joining the campaign.

States party to the treaty were required to meet annually and have done so. The first signatories' meeting was held in Maputo. Others have been held in Geneva, Nicaragua (which marked the signing of the 120th state), Geneva, and Bangkok. ICBL has continued its practice of holding parallel meetings as well as holding its own member meetings. It also holds specialty meetings, for example, to launch new projects such as "Adopt a Minefield" or "Adopt a Mine Dog."[9]

In 2004 it was estimated that more than 50 million landmines had been destroyed—17 million in Russia—a nonsignatory. Still, stockpiled landmines were estimated at 200 million, half of which were believed to be in China. Only two governments today acknowledge that they regularly use landmines: Myanmar and Russia. Others, like Burundi and Sudan, are under suspicion; and, of course, the United States uses them in South Korea. Also, nonstate groups continue to use landmines. This is especially true in Columbia, which reported more than eight hundred casualties from landmines in 2003–2004. Nevertheless, only fourteen countries, down from fifty-four, now produce landmines, and there seems to be little trade or exportation. Norms have changed.

More than a billion dollars has been allocated for landmine clearance since the treaty was signed. Nevertheless, eighty-two countries are still designated as "at risk," and sixteen of these have no demining program. Before the treaty was signed, it was estimated that there were 26,000 landmine accidents each year. It is believed that this number has now fallen by about a third. I should emphasize again that most of the casualties are civilians. In recent years the largest number of landmine victims have been in Chechnya, followed by Afghanistan, Cambodia, Columbia, and Angola.

Technical work and the collection of data remain critical. Part of the Nobel Peace Prize money has been used to prepare an annual "Landmine Monitor Report." This report, which has been published every year since 1999, can comprise one thousand to two thousand pages and seeks to monitor implementation and compliance throughout the world. It is a highly professional effort and is currently coordinated by Human Rights Watch. The report's goal is to make sure that every signer of the treaty adheres to the treaty's provisions. Rarely does a treaty have so independent and competent a watchdog. The countries that have ratified the treaty are well-informed about each other's compliance.

In addition to expertise, the ICBL has consistently shown itself adept at public relations. Princess Diana's visits to amputees in Angola and Bosnia in 1997 were important to capturing public attention. So was the support of Queen Noor of Jordan, Paul McCartney, Nelson Mandela, and Graça Machel. Photos of the "shoe mountains" built in more than a dozen cities (symbolizing shoes not needed because a landmine victim's foot or both feet had been blown off) found prime space in newspapers. A six-*ton* mountain of shoes was especially effective. ICBL visits were paid to Korea's heavily mined DMZ. An appeal was made at the Winter Olympics, then being held in Japan. Again, activity did not decrease; it increased.

Some issues remain. Demining is a tedious and dangerous process that can be expensive. Some demining experts argue that investing in sophisticated technology, using helicopters with radar, for example, is the best solution. Others argue that simple handheld detectors used by local people are the only sure way to clear a minefield, and that this method also provides employment and income to the local population, opportunities that might otherwise go to foreign contractors. There has also been debate about providing state-of-the-art prostheses to as many landmine survivors as possible versus using the simpler devices that may be customary in a particular survivor's society.

Williams has continued her work for peace. In 2003 she visited Myanmar to protest its use of landmines, and to visit Aung San Suu Kyi, who was

Jody Williams of the International Campaign to Ban Landmines gestures as she responds to questions about the United States' refusal to sign an international landmine ban while standing in front of her home, October 10, 1997. Courtesy of Reuters

temporarily free, bringing her messages of support from the other women Peace Prize Nobelists, and from Archbishop Desmond Tutu, Dr. Oscar Arias, Joseph Rotblat, and Norman Borlaug. The message she brought back from Suu Kyi was that outside pressure was, indeed, slowly bringing democracy to Myanmar. Suu Kyi meant by this that outsiders should continue to not make investments in or travel to Myanmar.

Today Williams is Distinguished Visiting Professor of Social Work and Global Justice in the Graduate School of Social Work at the University of

Houston. She continues to serve on the ICBL Coordinating Committee, and like two Cambodian amputees, she is an official ambassador for ICBL. She often appears on college campuses, and her message is clear: "Everyone can contribute in their own way," "Feelings without actions are irrelevant," and "Persist; there are no quick fixes." And while rejecting the likelihood of a utopia, Williams suggests that "progress toward a better world happens because you get up and take action to create the world in which you want to live."

As usual, Williams practices what she preaches. Believing that the importance of voicing an opinion is undiminished, even when doing so is described as unpatriotic, in March 2003 she and Mairead Corrigan allowed themselves to be arrested (along with sixty others) in a park just across from the White House while protesting against the Iraq War.

Lessons Learned: Ordinary People Can Achieve the Extraordinary

Williams took the high-school civic lessons she was taught literally. She then applied them in the international arena with passion and persistence. Her lessons are about ordinary citizens working together for the common good, about persuasion based on accurate information and reason, and about the responsiveness of government to informed public opinion. Even in the United States these lessons are not always taken seriously, and they have certainly not been a conventional route to success in the international arena. There the major forum for negotiation is the UN Security Council, a place where only a few may participate, and where a veto is available to even fewer.

Williams has always emphasized the importance of providing irrefutable information. The ICBL's data was gathered and regularly updated through old-fashioned drudgery. It proved so solid that nation-states as well as NGOs depended on it. Indeed, it and the campaign's reliability were crucial to forging the trust between NGOs and nation-states that made the Mine Ban Treaty a reality.

The close partnership between NGOs and a set of nation-states was new, and it evolved from their shared disappointment at the failure of the established disarmament machinery to deal effectively with landmines. This new model for diplomacy has created some enthusiasm, but we might be wise to reflect upon its potential for nation-states forming partnerships with NGOs that are devoted not to a general but to a special interest.

What may have been more important than having the ICBL sit at the negotiating table was the decision to invite only those countries that supported a ban to get together to create a treaty, one quite in accord with international law, but one that would be developed outside sluggish, superpower-dominated channels. Small and middle-size powers acted together. When they did so they became "a new kind of superpower." Even though the treaty was not signed by Russia, China, or the United States (which engaged in end runs and sought exemptions during development of the treaty), all three nations modified their behavior. A new international norm was established, and it did not depend on the major powers. Also, an independent system was established to monitor the compliance of signatories and the behavior of nonsignatory and nonstate actors.

The ICBL was a communications center. It linked some 1,200 NGOs that supported a landmine ban, but because there was no "there, there," each NGO devised and executed its own program. This model is similar to the vision McKeown had for Northern Ireland's Peace People. His efforts ended in disappointment. In fact, winning the Nobel Peace Prize may have accelerated the disintegration of Peace People. In contrast, it enhanced the success of the ICBL. Why? An important difference between the two organizations was Peace People's determined effort to be nonpolitical, even though it needed government action to achieve its goals of peace and justice. The ICBL, on the other hand, worked through and with government officials at every opportunity. Its goal also required government action, but it did not shy from working with diplomats and politicians. And because its goal was specific, clear, and nonnegotiable, the ICBL could work with officials without compromising its position.

Global civil society may, indeed, be finding its voice through interconnected NGOs. In the future NGOs may provide a systematic way of assessing and responding to global public opinion. At present, however, there are no institutions that give global public opinion a formal voice. The success of the Mine Ban Treaty has given hope to those who believe the world can be made safer and more just through the committed work of its citizens. But just as success begets success, success also stimulates opposition. In fact, three critiques of civil society are becoming commonplace. The first is that while NGO leaders may claim to speak for civil society, they do so without proof that they represent anyone's views but their own. Second, if they are not an accurate reflection of public opinion, what other grounds do NGOs have for claiming legitimacy? If an NGO prints up a letterhead and distributes a mission statement, what authority can it claim? Does expertise, an ability to raise money, or a facility at promoting smooth public relations confer legitimacy? Third, there is the question of transparency. Who directs particular NGOs, what is the source of their funding, and how are their budgets allocated?

Scholars of international relations are wrestling with these concerns and are trying to incorporate the concept of civil society within realist, idealist, and constructivist traditions. However, the simplest way to understand NGOs may be to understand them as interest groups, independent groups that permit concerned citizens to concentrate their energies and focus their efforts to get governmental institutions to be responsive to a specific concern. Again, the lobbying of interest groups in any democracy would seem to provide the best analogy for the work of global NGOs, and would also suggest a basis for their legitimacy. Such a basis was described years ago in de Tocqueville's analysis of that new form of government called a democracy. He emphasized the importance of independent citizen groups in maintaining democracy's health and responsiveness.

Once again, it should be noted that the grassroots, anonymous participants in the ICBL were largely women. When one can volunteer, when one can elect to act, women do so. When one has to be elected or appointed to act, as are national representatives, men predominate. Still, the lesson is that not having one's hands on the levers of power does not mean that one cannot be powerful.

Notes

1. The museum has U.S. Senator John McCain's flight suit on display as well.

2. Elections were held again in 1990 and this time Violeta Barrios de Chamorro and her party, the National Opposition Union (Unión Nacional de Oposición; UNO), were the winners. Ortega stepped down, but his brother was left in command of the military. In 1995 the second Ortega stepped down. Nicaragua had achieved a peaceful transfer of governmental and military power. Sadly, though, prosperity has not returned.

3. In thinking about the rapid responses by different countries, Williams has observed that governments have egos and that a number of them wanted to be seen as the leader on this issue. So when the United States announced its one-year ban, that motivated the French to call for the CWW review. Then Belgium jumped in with a complete ban, which stimulated others to action—a competition among governments propelled the issue. One might say a "disarmament race" had been created.

4. "Dumb" landmines are set off by pressure and do not expire. This means they are indiscriminate in their victims and dangerous for an indefinite period. Expensive, "smart" landmines expire at a particular time and are not supposed to be a long-term hazard.

5. Signing a treaty is only a first step. Countries must then ratify it by whatever process is required by their government. In the United States, two-thirds of the Senate must concur.

6. The treaty does not claim compulsory universal compliance. It binds only the states that sign it. In 2004 they numbered 143 of 190+ countries in the world. Nine additional states have signed but not yet ratified.

7. The treaty became law in 1999, so stockpiles should have been destroyed by 2003.

8. Russia, China, and the United States have not signed the treaty. The Clinton administration announced that the United States would sign the treaty by 2006, but this has not been done. In fact, in 2004 the Bush administration issued a new landmines policy that some see as moving backward because it calls for continued use of "nonpersistent" AP mines, and pledges to eliminate all "persistent" mines only by 2010. However, the United States apparently has adopted the norm of not exporting landmines. It has also pledged a 50 percent increase in funds for "mine action" (landmine removal). This brings the U.S. contribution for landmine removal to $70 million a year.

9. In Mozambique in May 2004 it was reported that a Belgian demining group had successfully trained rats to detect mines.

Shirin Ebadi. Courtesy of the Norwegian Nobel Institute

CHAPTER TEN

Shirin Ebadi: Muslim Judge

Persia

While Persia, known since 1935 as Iran, has long been a powerful nation, it has frequently been reviled by its neighbors to the west. The Old Testament did not have much good to say about the Persians, and in *History of the Peloponnesian War*, Thucydides recorded the defeat of an imperial and imperious Persia by the Greek city-states. But it is, perhaps, Montesquieu's satire of the French monarchy, *Persian Letters*, that most elegantly associates Persia with the themes of riches, tyranny, and the oppression of women. The West's critique, fair or not, of this country as authoritarian, unfriendly to women, and dangerous to its neighbors continues today.

While few in the West are familiar with Iran or speak its language, it has a rich and even a fabled history. About the size of Alaska, it has a population of 70 million. It is surrounded by Turkey, Iraq, Afghanistan, Pakistan, and the former Soviet republics of Armenia, Azerbaijan, and Turkmenistan. Almost every Iranian is Muslim, and 90 percent of them are, like most of those in Iraq, Shia. Of the total population, 80 percent are literate; 73 percent of women are also literate. The rate of GDP growth is 7 or 8 percent. GDP per capita is $7,000. The country is modern. Some 20 percent of its population is in agriculture, although agricultural provides only 12 percent of the GDP. Industry and services account for 25 and 45 percent of the labor force, respectively. Probably the best starting point for trying to understand Iran's politics is the beginning of the twentieth century.

The Qajar dynasty, officially founded in 1796, was still in power when the twentieth century began. In 1905, however, there was an uprising against the shah which resulted in the granting of a limited constitution that, for a limited time, created a Western-style parliament. Something similar occurred in neighboring Russia at the same time. But in 1908 oil was discovered in Iran, and everything changed. British and Russian rulers' interest and influence in the area, already strong, intensified. Iran remained neutral during World War I and was admitted to the League of Nations as a sovereign state, although it lost several northern provinces in the remapping of the region.

In 1921 a military coup was led by Reza Khan, an officer in the Persian Cossack Brigade. He quickly installed himself as shah and as the head of a new dynasty, the Pahlavi dynasty. This coup produced an authoritarian government that reduced the power of the tribes and provinces. Its thrust was toward the modern and the secular, as was a military government established in neighboring Turkey at about the same time. In contrast, twentieth-century Latin American coups have tended toward the traditional and have often enjoyed the support of church officials. One cannot predict the direction of a coup just because its leaders wear a uniform. However, one can expect that order will have a high priority.

In 1941 Iran was partly occupied by British and Soviet troops who wanted to ensure access to Iran's oil. The shah was replaced by his more compliant son, Mohammed Reza Pahlavi, who would rule until 1979. During World War II the United States sent supplies to the Soviet Union through Iran, and so the United States became a player there too. Still, the 1943 Tehran Declaration by the United States, the United Kingdom, and the Soviet Union guaranteed Iran's independence, although there was some difficulty when the Soviets were slow to withdraw their troops when the war was over.

Against the wishes of the shah, an elected, nationalist parliament led by Premier Mohammed Mossadeq nationalized the British-owned oil industry in 1951. The shah temporarily left the country but returned, and Mossadeq was arrested. The CIA got the credit both for the shah's return and Mossadeq's removal—perhaps its first regime change although the British played a role as well.

In 1961 the shah began his White Revolution, which was intended to modernize Iranian society and reform the system of landownership. It also included compulsory education and even the vote for women. With oil revenues to support it, the revolution moved quickly. Women became parliamentarians, pilots, physicians, police, and taxi drivers. The United States found the regime friendly and actively supported the shah.

However by 1978, opposition to the shah's excessive spending, his modernizing, his abolition of political parties and SAVAK (Sazeman-i Ettelaat va Amniyat-i Keshvar), an internal security and intelligence service, led to yet another revolution and to the shah's abdication. Ayatollah Ruhollah Khomeini returned from fifteen years in exile to establish a theocratic republic. Americans took note because after the deposed shah was admitted to the United States for medical treatment, revolutionary students seized the American embassy in Tehran and held its staff captive for more than a year. At the same time, Iraq tried to take advantage of the revolution's disarray by launching a war against Iran. This challenge may actually have united Iranians and solidified the revolution. For eight years the two countries struggled. Perhaps a million died, and both sides probably used chemical weapons. When the war was finally over, Iran's new government was firmly in control of the country, and religious leaders were firmly in control of the government.

Today the Assembly of Experts, an elected body of eighty-six senior clerics, selects a religious leader as Supreme Leader for a lifetime term. Since 1988 the Supreme Leader has had "absolute general trusteeship" over the government. Besides having control of the media and judiciary, he can dismiss the president, and he is commander-in-chief of the armed forces. The Guardian Council is composed of twelve judges, six of them clergy, six of them lay jurists. It has the power of review and veto of all legislation, and it supervises elections. Recently it assumed responsibility for certifying candidates for election.

Governmental institutions in Iran have a democratic look. There is an elected president and an elected parliament, the Majlies. However, by 1997 the elected bodies were not in step with the clerics. Reformers won the presidential election that year and again in 2001. They also won the Majlies. The clerics dealt with this problem by simply disqualifying large numbers of candidates in the 2004 elections for the legislature. Competing mostly against each other, the candidates backed by the clerics won. More recently, a religious conservative was elected president. Full control by religious leaders has been reestablished in Iran.

Since the shah's abdication, Iran's relations with the United States have been rocky. During the Reagan administration, the embassy hostages were recovered, and later the Reagan administration sold weapons to Iran as part of a deal to recover a hostage held elsewhere and to channel money to the Nicaraguan Contras. However, by the time of the Clinton administration, diplomatic relations had been suspended over two issues. One was Iran's alleged support for terrorists. The second was its apparent plan to develop nuclear weapons. Neither of these issues has been resolved, and President George W. Bush has famously described Iran as a member of an "Axis of Evil."

The press in Iran, which flowered after the 1997 election, is again experiencing a variety of restraints. There is unrest among students, and women fear that the new regime will be increasingly restrictive. Many of the educated elite have found their way to Paris, London, or Los Angeles. One family that stayed was that of Shirin Ebadi, once a judge, now a defendant's lawyer.[1]

The Prequel

Shirin Ebadi was born in Hamedan, Iran's oldest city, in 1947. She had two sisters and a brother. One sister became a dentist while her brother, who got a PhD in Economics from the University of California, Santa Barbara, became a professor. When Ebadi was still an infant, her family moved to Tehran. Her father, Mohammad Ali Ebadi, a professor of commercial law, and her mother, Minu Yamini, a homemaker, named her *Shirin* or "Sweet," a name that does not suggest the strength of character she has consistently displayed. Ebadi was a teenager when the White Revolution, which featured land reform but which also included new opportunities for women, began. This made it possible for women to serve in the parliament and as government ministers. It also made it possible for Ebadi to enroll in and graduate from the University of Tehran's School of Law. Ebadi did not travel abroad as a young woman, and although she admires the work of William James, her education was in Iran and her important referent figures are Iranian, for example, Prime Minister Amir Kabir, who in the late nineteenth century brought many Western ideas to what was then Persia.

After receiving her law degree, Ebadi chose to continue her legal studies and she obtained a master's degree in 1971. She also took the examination for a judgeship and became a judge in 1969. At the age of twenty-eight, in 1975, she became president of the City Court of Tehran, a judicial first for a woman. The jurisdiction of the city court is commercial and civil law. However, Ebadi sometimes did extra work in the evening related to family law. She served as a judge for only four years because those who led the 1979 revolution demoted her and other recently appointed women judges to positions, first as secretaries, and later to slightly higher positions as "law experts." The new government argued that women were too emotional to serve as judges—that they lacked the capacity to reason in accord with legal principles.[2]

Ebadi took early retirement in 1984 and applied for a license to practice law. It took eight years to obtain that license. However, the revolutionary government had made many changes in Iran's laws almost overnight, and many of those changes involved restrictions on women. These included a requirement that hair be covered in public and that women wear the chador,

Shirin Ebadi. Courtesy of Nayereh Tohidi

a traditional Iranian garment. The government also lowered the legal age of marriage from eighteen to nine, legalized polygamy, reinstated stoning as a legal punishment, and repealed the Family Protection Act, which had afforded protection to women in such matters as choice of spouse, divorce, and financial support.

Ebadi did not pine while she waited for her license. She had married Javad Tavassolian, an electrical engineer, in 1975 and was raising two daughters. One of her daughters studied law in Iran while the other studied electrical engineering in Canada. Although Ebadi insists that she did not have a role model and that she does not believe in them for others, she wanted to have a cultural environment in her home. No TV was permitted, and Ebadi frequently worked at home so her daughters would see what hard work meant.

She also did some work for a private law firm. She wrote reports, articles, and books. Concern for children was particularly high on her agenda, and in 1994 she helped found and lead the Society for Protecting the Rights of the Child. The society's purpose was to persuade the parliament to reform Iranian law in accordance with the UN Convention on the Rights of the Child. The Iranian government had accepted that convention. Thus, Ebadi's and the organization's efforts were focused not on ratification but on implementation. The society was an organization of and by Iranian women both in and out of the country. While they did not seek support from non-Iranian sources, Ebadi and many other Iranian women knew about and participated in a variety of UN programs directed toward women and children. The establishment of UN norms can be very helpful to domestic reformers, even though there is no mechanism for their enforcement.

Among the society's activities was the establishment of a "Helpline" for children and parents. The group published a journal, and it also established kindergartens and homes for street children. In one instance, Ebadi represented a divorced mother who had lost custody of her six-year-old daughter. This was in accordance with traditional law, and the judges were not moved to rule in the mother's favor even though she was able to provide evidence that the child was being abused in her father's home. Again and again the mother sought custody. Eventually the abuse resulted in the child's death. The public was so outraged by this tragedy that custody law in Iran was amended in 1998 to favor women. Like many of Ebadi's victories, this one was bittersweet, for it occurred only after a six-year-old died. It is, however, an example of Ebadi's approach to social reform, which is to use the legal system and never, ever, be associated with any kind of violence.

Another success for the society was a change in the minimum legal age for marriage. In 2002 the policy was changed to require court approval for the marriage of a girl under the age of thirteen or of a boy under fifteen. The legislature had tried to raise the ages to fifteen and eighteen, but that was blocked by the Council of Guardians, and the new legislation represented a compromise.

Ebadi has continued her work on children's rights. She authored the first draft of a law passed in 2002 that forbid the physical abuse of children. She has also written about children's rights, arguing among other things that the laws under the first Pahlavi shah were more generous toward children than are today's laws. She has written about the Court for Juvenile Delinquents and about the Reform and Training Center. Her major and prize-winning work about children is *The Rights of the Child: A Study of Legal Aspects of Children's Rights in Iran* (1994), which has been published in English with the support of UNICEF. She has also written *Comparing Children's Rights*, in which she compares the rights of Iranian children to those guaranteed by the UN Convention on the Rights of Children.

Ebadi has also been active in women's rights. Her major publication in this area is *Women's Rights in the Laws of the Islamic Republic of Iran*. She is not hesitant to accept the title of *feminist*, or at least *Islamic feminist*. In a talk in May 2004 she noted that at the beginning of her activism on behalf of women, her strongest detractors were often other women, but that in recent years that resistance had decreased. Indeed, some women have begun to criticize Ebadi as being too conservative because she works within a legal and Islamic framework.[3] Her position is that the principal injustices suffered by women are not required by Islam, but derive from a much earlier patriarchal system that has no necessary connection to Islam. An indicator of such a system in another culture might be that, like most Muslim women, Orthodox Jewish women also cover their hair. However, instead of wearing a scarf they cover their hair with a wig.

As Iranian women have become more likely to support issues related to their rights, they have also begun to exercise them. They are an important voting bloc, and today a majority of university students in Iran are female. In fact, three Iranian universities have recently begun Women's Studies programs. Ebadi is associated with the one at Allameh Tabatabai University.

One issue Ebadi has pursued for years is the weight to be given to women's legal testimony. At present, a woman's testimony is valued at only half that of a man's. Another issue involves "blood money." According to traditional Iranian law, a person responsible for another's death must pay the bereaved a certain amount of money, which is thus known as "blood money." Also, the value (or judged loss to the bereaved) of a female death is only half that of a male death. The results of these two principles can sometimes be bizarre. Take the case of an eleven-year-old girl named Leila Fathahi. She was raped and killed. Three men were convicted of the crime. One confessed and killed himself. The other two men acknowledged helping to bury the body of the girl, and they were convicted and sentenced to death. Their conviction was upheld on appeal, but, the Fathahi family was required to pay blood money for their execution—money the family did not have even after selling their home. Ebadi is the lawyer for the family, and she is trying to get the courts to abolish the requirement for blood money in criminal cases, and also to value women's lives the same as men's. In the Fathahi case, the judiciary has agreed to reduce the blood money payment by a third, but the case is not yet settled.

Another success involved the parliament's approval of the UN's Convention on the Elimination of All Forms of Discrimination against Women (CEDAW). That success proved of little consequence, however, because the Council of Guardians declared the convention at odds with Islamic law, Sharia, and therefore unacceptable. Many restrictions on women in Iran continue. For instance, although Ebadi is able to travel freely to advance women's rights, it is only because her husband permits it. She, like all Iranian women, can only leave the country with the written permission of her spouse or guardian.

Ebadi's concern for the rights of women and children is broad-based; for instance, in *Refugee Rights in Iran* she has written about the rights of laborers and of refugees.[4] Further, as her view has expanded, she has begun to think about the rights of men as well. After extensive debate, the UN has also decided that women's rights are human rights. Thus it is not surprising that Ebadi's work on behalf of women's rights led her to a more general consideration of human rights. When she did so, her work became risky.

Doing Dangerous Work

Ebadi is a defense lawyer. She describes her work as being the speaker for "silent people." She rejects any portrayal of her work as political, and rejects any suggestion that she might eventually seek or accept political office. Nevertheless, her work has political consequences, for while some of those she represents have simply displeased the Iranian government, others have been actively political. She has had an important role in three kinds of cases. In the first, she has represented the families of dissidents who have been killed at the direction of government officials; in the second, she has represented students who have been arrested by the government; and in the third kind of case, she has represented members of the press whose papers have been closed and who may also have been arrested.

After the end of the war with Iraq in 1988 and the death of Khomeini in 1989, government control eased and attention was even given to developing congenial relations with other countries. In fact, after his election as president in 1997, Mohammad Khatami called in a CNN interview for a dialogue with the American people. He also supported a variety of democratic institutions and the rule of law. Almost immediately a "press revolution" began. In Tehran alone a dozen major, independent newspapers appeared. One kind of story that had not been seen before involved reports of state-sponsored assassinations. One well-documented case involved the murder of four Kurdish nationalists in Berlin in 1992. German courts tied the deaths directly to Iran's top leadership. Other reports of assassinations and threats of assassination were reported, including an effort to drive a minibus of secular intellectuals off the road and into a ravine. At one point the president's brother publicly stated that there were at least eighty unsolved deaths or disappearances of secular intellectuals and political dissidents.

In late 1998, a series of apparently connected or serial killings and disappearances occurred. They are collectively referred to as "the Chain murders," and they included the disappearance of Pirouz Davani, a dissident intellectual, as well as the murder of three secularists, Javad Sharif, Mohammad Mokhtari, and Mohammed Jafar Pouyandeh, who was killed on the very day that his translation and history of the Universal Declaration of Human Rights was published. Then nationalist leaders Dariush and Parvaneh Forouhar were stabbed to death in their home. Listening devices planted by a government security service allegedly recorded the sounds of the killing. The victims were intellectuals, residents of the capital, and known to many. The string of murders shocked and frightened the public, and the newly free press headlined the killings. Story after story appeared. The press demanded that government security forces find and punish the killers, and suggested that if they did not do so, it could only be because government officials were directly or indirectly responsible.

Astonishingly, in January 1999 the Ministry of Intelligence admitted that "rogue" agents had indeed been responsible for the "catastrophe." The minister of intelligence resigned, and the bureau was reorganized. Continued criticism and allegations of the complicity of high-ranking clerics helped reform forces win a solid victory in the next election for the legislature.

Ebadi's role in all this included representing the families of Pouyandeh, of the Forouhars, and of other victims of the government. These were cases that most lawyers feared to take. When asked why she took them, Ebadi's answer was "Who else would do it?" If no one else would accept a case because of the danger involved, Ebadi believed she had a special responsibility to step forward.

Universities are rarely quiet during periods of social upheaval. In 1999, peacefully demonstrating students at the University of Tehran were attacked by vigilantes in the presence of police. At least one student, Ezzat Ebrahim-nezhad, was killed. The government's response was to arrest hundreds of students, but not their attackers. Ebadi offered to represent Ebrahimnezhad's family without compensation after she read that his father was going to sell the family home to raise the money to pay for a lawyer. The family selected Ebadi's offer from several offers for assistance that they received. The choice was made because the only family member who could follow each step of the case was the dead student's sister, and she preferred a woman lawyer. Ebadi's investigation bore fruit. Many onlookers had suspected that the vigilantes were members of government security forces or were being paid by them. One result of Ebadi's investigation was to provide evidence that this was, in fact, true. A second result was that Ebadi was jailed and disbarred.

The issue involved evidence uncovered by Ebadi and the use to which it was put. Specifically, Ebadi obtained a videotaped confession from a participant in the beatings. He said that prominent conservative figures were behind the attacks on the students and reformers. The tape reached the public, although Ebadi said that she had planned to use it only for evidence in the student trials. After the tape became public, the agent who had confessed on the tape was arrested. While he was in police custody he recanted, saying that the tape represented a "forced confession" made during a previous arrest. The distribution of the tape was deemed illegal by the government on the grounds that it "disturbed public opinion." Ebadi's assertion that she had only taped the confession as part of her responsibility as a defense lawyer was rejected. She was convicted in closed-court proceedings and received a fifteen-month jail sentence, which was then suspended. She also lost her license to practice law for five years. However, it was soon restored.

Ebadi did serve time in jail, but she served it *before* her trial and conviction. When she was first arrested, she was placed in solitary confinement for twenty-five days. There she had no one to speak to and was at first forbidden access to any books except a prayer book she had taken with her when she was first summoned for questioning. Also, the Koran was provided in the cell. After two weeks she was allowed to use the prison library, that is, someone could bring books to her, but she (as was the case with every woman prisoner) could not go to the library herself. It was a difficult time. She had back pain, but worse than this was not knowing what would come next. She was determined not to complain, but she admitted that during this time she would grit her teeth and flex her fingers until the nails turned blue. Both Henry David Thoreau's and Martin Luther King Jr.'s accounts of their days in jail suggest that the impact of even a brief confinement can be significant. Sometimes it can be empowering.

In addition to cases involving dissident intellectuals and students, Ebadi accepted cases on behalf of the many periodicals that were banned after the clerical backlash began. *Jameah* was one of the first and most successful of these newspapers. It began publication in early 1998 with a commitment to independent professionalism and to civil society. Within months it had achieved a circulation of 300,000. It flatly asserted that one could criticize an Islamic government and remain a good Muslim. It reported that the head of the Revolutionary Guards had said that the "necks and tongues" of political opponents should be severed. But by June of the same year its license had been revoked for the undermining of religious and revolutionary values. Its editors continued to publish for a short time under other names and with other licenses, but it soon became clear that the clerics were not ready for a free press.

More than 140 licenses to publish had been awarded during President Mohammad Khatami's first term, but while a host of other papers continued to publish, the repression of *Jameah* cooled editors' ambitions. Many of the papers were political, and many supported Khatami and his reformers.

Even so, many of these papers and magazines were closed in the next eighteen months. Supporting the elected government did not make one immune to punishment, for the clerics, not elected officials, decided both the meaning of the law and the nature of the changes that were or were not to be permitted.

As a result, many editors and reporters found themselves in jail. In 2000 and just before the new, reformist legislature was to be sworn in, new press laws were passed. No criticism of the Islamic constitution was to be permitted. And journalists would, in effect, have to pass a security review. In April of that year, no less than fourteen reformist publications were closed. When the new parliament took office, it quickly began a revision of the repressive laws. But the Supreme Leader then declared that amendment of the press law and similar actions were "not [religiously] legitimate and not in the interest of the country or the system." The reformists who had consistently campaigned for the rule of law were hoisted by their own petard, because law permitted the Supreme Leader to make such decisions.[5] Many journalists remain in prison today. In May 2005 one of them, Akbar Ganji, who had accused senior officials of complicity in the Sevialor chain murders, began a hunger strike. He will receive the Golden Pen of Freedom award from the World Association of Newspapers in June 2006.

Ebadi does not accept theocratic rule. Her belief is that democracy and human rights are fully compatible with Islam. To her, a government that violates the rights of its citizens and then seeks refuge in the argument that freedom and democracy are not compatible with Islam is, simply, wrong. In her view, many of the cases she defends represent the use of Islam to thwart democracy. Nor does Ebadi accept the validity of the argument that Iran's is a special culture. Democracy is simply the "people's will"; there are no different models of democracy, there is only democracy. In the same way, she believes that human rights are universal, that they are a component of every religion and of every civilization. Justice and rights are fundamental.

One of Ebadi's most recent cases involved Canadian and Iranian photojournalist, Zahra Kazemi. In July 2003 Kazemi was arrested while she was taking pictures at a student demonstration. Within a month of her arrest she died in an Iranian prison. She was fifty-four. At first it was reported that she had died of a stroke. Then a prison guard was charged with beating her to death. He was acquitted. The court then declared that she had died as the result of an accident—that she had fainted and hit her head when she fell. The circumstances were sufficiently suspicious that Canada broke diplomatic relations with Iran, and the Khatami government charged that the guilty person was known and should be arrested. Ebadi represented the family and also believes that a known senior official was responsible. In late 2005 yet another investigation was ordered.

Among her other efforts, Ebadi also helped to establish the Center for the Defense of Human Rights, published *Rights, History, and Documentation of Human Rights in Iran* (2000), and has been recognized by Human Rights Watch.

The Prize

By 2003 the reformers were firmly in control of the Iranian legislature and the presidency, but their programs were being regularly blocked by either the clergy-appointed judiciary, the Guardian Council, or even the Supreme Leader. Those who had committed themselves to democratic, peaceful change were discouraged. That fall, the Norwegian Nobel Committee made a surprise announcement: the Nobel Peace Prize for 2003 would go to Iranian lawyer and human-rights activist Shirin Ebadi.[6] The committee commended her as a representative of Reformed Islam who argued for interpreting Islamic law in harmony with democracy, equality before the law, religious freedom, and freedom of speech. The committee particularly praised her courage in defending individuals and groups who had fallen afoul of a system that legitimated its power as deriving from Islamic law.

Ebadi was in Paris attending an Iranian film festival when the prize was announced. She was stunned, but collected her thoughts at a news conference to assert that the most important change needed in Iran was freedom of speech accompanied by the release of political prisoners.

Although Lech Walesa harrumphed that the Pope should have won, Westerners were mostly curious about this unknown Muslim woman. The response in Iran varied. The government media first said nothing, and then made a brief announcement. The media controlled by reformers praised the award. Since Ebadi was in Paris at the time of the announcement, her homecoming reception at the Tehran airport became a measure of Iranians' feelings. She was greeted by a crowd of thousands organized by NGOs, a lawyers' association, and a writers' association. Most were women who wore white headscarves and carried white flowers. She was officially met on the tarmac by two of President Khatami's deputies and a group of legislators, including all the Iranian parliament's women legislators. Zahra Eshraghi, granddaughter of Ayatollah Ruhollah Khomeini and sister-in-law of President Khatami, gave her a garland of flowers.

The next day, however, conservative newspapers blasted Eshraghi's act as a betrayal of her grandfather and declared that she must have been manipulated by her reformist husband. At prayers that Friday many clergy denounced Ebadi and the prize. In the religious center of Qom, a declaration was issued saying that the prize was "the latest plot of the Global Arrogance" to undermine Islam. It urged a serious revolutionary confrontation with the infidels whose tongues should be "cut from their mouths and the poisonous pens broken in their hearts." A prominent legislator said awarding the prize to Ebadi was like rewarding Salman Rushdie, the Zionist regime, or U.S. leaders. President Khatami observed that the Nobel Peace Prize is "not important and is political." State television did not broadcast Ebadi's Nobel lecture because she gave it without a headscarf. Some conservatives dismissed her as a "Western mercenary."

Overnight Ebadi, a short woman whose presence fills a room and who covers her hair in Iran but not while traveling abroad, became an international celebrity. Her character emerged. The limelight revealed a hard-working, practical professional who was respected for her honesty, her consistency, and her bravery. From the day of the announcement on, Ebadi's public appearances would command a worldwide audience. Because her Nobel lecture first defined her for the international community, that speech merits attention.

She began with a call for restoring the rights of women, which had been taken away from them "through the passage of history"—a situation resulting from a patriarchal culture that "cannot continue forever." She then noted that her lecture coincided with the fifty-fifth anniversary of the Universal Declaration of Human Rights, a declaration that provided for protection from fear and poverty as well as for rights, freedom, justice, and peace. She noted UN data showing that 1.2 billion people in the world lived on less than a dollar a day, that AIDS had claimed 22 million lives and orphaned 13 million children, and that a quarter of the world's countries were then engaged in war or had recently suffered a major natural disaster. There was work to be done.

Ebadi went on to note that "some states" had used a war on terrorism to introduce new regulations restricting human rights, and that they had set up special bodies and extraordinary courts making fair adjudication "difficult and at times impossible." She said that while some states had long opposed human rights in the name of cultural relativism, others, traditional supporters of human rights, were now violating their own principles. Her primary example involved prisoners held by the United States in Guantanamo Bay, Cuba. Also, Ebadi asked why some UN Security Council resolutions were promptly acted on, for example, that related to Iraq and the first Gulf War, while others, those related to the Palestinian territories, for instance, languished for decades.

She proudly declared herself an Iranian, a descendent of Cyrus the Great who promised religious freedom to his people and declared he would not rule without the people's consent. She also declared herself a Muslim, a Muslim whose religion had been imbued with humanitarianism especially through the Gnostic literature. As a Muslim, she also argued that it was not necessary for Islam to "lag behind the caravan of civilization, development, and progress," and that just as a war against "terrorism" masked Western violations of human rights, so obedience to "Islam" masked patriarchal violations of women's rights and also masked violations of democracy and freedom for men as well.

She concluded that a commitment to international human rights law required that nations have the right to determine their own destinies, and to enjoy their territorial integrity and political independence. The "sluggishness of the South," she declared, did not justify intervention in the region with claims to be advancing human rights and democracy. That was the responsibility of the people of the South themselves.

While Ebadi acknowledges that she now has more platforms from which to speak, especially outside the country, she asserts that winning the Nobel Peace Prize has "changed nothing in my life." She does not feel safer. Even after she won the prize, conservative women students disrupted and forced the cancellation of a talk she was scheduled to give.

Since winning the Nobel Peace Prize, Ebadi has made a number of visits to the United States. Several themes recur in her appearances. One is that she is a Muslim and that she has no quarrel with Islam.[7] Her quarrel is with an Islam that uses the power of the state to impose particular interpretations of the Koran and of Sharia, many of them centuries-old and narrow. Islam, she asserts, does adapt. The most obvious example concerns slavery, which is assumed in the Koran, but is no longer considered fundamental to Islamic society. Adaptations can also be made to location. For instance, during Ramadan the devout Muslim is supposed to fast from sunrise until sunset. At certain times of the year in the Arctic, however, the sun never sets. Thus, a reasonable interpretation of the rule might be to require fasting for a certain number of hours instead. Further, Shiite Islam, which is Iran's dominant version of Islam, has a tradition of theological discussion, even though this is not the case in today's Iran. Some Muslims claim that debate and discussion are the real Islamic tradition.

Ebadi is not one who says, "I'm not a feminist but...." She is willing to accept the label. But it is qualified; she is an Islamic feminist. One point that she makes to Western audiences is that rights and freedom are essential. The chador, the headscarf, the veil that many Westerners see as a symbol of repression is for many Muslim women a symbol of their faith. She would prefer that wearing the chador be voluntary rather than mandatory, but she also prefers that women and girls not be forbidden to wear the chador or headscarves as they are in French schools. Ebadi does not see ending compulsory veiling as a priority.

In her talks in the United States she has emphasized Iran's long history and the degree to which it continues to develop. She praises reformist president Khatami, although she believes that he missed important opportunities for change by being too accommodating. But changes in Iran, she emphasizes, are the responsibility of Iranians and of no one else. She regularly criticizes U.S. policy related to terrorism. "One day they help the Taliban rise to power and the next they attack Afghanistan with the excuse of ousting them." Other recurring themes include (1) The war on terrorism has not reduced the number of terrorist acts; (2) The violation of the rights of prisoners is unacceptable; (3) Violence begets violence; (4) Terrorism must be defeated by attacking its two pillars: injustice and certainty of belief, and a crucial weapon against both is education; (5) We must recognize that there are some who benefit by war; and (6) The United States is in Iraq now because of its ignorance of the region and because of oil. "How I wish the Middle East had more water and less oil," she has lamented.

Ironically, Ebadi finds that when she argues on behalf of human rights at home, she is charged with being an ally of President George W. Bush. But she does not believe that human rights activists can ever be in the same camp with President Bush. Nor can supporters of democracy be supporters of President Bush. She has said that "you cannot drop democracy down like bombs!" that "democracy cannot be served on a golden platter," and that democracy cannot "be enforced with the use of weapons of war."

Ebadi plans to write a memoir. It will surely reverse any stereotyped opinion Westerners may have of Muslim women as docile and controlled. It will argue on behalf of human rights and democracy. She is not likely to be able to publish it in Iran. But will it be published in the United States? At first this seemed doubtful.

Although federal law prohibits the embargo of information, the Treasury Department's Office of Foreign Assets prohibits the publication of works from Iran, Cuba, and the Sudan not already "fully created and in existence." This

Judith Stiehm (l) and Shirin Ebadi (r). Courtesy of the author

would have made it impossible for Ebadi to work with a U.S. publisher or translator. Violation of the law could have resulted in a fine of $1 million and ten years' imprisonment. So what would a rights lawyer naturally do? Refusing to accept an "enforced silence," Ebadi filed a lawsuit in federal court in New York City. The rule was quickly changed.

What Will Be the Sequel?

In the last quarter century Iran has endured a revolution and an extended war. Few are interested in further violence. The current constitution provides for a government with democratic-looking institutions, but the Supreme Leader and the Council of Guardians have ultimate power. They are chosen by the Assembly of Experts, who are elected in national balloting. There appears to be room for evolution in the direction of democracy. However, nations under threat typically narrow rather than loosen the reins, and Iran feels threatened.

The government does not let its citizens forget the CIA's regime change of the 1950s or President George W. Bush's labeling of Iran as one of three members of an "Axis of Evil"—one of which the United States has since invaded and occupied.[8] Apart from the issue of support for terrorists in the Middle East, the issue involves Iran's development of nuclear power and its possession of nuclear weapons. The United States, Europe, and Israel are determined that Iran not get such weapons. Iranian officials, unsurprisingly, see this as an infringement on their sovereignty, and see that many neighbors within missile distance already have them (China, India, Pakistan, Russia, and Israel).

Ebadi's initiatives have always been taken within Iran's legal and religious framework. She is no revolutionary. But in a nation under siege, even to ask questions, to publish factual material, or to mount an effective legal defense can be perceived as endangering the state. Ebadi has reason to fear. However, as she has explained, she has trained herself to live with fear because "Every time I am fearful I think to myself, the reason they do this is to discourage me from doing what I do. Hence, if I discontinue my work I will have succumbed to my fears. Finally, I believe in God. This helps make me strong."

Ebadi supports and is supported by UN principles. What is tricky for her is support by outside governments and NGOs. She does not want to become the reviled Jane Fonda of Iran. For the U.S. government to endorse her would be to damage her acceptance at home. This may be part of the reason she is so publicly critical of U.S. policy and behavior. Even Norway's awarding her the Nobel Peace Prize was seen by some as meddling in Iran's domestic politics. And there are grounds for this belief. In its citation, the Norwegian Nobel Committee said that democracy and human rights had been advancing in various parts of the world and that in making its awards the committee "has attempted to speed up this process." Moreover, the award came at a time when reformers in Iran were losing ground. It was heartening for them. Indeed, Ebadi's husband was quoted as saying, "The reform movement is reborn."

Strong electoral support in Iran for the reform movement has shown that the population may be ready for change. To contain reform, religious rulers have had to exercise their vetoes and justify the use of force. Some observers have even suggested that the clerics' real concern is not with religion but with staying in power. However, discussion and dissent among religious leaders and by religious laypeople may be necessary before change can gain any momentum. This is unlikely to surface if Iranians believe they must be unified in the face of an external threat.

Much as Ebadi discounts the concept of role models and urges individuals to express and act on their individuality, she has, nevertheless, become an inspiration for both Iranian women and others committed to social justice. She can be expected to continue her advocacy through her writing, her teaching, and her work as a defendant's lawyer, even though any changes in the direction of democracy and human rights in Iran may be slow in coming. The cases Ebadi accepts are largely those of people who have suffered or who are suffering, or are those of families who have lost loved ones. It is crucial and important work, but it is not work that gives her much joy or many victories. Like that of Mother Teresa, Ebadi's work is continuous. As does Aung San Suu Kyi, she challenges a well-entrenched government, and one that elected a conservative president in late 2005. Keeping her spirits up is sometimes difficult. When I asked Ebadi what she did when especially disheartened, she replied, "I eat chocolate and take walks." I hope someone is making sure that her chocolate will never be in short supply.

Notes

1. There are no substantial works on Ebadi in English. Most of this chapter is based on an interview held in New York City on June 8, 2004.

2. After sustained and energetic lobbying, women have won a reversal of the no-women-judges policy. Ebadi points to this as an example of something that was once forbidden as un-Islamic and that has now been found to be in harmony with Islam. She argues that there are many other policies that might be altered if they were carefully reviewed.

3. This is especially true of women in the exile community. Ebadi's response is "If I am so tolerant of the clerical regime why have I lost my judgeship, why have I been in jail, why have I had assassination threats? Do I need to be killed to prove I am brave?"

4. Iran took in as many as 3 million refugees from Afghanistan after the Russian invasion.

5. Although Khatami ran on a platform of democracy and the rule of law, he is also a cleric. It is important to understand that while Islam has different sects, most importantly Sunni and Shiia sects, becoming a cleric is a matter of extended, recognized scholarship and the acquisition of followers. There is no hierarchy equivalent to that of the Roman Catholic Church. Thus, any number of clerics can issue a fatwa, an authoritative religious decree. In some sense, a cleric's authority derives from the acceptance of his views. This means that different senior clerics, even within a sect, may hold different beliefs.

6. Her mother cried at the news. Only twice before had she done so—once when Shirin graduated from law school, and once when she was jailed.

7. Two other Muslims have won the Nobel Peace Prize: Anwar el-Sadat and Yasser Arafat.

8. Iraq is Iran's neighbor to the west. The United States has also invaded her neighbor to the east, Afghanistan, is exerting influence in the former Soviet republics on her northern border, and has built a major military base in Qatar to Iran's south. Essentially, Iran is encircled. The United States is also exerting a variety of negative pressures on Iran, for instance, preventing her from joining the World Trade Organization (WTO). One can understand a belief that having a nuclear weapon that could be delivered at some distance would be seen as insurance against invasion.

Wangari Muta Maathai. Courtesy of the Norwegian Nobel Institute

༄

CHAPTER ELEVEN

Wangari Muta Maathai: Kenya's "Green" Doctor

A Different African Story

Wangari Muta Maathai is not the first Nobel Peace Prize winner from Africa. Egypt's Mohamed Anwar el-Sadat won for his support of peace with Israel (and was assassinated for doing so); Kofi Annan of Ghana won for his leadership as secretary-general of the United Nations; and South Africans Albert John Lutuli and Desmond Mpilo Tutu, and Nelson Mandela who paired with Frederik Willem de Klerk, all won for bringing an end to apartheid and civil conflict in their multiracial country.

Maathai is different. She is East African. She holds a PhD. Her base was indigenous, mostly women's and environmental organizations, and her Nobel Peace Prize came not for efforts related to war or civil conflict or even politics. She won for her efforts to "green" sub-Sahara Africa.

Let us begin with Kenya's story. It is an ancient one, for anthropologists believe that human beings may have had their origin there some 2.6 million years ago. Indeed, it has been called "the cradle of humanity." The Sahara limited communication between Europe and Mediterranean Africa and the southern portion of the continent. East–west travel was also difficult. Still, Arabian traders did find their way down the eastern coast by the first century AD. Kingdoms, some of them mighty, came and went over the centuries, and tribal groups migrated over extended distances. Still, for many in the West, African history begins with its discovery by Europeans.

The first Western explorers were Portuguese, who rounded Cape Horn at the end of the fifteenth century. They staked a claim to what is now coastal

202 ⌒ Chapter 11

Kenya, but were displaced by two Arab dynasties established in the early eighteenth century. The early Europeans did not come to stay, that is, they did not come with their families. Most were traders, many of them slave traders. However, some Europeans not only came with their families, they moved from the coast to the interior and made Africa home. This happened in what is now South Africa. One result was that the region became home to African, mixed-race, and also Caucasian populations, all of whom can claim many generations of residence there. Another result was the continued conflict that led to Nobel Peace Prizes for four South African men.

Kenya was different. Bounded in the north by Sudan and Ethiopia, in the west by Sudan and Uganda, in the south by Tanzania, and in the east by Somalia and the Indian Ocean, Kenya's coastal region long included an Arab, Islamic culture. Europeans did not begin inland exploration there until the mid-nineteenth century, about the same time European nations began staking out African spheres of influence. Although Germany first claimed today's Kenya, by the end of the nineteenth century England had won control. A railroad was built from the coast to the western border, and Europeans moved inland to farm the highlands.[1] They were followed by Indian traders, and Kenya was on its way to becoming what we now know it to be.

The displacement of Africans by European farmers, and laws that forbid Africans to raise cash crops, led to protests and conflict. Members of the Kikuyu tribe led insurgents in what England called the Mau Mau Emergency and what Africans called the War for Independence. The insurgency peaked between 1952 and 1956 and was put down by 1959. However, while only some one hundred Europeans died in contrast to the more than thirteen thousand Africans who also lost their lives, the English soon elected to leave. Independence was granted in 1963, and the first president was Jomo Kenyatta, leader of the Mau Mau. Because many Europeans and Indians had then or subsequently left the country, Kenya did not become as multiracial as South Africa. But the Europeans left their mark. Today two-thirds of the population is Christian. It is estimated that 40 percent is Protestant and close to 30 percent is Roman Catholic. (Muslims make up 10 to 20 percent of the population.) Also, English is one of the two official languages.[2]

One reason English became an official language is that Kenya encompasses many different tribes and languages. Tribal identification and tribal lands are important to individuals, but no tribe is numerically dominant in Kenya. The three largest tribes are the Kikuyu, with an estimated 22 percent of the population; the Luhya, with 14 percent; and the Luo, with 13 percent. Collectively the three do not make up quite 50 percent. Kenya is a multi-African nation.

In 1978 after President Kenyatta's death, Daniel Arap Moi, a Tugen but a member of Kenyatta's political party, the Kenya African National Union (KANU), became president. Moi held that position for twenty-four years. Opposition parties were allowed to form and compete for the first time in 1992. In 2002 the KANU suffered its first electoral defeat. Mwai Kibaki of the National Rainbow Coalition defeated Kenyatta's son, who was KANU's candidate for president. Kibaki won 63 percent of the vote. He is the president today.

Under Kenya's constitution, the presidency is the center of political power. An interesting constitutional provision does help to insure that he or she does not represent a single constituency. To win the presidency, a candidate must receive both the largest number of votes and at least 25 percent of the vote in five of the country's eight administrative units.

By European standards, Kenya is not prosperous. Still, its GDP per capita is over $1,000. Its literacy rate for males is 91 percent, and for females 80 percent. Life expectancy is forty-eight years, in spite of the HIV/AIDS epidemic. But as much as 40 percent of the country's population of 34 million is un- or underemployed. Kenya's capitalist economy has not been able to provide work for the country's citizens. The desperate need for work contributes to what has been a history of corrupt government. Efforts to capitalize on tourism and to exploit Kenya's game parks and beaches have provided some work, but tourism does not provide the kind of jobs that build GDP.

Enter Wangari Muta Maathai

Wangari Muta Maathai was born in April 1940 in Tetu, Nyeri.[3] Her parents were farmers, and she was the third of six children. Some of the world's best coffee comes from Tetu, which is located in the heart of the highlands. At an altitude of more than 5,000 feet, Nyeri has a pleasing climate and is nestled at the foot of the Aberdare Mountains. In the other direction, Mount Kenya can be seen on the horizon. Nyeri is both a market town for the region and a jumping-off place for game-watching at tourist sites like the Tree Tops and the Ark.

Maathai began school at age eight at Itithe Primary School. From age twelve to fifteen she attended St. Cecilia's School in Nyeri, and she was then chosen to attend Loreto Girls' School in Limuru. The Catholic Church had long been active in Kenya, and Maathai's convent schooling by foreign missionaries provided her with a solid education.

Nyeri is the heartland of the Kikuyu and was the center for Mau Mau resistance to the European settlers and their government.[4] Maathai was a young

Wangari Maathai as a student at St. Scholastica College (now Benedictine College). Courtesy of Florence Conrad Salisbury

teenager during the worst of the struggle. But she was also a direct beneficiary of the conflict for she was awarded a scholarship to attend college in the United States. The Kennedy administration believed that when independence came, the new nation would benefit from a cadre of young people who possessed U.S. college degrees. Maathai was one of some three hundred students chosen for the scholarship program.

At age twenty, after a Greyhound Bus trip from New York City where she saw her first skyscraper and her first escalator, Maathai arrived at Mount St. Scholastica College in Atchison, Kansas, on the Missouri River. Atchison was an agricultural community, and the schooling was Catholic and for women only. Little else was familiar to Maathai. The college was small but well-established. It had been founded by seven Benedictine sisters in 1863 as an academy for young women. In 1924 the sisters had inaugurated a college curriculum, and by 1934 the college was offering accredited, four-year liberal arts degrees. Mary Jo Wangari Maathai won a bachelor's degree in biology in 1964. In 1989 she was awarded the school's Offeramus Medal as an outstanding graduate.[5]

A good student, Maathai chose to pursue more education before returning to her newly independent country. The University of Pittsburgh was her next destination, and biology continued to be her subject. The fact that Jonas Salk and his team had recently developed a vaccine for polio at Pittsburgh must have been an attraction. With a master's degree in hand and after six years of studying science in the United States, Maathai continued her studies in Munich before heading home. There she found a position as a research assistant at the University of Nairobi. Five years later in 1971, she had become a wife and a mother, and she had a PhD in anatomy. In fact, she was the first woman to earn a PhD in Kenya and was made a faculty member in the university's well-regarded Department of Veterinary Medicine. She became chair of veterinary anatomy in 1976 and associate professor in 1977. Both were firsts for a Kenyan woman.

Maathai appreciated the educational opportunities she had enjoyed, and busy though she was, she joined the National Council of Women of Kenya (NCWK) to advocate for women's rights and education. She was also active in the National Association of University Women, the Kenya Red Cross, and the Environment Liaison Center.

In addition to her academic position, Maathai enjoyed a certain status as the wife of a new member of parliament. After her husband's winning campaign, Maathai took an interest in his poor constituents. In fact, her first environmental effort involved trying to create a tree nursery and planting program to provide work for those constituents. For a variety of reasons the effort proved unsuccessful, but in 1977 Maathai was invited to give a lecture to the general meeting of NCWK about a UN Human Settlements Program (UN-HABITAT) meeting she had attended in Vancouver the year before. She was a hit and was soon elected to NCWK's executive committee and to its Standing Committee on Environment and Habitat. When NCWK adopted Maathai's tree nursery and planting program as its own, Save the Land Harambee, the precursor to the Green Belt Movement was launched. The first seven trees were planted that June. From the beginning the emphasis of the program was on *harambee*, meaning "let us pull together." The goal was to have individuals make a commitment, assume responsibility, and take action.

Sadly, Maathai found that pulling together didn't always come easily. In fact, in the early 1980s her husband sued for divorce, publicly accusing her of adultery. She opposed the divorce. When the judge ruled against her, Maathai declared that to reach the decision he had reached the judge must be either incompetent or corrupt. She was quickly sentenced to six months in jail for contempt of court, although she was released after several days when she promised to apologize. This was her first but not her last stay in jail.

Maathai decided to run for parliament herself. She resigned from her academic position to do so, but election officials disqualified her on a technicality. The university then refused to reinstate her. Her days of research on East Coast

Fever, a fatal cattle disease, were over. Her energies would now be devoted to environmental work. Neither the government nor the university could have foreseen the force they had unleashed. And a prophecy her former husband had once made proved correct. During the divorce proceedings, he had said Maathai was "too educated, too strong, too successful, too stubborn, and too hard to control."

Maathai's childhood memories included being able to drink from a spring close to her home. They included a giant fig tree so beloved by her mother that she did not even collect its fallen twigs for firewood. She remembered a healthy and well-fed community of subsistence farmers. But when she returned from abroad, she found the spring and the fig tree gone, and the land converted to tea plantations. At first she thought that earning a cash income would have a positive effect. However, there was an unintended negative consequence; there was not enough food to buy. There was not enough firewood to cook meals either. What Maathai realized was that her home district's independence and participation in a cash economy had resulted in a deterioration in the quality of life. Further, from her fieldwork Maathai realized that erosion, deforestation, and malnutrition were not confined to her home district—the deterioration of the environment was occurring throughout Kenya and in other parts of sub-Sahara Africa as well.[6]

Maathai did not attend the 1975 UN Women's Conference held in Mexico, but others from NCWK did. Their reports reinforced her conviction that one of the most important issues of the day, especially for African women, was access to clean water and energy. Another idea that came from that 1975 conference was the concept of a Voluntary Fund for Women. That idea would be developed by Margaret Snyder, regional advisor to the UN Economic Commission for Africa (ECA), and the Voluntary Fund would eventually become the UN Development Fund for Women (UNIFEM). Also, Snyder would later become a friend and an important supporter of Maathai's Green Belt Movement.

To village women, energy meant firewood, and clean water required mountains and forests. But the forests were gone. What was to be done? Search for new sources of fuel? Create irrigation projects? Build water treatment plants? Maathai believes that one important result of her education is her capacity to identify a problem and to then think through to a solution. Another important characteristic of her thinking is her ability to offer a simple solution. If deforestation resulted in a loss of access to energy and clean water, the obvious remedy was—reforestation. Plant trees. Her solution was not only simple; it was something virtually every Kenyan could help realize. The poor and uneducated could plant and nourish a tree as ably as a PhD. Further, they would have the experience of taking an action that would change their lives for the better. And they could enjoy the beauty of a tree's growth and flowering. Thus, trees were a solution, but they also became a symbol of hope.

Maathai's Harambee project gained momentum in the fall of 1977 when the Kenyan subsidiary of Mobil Oil and several other donors gave the project money in conjunction with a UN Conference on Desertification held in Nairobi. The money was used to develop tree nurseries. More importantly, the media gave Harambee attention and support. Among the first to be mobilized were children. Maathai went to the schools. She gave children seedlings to take home, plant, and nurture. By the time the children had finished school, their trees were established and no longer required careful attention. Today children in thousands of schools throughout Africa are involved in the Green Belt Movement.[7]

It was rural women, though, who provided the sustained energy for the tree-planting campaign. As the chair of NCWK from 1981 to 1987, Maathai mobilized its large, widespread, grassroots membership. Her goal was to plant 15 million trees (Kenya's population at the time). Her efforts were greatly assisted by "seed money" from UNIFEM, which made it possible to establish hundreds of nurseries, most of them in rural areas. The nurseries then provided thousands of women with millions of seedlings. The seedlings were donated; if they survived for three months, the person who planted the seedling was given a (very) small sum. It is estimated that 80 percent of the trees reached maturity.

When the Harambee project began planting belts of a thousand or more trees, its name evolved to the Green Belt Movement. As its projects grew larger, the movement's sometimes advantageous, sometimes awkward relationship with government foresters gave way to a movement decision to build its own nurseries and to train its own participants. By 1999 it was supporting six thousand nurseries.

In 1986 the movement went international. The Pan-African Green Belt brought together women from neighboring countries like Tanzania, Uganda, Malawi, Lesotho, Ethiopia, and Zimbabwe. Women from as many as thirty countries have by now worked with the movement or have created similar organizations of their own. As many as 30 million trees have been planted.

The movement's stated mission is "to mobilize community consciousness for self-determination, equity, improved livelihood securities,[8] and environmental conservation using trees as an entry point." Again, planting trees is only the first step. From the beginning Maathai's goals were larger. They included giving women confidence, generating income, empowering women, and demonstrating their capacities.

The Movement Expands

Efforts were made to educate women about nutritional requirements, family planning, and farming techniques almost from the beginning. However, as women acquired information and experienced success, they began to ask questions like "Why were the trees cut down in the first place?" "Don't we have a right to a clean and healthy environment?" "Shouldn't our government be helping us?" and "How does the government decide what to do?" These were not the kind of questions that the one-party, one-man government of President Moi was used to hearing. Environmental issues soon melded into political issues over land usage. Programs for civic education and advocacy were formally adopted. "Land grabbers" and corruption became targets of the movement.

An important confrontation occurred in 1989–1990. President Moi, unchallenged in office for more than a decade, decided to make downtown Nairobi's Uhuru (Freedom) Park the site of a sixty-two-story office building in the service of his own prestige. In front of the skyscraper there was to be a four-story statue of—yes, Moi. The building would have been twice the height of any other building in Nairobi and the tallest building in Africa. The budget estimate was close to $200 million and would have required foreign financing.

Maathai and women in the Green Belt Movement protested vigorously. Maathai said, "We can provide parks for rhinos and elephants, why can't we provide open spaces for people? Why are we creating environmental havoc in urban areas?" Green Belt members protested to parliament, where they were denounced and derided. Maathai was ridiculed as an adulterous divorcée. She filed a lawsuit to block the development. Her action was called "ugly and ominous." The suit was dismissed. She applied for a license to hold a demonstration. It was denied. Not a single government official questioned the project. Finally, the movement was forced out of its offices in a government building, and there was talk of banning it for trying to "destabilize" the government.

The struggle caught the attention of the international press and that of environmental and human rights groups as well.[9] Maathai's protests also reached the international financial community. A scaled-down version of the building was announced. Then, without announcement, fencing in the park came down. The financial community had decided not to invest. Uhuru Park remains downtown Nairobi's jewel. Moi's government had experienced its first defeat. Shortly thereafter, it authorized the country's first competitive elections.

The Green Belt Movement had added democracy to its agenda, and the tree became a symbol of democracy as well as of hope. Soon a demonstration began on behalf of political prisoners. Maathai joined a group of mothers of some of those prisoners in a three-day sleep-in and hunger strike in Uhuru Park at what is now called Freedom Corner. The demonstrators were rural women and few in number, but they attracted large antigovernment crowds and the media. People told stories about their arrest and torture. All-night prayer vigils were mounted. Musicians performed. Then the police attacked with batons and tear gas, and there was a lengthy struggle before they could reach the protesting women. Maathai was knocked unconscious and taken to a hospital in critical condition. Some of the infuriated women stripped off their clothes as a sign of their disgust and contempt for the police. Some women were sent to the hospital; others were taken to their homes. The tree began to symbolize not only democracy and hope, but human rights too.

The next day, the women gathered in the basement of an Anglican church near the park to resume their vigil. The government sent five hundred armed men who laid siege to the church for a week. Then an agreement was brokered. The police would leave and the women would agree not to receive visitors. Theirs became a campaign of silence, but one that proved effective for within a year the government had released all but one of the more than fifty arrested.

Maathai continued her criticism of Moi's repressive government. In 1997 she challenged the government by running for president. However, it was falsely reported that she had withdrawn from the contest, and her candidacy failed. She stood for parliament in the same election, but that candidacy also failed.

The next year there was another confrontation. Again it involved an environmental challenge to the government. This too would become violent. A third of Karura Forest on the outskirts of Nairobi had been sold to developers backed by President Moi. Clearing of the land had already begun and violence had already occurred when Maathai led a group of supporters to the site. The group, which included twelve women and six members of the Kenyan parliament, planned to plant a small number of trees. At the site they were met by two hundred men dressed in civilian clothes and equipped with whips, clubs, and, allegedly, bows and arrows. When Maathai tried to plant a single symbolic seedling, the men attacked. Maathai and ten other protestors were injured, three of them seriously. There were no arrests of either the demonstrators or their attackers. Nevertheless, the development was stopped.[10]

The Green Belt Movement's Civic and Environmental Education Program specifically linked environmental mismanagement to bad government and corruption. Maathai and her colleagues showed rural women and men that the colonial system of commercial agriculture had damaged the environment and impoverished them. In addition, they pointed out that the system did not come to an end when the country became independent. It was simply taken over by a small number of Africans. The only difference was that African guards replaced white guards. The education project taught that the only way to change the system was to support a pro-democracy (antigovernment) movement.

The government retaliated with a series of actions designed to undermine the movement. The Green Belt response was an innocent "Us? But all we are doing is planting trees." In a similar way, when Maathai wrote reports critical of the government, she would say, "Oh, no, I am not criticizing the government, I am just writing a standard report for the United Nations."

By the middle of the 1990s in Kenya the environment was no longer just an issue for the countryside and for children, women, and poor men. It had been elevated to a national, even an international issue. Nor was land use simply a matter of trees versus development. It was a matter of democracy—who should decide how land was to be used? It was a matter of corruption—public land should not be sold to developers by officials with a stake in the development or who received fees from developers. It was a matter of rights—private and tribal land claims were not to be manipulated, and beatings and arrests of protestors were unacceptable.

Maathai was not one who had to be persuaded that human rights included women's rights. She had too often taken the knocks that accompany being first and speaking one's mind. In her early struggles, both men and women condemned her for violating African tradition by challenging men, especially male officials. She recalls being told over and over again that she should not have a career and that she, like all women, needed a "master." Importantly, even though she is one of the most educated women in her country, Maathai has always worked with poor and uneducated women. She has always believed that information and common sense can help ordinary people accomplish great things. She refers fondly to her Green Belt women as "foresters without degrees." One might add, "but with information."

It might be thought that Maathai's six years in the United States and Germany account for her belief in individual responsibility and in the importance for women of being strong. However, in arguing that African women need to be liberated from fear and silence, she has said that the most important thing for them is to "decolonize their minds." That is, to shake off the patronizing and exploitive cultural stereotypes imposed by the West. It would seem that Maathai sees both Western culture and traditional African culture as harmful to women.

Even as she has exercised leadership and power, however, Maathai has acknowledged that many women seem happiest when serving. She has even described herself as happiest and at her best when serving. But she is not naive. She sees that those whose goal is service rather than the acquisition of power are disadvantaged when they are competing with men whose only goal is power. She understands too that when the powerful are threatened, even those who only wish to serve are seen as a threat, as dangerous. But Maathai has never been one to back down. As she said during the Uhuru Park campaign, "They think they can embarrass and silence me with threats and name-calling. But I have an elephant's skin. And somebody must raise the voice. I might as well have been doing nothing if I did not raise my voice." Maathai has been jailed a number of times, and has been hospitalized after physical attacks. She has received death threats and periodically has found it necessary to go into hiding. Nevertheless, her voice has always been heard.

Maathai's recent participation in electoral politics has been as a leader of the Mazingira Green Party, which was one of seventy-two parties that founded the Global Greens Federation in Canberra in 2001. The Greens' next international convention will be held in 2007 and 2008 in Kenya; Maathai will be its official hostess.

In 2002 a coalition she supported defeated the KANU candidate for the presidency. The challengers ran on a platform of democracy, human rights, and clean government. The transition was peaceful, and one of the new parliamentarians was Maathai, who won 98 percent of the vote in her home district of Nyeri. Not only did she join the parliament, she was appointed deputy minister of environment, natural resources, and wildlife.

It should be remembered that Maathai was a well-known international figure long before she won the Nobel Peace Prize. She had received honorary degrees from Williams College, Hobart and William Smith Colleges, Yale University, and the University of Norway. Among her prizes and awards were Woman of the Year (1983), Right Livelihood Award (1984), the Better World Society Award (1986), the Windstar Award for the Environment (1988), Woman of the World (1989), the Goldman Environmental Prize (1991), the UN's Africa Prize for Leadership (1991), the Jane Addams Leadership Award (1993), the Edinburgh Medal (1993), the Golden Ark Award (1994), the Juliet Hollister Award (2001), the Excellence Award from the Kenyan Community Abroad (2001), the Outstanding Vision and Commitment Award (2002), and the WANGO Environment Award (2003). In the same year that she won her Nobel Peace Prize, she also won the J. Sterling Morton Award (2004), the Petra Kelly Prize for the Environment (2004), the Arbor Day award (2004), the Sophie Prize (2004), and the Center for Environmental Research and Conservation's Conservation Scientist Award (2004).

Further, Maathai was cochair of the Jubilee 2000 Africa Campaign, which advocated cancellation of the large foreign debts owed by African countries. She has served on the Secretary-General's Advisory Board on Disarmament, and also on the boards of the Jane Goodall Institute, the Women and Environment Development Organization, World Learning for International Development, Green Cross International, Environment Liaison Center International, and the WorldWIDE Network of Women in Environmental Work. The Nobel Peace Prize may have been a surprise, but Maathai was by no means an unknown.

The Tree as a Symbol for Peace as well as for Hope, Democracy, and Human Rights

The Norwegian Nobel Committee's announcement of the 2004 Nobel Peace Prize cited Maathai for her holistic approach to development, an approach that embraced democracy, human rights, and women's rights, and it praised Maathai for thinking globally while acting locally. She was cited as a strong voice speaking for "the best forces in Africa to promote peace and good living conditions on that continent." The chair of the committee noted that "peace on earth depends on our ability to secure our living environment."

Maathai agrees: "When our resources become scarce, we fight over them. In managing our resources and in sustainable development, we plant the seeds of peace."

In her Nobel lecture, Maathai emphasized that her work began in response to the problems identified by rural women, women who had seen the quality of their life deteriorate with the expansion of commercial agriculture. A crucial first step was helping these women understand the reasons for that deterioration and helping them identify solutions they could implement themselves. Green Belt education urged villagers not to wait for "the outside" to help. It even suggested that "the outside" (the government) was contributing to their problems rather than solving them.

Maathai expanded in her lecture on the theme of the tree as a symbol of peace by observing that during the contentious rewriting of Kenya's constitution, trees of peace were planted throughout the country.[11] Trees were also used to reconcile disputes between ethnic communities. She noted that in Kikuyu tradition, an elder would place a staff (made from a tree) between disputing parties as a sign that it was time to reconcile.

Several times in her address, Maathai called for preservation of African traditions and "cultural biodiversity." Still, she noted that all cultures must change, and that retrogressive practices like female genital mutilation must be discarded while positive elements from other cultures, like elections, must be accepted.

While she called for the mobilization of the grass roots, of civil society, which she considered essential to maintaining government's checks and balances, she also called on citizens to accept their responsibilities even as they campaigned for their rights.

Global corporations were not forgotten. She sternly reminded them that their mission must not be "profits at any cost." Economic justice, equity, and ecological integrity were of "greater value."

When the prize was announced, the Green Belt Movement had already developed a strategic plan and had declared that it was about to enter phase 2 of its existence. One important element of the plan was to wean the organization from its dependency on donors, many of whom were Western. The movement itself wished to be sustainable. A second goal was to educate the rural poor about the reasons for their poverty and to empower them to change their status.

Under the new plan the core activities of the movement were to be unchanged. It would continue planting trees, particularly on public (as opposed to private) land, and promoting food security at the household level, civic and environmental education, and advocacy. But instead of paying people to plant seedlings, the movement now plans to sell the seedlings in order to support itself. More attention will also be given to teaching farming methods that increase yields, and to the raising of crops that lead to a balanced diet.

The education program is to be broad based. In addition to environmental education, it will specifically include an emphasis on (1) basic human rights, (2) knowing one's roots (one's culture), (3) good governance, (4) Green Belt Movement values, (5) issues of equity, (6) natural-resource base values, and (7) responsibility toward future generations. It is not a modest undertaking—and it is to be self-taught. Professional educators will not be required. A variety of means will be used. These will include seminars, radio broadcasts, leaflets, cultural exchanges, audio cassettes, and school projects.

Advocacy programs need not be limited to the local or even the national. There is often a clear intent to enlist international public opinion and, today, to employ the Internet. For Kenya, international advocacy is facilitated by the many Western tourists who come to visit its game parks. However, much of the movement's energy will now be directed toward pan-African activities. New emphasis will also be given to the protection of rare, indigenous plant and animal species and to sites of cultural significance.

The movement now provides a very specific ten-step procedure for establishing and running a Green Belt campaign. It also provides concrete advice about replicating the Green Belt Movement in other countries.

Finally, its business development plan includes provisions for making a profit on some of the movement's education and safari programs, and it also attempts to increase local fund-raising. Building the movement's capacity for planning, personnel development, public relations, record keeping, and financial management is also on the agenda.

In the last several years Maathai has had to make an adjustment to being a part of the government—but only a part—and to being only a deputy in the area of her primary interest. There is a long way to go to reach the movement's goal of 10 percent forest cover since the present cover is less than 2 percent.[12]

New projects include incorporating handicapped individuals in the seedling program and establishing a center for battered women and children. The latter promises to be an uphill battle, for abuse of women and children is not widely seen as either illegal or wrong in Kenya.

Maathai has always emphasized the individual's capacity and responsibility. She has fought passivity and acceptance of apparent power, whether that power was exercised by government, or by an even higher power. Thus she explains her widely quoted statement that "AIDS is not a curse from God to Africans or the black people. It is a tool to control them designed by some evil-minded scientists" by saying that she was trying to counter the widespread belief in Kenya that AIDS was God's will. Even after the Norwegian Nobel Committee had announced her award, she was quoted as saying, "I may not be able to say who developed the virus, but it was meant to wipe out the black race." She later explicitly denied saying or believing that white people were trying to destroy African people. Still, she noted that the belief that the cause of AIDS was a failed scientific experiment was widespread, and that she hoped scientists would find conclusive evidence to the contrary.[13] The Norwegian Nobel Committee acknowledged that it did not know about Maathai's views on AIDS when it made its selection.

And Tomorrow?

Some complained that the 2004 Nobel Peace Prize should have gone to the Pope. Others were appalled that the holder of a PhD in science, and with much of her training in U.S. or German laboratories, would give credence to a theory featuring evil scientists and a biological weapon of mass destruction. Others thought trees had little to do with peace.

The criteria stated in Alfred Nobel's will call for the prize to go to the person who has "done the most or the best work for fraternity between nations, for the abolition or reduction of standing armies and for the holding and promotion of peace congresses." It is true that Maathai does not fit the criteria well. However, the Norwegian Nobel Committee long ago gave up a strict interpretation of the criteria. Almost from the beginning the prize has been given to organizations as well as to persons. Many times it has gone to those working within a country rather than to those working to resolve conflicts between countries. While some winners have sought to eliminate or control nuclear weapons and to prevent the use of standing armies, no one has won for trying to abolish armies altogether, and few have won for holding a congress. Some, like Mother Teresa and Albert Schweitzer, have won just for doing good. Further, the idea that enhancing the food supply contributes to peace is not new. In 1970 the Nobel Peace Prize went to Norman Borlaug, a U.S. scientist considered the father of the Green Revolution. His discoveries greatly increased agricultural productivity, which in turn reduced periodic famines.

Maathai is a proud Kenyan who urges her people to shake off all remnants of colonialism. But she is also highly educated and worldly. She has lived abroad and traveled the globe; she has been supported by donors from many countries; the UN has given her legitimacy, contacts, and support. But her life has not been easy. For years she has been assailed verbally. She has been attacked physically. She has been jailed. But she comes back. Her resiliency is remarkable and gives credence to her consistent advocacy of hope even in the darkest hour.

A Nobel Prize can only go to the living. But how can a Nobelist follow his or her own act? Sometimes the prize comes late in life, and the winner can simply enjoy the honor. Two examples would be Jane Addams, and Emily Balch. Sometimes it comes in the midst of the work and provides support for the work's continuance, as it did for von Suttner, Mother Teresa, and Alva Myrdal. Sometimes, though, winning entraps. Even if there is little prospect of success, a winner cannot abandon her efforts because it would gravely disappoint her followers and a world audience as well. This is true for Aung San Suu Kyi and, perhaps, for Shirin Ebadi. Sometimes the prize brings enhanced opportunity to someone whose honored accomplishments must necessarily be followed by less dramatic work, but work that is consistent with what has gone before. This has been true for Rigoberta Menchú, Jody Williams, Betty Williams, and Mairead Corrigan (now Maguire).[14]

Although sixty-five, Maathai has no intention of resting on her laurels or of simply being a role model.[15] Her prize money of $1,369,000 will go to a foundation to support tree planting and women's rights. Still, Maathai is in a difficult position because she is now part of the government. Her ideals may not be compromised, but her position is different. She can no longer be the critic, the leader of outsiders. She might have been able to play that role as a mere member of parliament, but she is a deputy minister. She is constrained as a deputy. In fact, the day before the prize was announced, she threatened to resign over the prospect that forests in her own constituency would be cut down to create more crop land. She is also discovering how constrained any government is by lack of resources, lack of unity, or lack of public support.

Wangari Maathai planting trees with a member of the Green Belt movement, Kenya.
© William Campbell / Peter Arnold, Inc.

Maathai is connected to her Nobel sisters. She benefited from an education by the Loreto Sisters, Mother Teresa's order. She won a Jane Addams Prize. She worked with the UN, as did Alva Myrdal. Like Rigoberta Menchú, she came from humble beginnings. Like Aung San Suu Kyi, Shirin Ebadi, and Jody Williams, she challenged her own government. Like Emily Balch, Mairead Corrigan, and Betty Williams, she worked primarily with women. Like Bertha von Suttner, she worked internationally and understood well the need to be raising funds constantly.

Her message is clear. Each of us can make a difference. It may take forty, fifty, or sixty years, but one must have hope and patience and work with others as a team. Or in Wangari Muta Maathai's words, "No matter how much we fail, we must recognize that there is hope. Especially in my region, with all the recent slaughter in Rwanda, for even there, the sun will rise, and we continue to hope that we can overcome our suffering."

Notes

1. One settler was Isak Dinesen whose *Out of Africa* recounts the life of European settlers.

2. The other is Kiswahili or Swahili. It is interesting that in the 1960s some African Americans who identified with their African roots and with "black pride"

began learning Swahili, even though their roots were far more likely to have been in West rather than East Africa.

3. President Kibaki was also born in Nyeri.

4. There is a monument in Nyeri to the Kikuyu warriors who fought for Kenya's independence. Another site of interest is a statue of Lord Robert Baden Powell, founder of the Boy Scouts, who retired there in 1938.

5. In 1971 St. Scholastica merged with St. Benedict's College, a nearby men's college, to become Benedictine College.

6. A UN report issued in 1989 stated that in Africa only nine trees were being planted to replace every one hundred trees cut down. This was after the Green Belt Movement had been at work for a decade.

7. Foresters had encouraged the planting of eucalyptus and evergreens, which grew rapidly, but Maathai's program emphasized indigenous trees such as baobabs, acacias, cedars, and thorn trees for their firewood, and citrus, papaw, and fig trees for their fruit.

8. The term *improved livelihood securities* refers to raising enough food, and raising food that provides good nutrition.

9. Moi called Maathai "a mad woman" and "a threat to the security of the country." Other officials referred to her as "an ignorant and ill-tempered puppet of foreign masters," and "an unprecedented monstrosity." The *New York Times* said Maathai was enduring a "vilification unusual even in the highly personalized politics of Kenya."

10. In 2001 the government proposed building housing for homeless squatters on forested land. Clearly this was an electoral appeal to those who usually supported Maathai. She remained true to her principles of opposing any development that required deforestation.

11. In November 2005 a proposed constitution was rejected in a national referendum because it maintained a strong president. It had included a strong bill of rights and gave one-third of the three hundred parliamentary seats to women. The colonial constitution of 1963 remains in force.

12. That 10 percent goal includes reforesting areas with indigenous trees, but also permits growing exotic trees in plantations for commercial purposes.

13. A British journalist has suggested that a polio vaccine used in West Africa might have been the source. Most scientists believe that hypothesis has been disproved.

14. Once in the public view does not mean always in the public view. During the protests preceding the Iraq War, Mairead Corrigan Maguire and Jody Williams were arrested in Washington, D.C. Their civil disobedience went virtually unnoticed.

15. Every famous person gets the role-model question in an interview. This is Maathai's answer: "A role model? I think women were thrilled because I represent an ordinary woman—it's very different from coming into a position because of your inheritance. I'm coming from any Dick and Harry. I'm a Dick and Harry of a woman."

❧

Champions All

The women whose stories you have just read have earned our admiration. But do their stories offer lessons as well? Do they give us guidance as to what we might do? Withholding sex and seizing the treasury like the women in *Lysistrata* are appealing tactics, but are there measures better suited to our time and place? And do their stories make us want to do our part?

The lives of these women Nobelists span more than a century. Their homes are in Asia, Africa, Central America, Europe, and the United States. One was born with a title and another in a village accessible only on foot. Some tried to avert or halt wars between great empires; others tried to end a civil war or just tried to get recognition for the results of an election. A woman was included in each of the five prize categories described in the introduction. Yes, there is great diversity among them, but there are some commonalities worth remembering.

Twenty-five Nobel Peace Prizes went to individuals who worked within national and with international organizations to advance peace between nations through mediation, arbitration, and international agreements. But only one of these prizes went to a woman, Alva Myrdal, and she had special visibility as a Swede and as the wife of another Nobel Prize winner. Winners in this category clearly did the kind of work anticipated by Nobel, but in spite of their official positions, these leaders could not prevent two World Wars that were separated by only twenty years.

The largest category of prize winners is made up of peace activists. These individuals did not hold high office although some of them, for example Fridtjof Nansen of Norway and Jane Addams of the United States, were well-known public figures. These winners are distributed over the century. Some were principled opponents of violence, but others were not. Some were popular in their homelands, while others were reviled. These winners did not necessarily work within existing structures. In fact, *all* the women in this category worked through organizations they founded or cofounded. These individuals *chose* to act. In the previous category, individuals were *chosen* to act by election or by appointment. Further, these activists' appeals were often to their fellow citizens rather than to officials. Although some did hold congresses, they were for the purpose of influencing governments. Their congresses were not assemblies of officials. And while the elimination of standing armies was on no one's agenda, a number of these activists' efforts were directed toward the control of nuclear weapons and, of course, to the banning of landmines. Note that both the antinuclear and landmine campaigns targeted weapons that especially harm civilians. Thus, their appeal addressed citizens' and civilians' self-interest. These women activists include von Suttner, Addams, Balch, Corrigan, Betty Williams, and Jody Williams.

The prizes given to leaders who sanctioned or exercised force but then agreed to stop fighting have been controversial. In the last quarter century, five pairs of antagonists have been honored when a peace agreement was reached or about to be reached. In these cases the Norwegian Nobel Committee seems to have been trying to have an effect on peace. The last two prizes awarded in this group—to leaders in Israel and representatives of the Palestinians (1994), and to opposing leaders in Northern Ireland (1998)—have had little measurable result. Rigoberta Menchú fits in this category in that she supported the Guatemalan guerrillas' violent resistance and was present at the peace settlement. She does not fit in that her crucial contribution was not in calling a halt to violence but in exposing it through her autobiography. That volume was a catalyst to the peace process because it brought outsiders into the negotiations. The process ended with a set of remarkable provisions, including the down-sizing of the military, land redistribution, and the compilation of evidence related to human rights violations. Even though many of the treaty provisions have not been carried out, the accord represents a serious effort to create a positive, just peace.

A similar number of awards went to individuals who did not seek peace directly but sought justice, freedom, democracy, security, or rights through peaceful means. The argument is that without such conditions, peace cannot be maintained. All these awards have been made in the last half century, and have been given to individuals around the globe. These prizes may not fit the original Nobel criteria, but because they advocate nonviolent means, they do seem to fulfill the Nobel spirit. Three in this group, Suu Kyi, Ebadi, and Maathai, are women.

Finally, some would say that Mother Teresa's "exemplary service" had nothing to do with peace, and that her acts of mercy were religious in intent and were only an attempt to give immediate relief in horrific circumstances. Others would argue that her efforts increased "fraternity," albeit between individuals not between nations.

One characteristic of all these women, however, was their optimism. In most cases they also showed great perseverance. Further, each knew or soon learned that peace is not necessarily popular.

Another important lesson to be learned from these Nobel Peace Prize winners is that we can start to work for peace at any time in our lives. Many of them did not become engaged in peace work until their forties or fifties. The only ones who were involved as young women, Menchú, Corrigan, and Betty Williams, were women actually living amid violence. Jody Williams, Mother Teresa, Addams, Balch, Ebadi, and Maathai were engaged in civic life for years. However, they only began to work for peace in middle age. Von Suttner and Suu Kyi also came to their work later in life, and Myrdal began her work on disarmament at age fifty-nine. It is never too late.

Addams, Balch, Mother Teresa, Menchú, Jody Williams, and Corrigan were single during their active advocacy. Von Suttner was married but childless. Only four were married and had children: Betty Williams, Myrdal, Suu Kyi, and Ebadi. The fact that Suu Kyi and Ebadi were from prosperous backgrounds undoubtedly made combining their motherhood and peace activities easier. However, even with a comfortable income that task is challenging, which may be one reason so many Nobel Peace Prize–winning women began their work later in life.

Betty Williams, Corrigan, Mother Teresa, Maathai, and Menchú did not come from privileged families, and Menchú's was poorer than the rest. Jody Williams, Balch, Addams, Myrdal, and Maathai were college-educated women who were not from elite families but who were free to make choices without being governed by economic need. Suu Kyi's father was a national hero, and von Suttner was an aristocrat with style but no fortune. For the Nobel women, social class was not a bar.

Were these women feminists? Did they advocate women's equality? Did they value women's special roles? And were they willing to say so? Suu Kyi may be the only one for whom women were not a special concern. Mother Teresa also was not interested in rights for women, though she founded an all-women organization while observing a vow of obedience within a hierarchical and patriarchal organization. She was also devoted to girls' education, and clearly she honored motherhood. Corrigan and Betty Williams appealed to and mobilized women, but on behalf of peace and not women's rights, although later their efforts might have been described as action opposing violence against women. After the prize was awarded to them, both continued to work on behalf of children and prisoners, but again, not specifically on behalf of women. Jody Williams focused on issues that gravely affected women, and ICBL activists were largely women, even though the campaign was initiated by Vietnam War veterans. Still, even if these women were not feminists per se, each worked with women and each has been an inspiration to women.

In contrast, while the bulk of von Suttner's work lay in appealing to men and working with them, she was responsive to women and their organizations and she campaigned for women's suffrage. Balch and Addams also supported suffrage. Both worked largely within women's institutions that they themselves helped build, but they tried hard to influence men and their political institutions. Myrdal, Menchú, Ebadi, and Maathai were or are specifically committed to women's rights.

Did these women break out of traditional roles? Mother Teresa operated within a long-established woman's role but carried its practice beyond the ordinary. Myrdal fulfilled both a woman's traditional role and a role that was then reserved for men. Suu Kyi's challenge to a military government for so sustained a period was not traditional, but elite Asian women have led their countries in India, Pakistan, Bangladesh, the Philippines, and Sri Lanka. Ebadi's legal leadership in a Muslim country is not traditional, but it is not unique. Muslim women have been elected to lead the governments of Pakistan, Bangladesh, Turkey, and Indonesia. Betty Williams and Corrigan broke boundaries because they came from the working class to lead an organization drawing women and men from all classes. Addams, Balch, and Maathai broke tradition by going to college, establishing important work for women, working internationally, and making the transition from the adored to the criticized and back to the adored without compromising their principles. Von Suttner's status may have given her a sense of impunity, but she did not use her talents and energy to pursue conventional goals. Jody Williams worked within a tradition of volunteer organizations but achieved remarkable breadth (working with Princess Diana and Vietnam veterans), and she and ICBL pioneered the technology of the Web to create a collective will. Menchú, though, may have broken the most boundaries, those being class, ethnicity, and country size.

As I've noted, the Norwegian Nobel Committee's deliberations are kept secret for fifty years. We know that many deserving candidates are considered and not chosen for the Nobel Peace Prize, and that campaigns are even waged on behalf of some of them. Among the women "might-have-wons," one would surely have to include Eleanor Roosevelt for her work on the UN Declaration of Human Rights; Australia's Helen Caldicott for her work against nuclear weapons; the Madres de la Plaza de Mayo of Argentina for witnessing on behalf of the *desaparecidos*, the "disappeared"; the Black Sash women of South Africa for demonstrating their opposition to apartheid; the Israeli and Palestinian women's Women in Black, whose vigils have become an international phenomenon; and the women of Greenham Commons Women's Peace Camp in England.

And what is the take-home message? Surely it is that we can all be champions for peace. From *Lysistrata* we learn that it is important to be creative, to take action, to organize women, and to think beyond national boundaries. From the laureates we have learned to be optimistic, to persevere, and to expect criticism and sometimes physical attacks and jail.

If I were a member of the Norwegian Nobel Committee, I would not support candidates in two of the Nobel Peace Prize's current categories: that of exemplary service, and that of leaders who have used or sanctioned force but who have agreed to stop using it. In *Nonviolent Power* (1972), I have expressed my respect and hopes for the effective use of nonviolence on behalf of peace and social justice. In doing so, I have described two quite different philosophies of nonviolence. One, *conscientious nonviolence*, is based on the belief that there is a natural human harmony of interests and that every human has a conscience, a potential for good. This kind of nonviolent action is directed toward reaching an agreement or reconciliation without the use of violence, threat, or coercion. Among its tools are surprise, empathy, and self-sacrifice. This individualistic, perfectionist formulation often has a religious foundation. It is a way of life and is sustained over the years by groups like the Quakers, the Society of Friends. The second philosophy, one of *pragmatic nonviolence*, assumes that because violence begets violence and humans have a capacity for horrendous deeds, it is important not to unleash violence. It judges violence not so much as "wrong" as ineffective, and uneconomic. While nonviolence remains the strategy, the tactics of this philosophy can be coercive. They can include massive demonstrations, sit-ins, boycotts, appeals to public opinion, and calls for third-party intervention. Practicers of this second form of nonviolence may consider it a winning strategy without committing themselves to it as a way of life. Adherents to both schools, however, understand that nonviolent action can involve risk and sacrifice.

In successful nonviolent campaigns, followers of the first kind of nonviolence play a crucial role, but inevitably many participants adhere to the second perspective. For me, there is only one sticking point. If I were in a position to offer protection—certain protection—by using violence against, for instance, a terrorist, I would feel I should do so. The role of protector is not to be taken lightly. That brings us to a final point.

In becoming champions for peace, in setting goals, and in adopting strategies, we must remember that the point is not to express or to absolve ourselves; it is to change men's behavior. After all, most violence is done by men and particularly at the direction of governments. Officials tend to believe that one of their most important roles is that of the protector. Officials also tend to believe that violence is effective. Where they are elected to office, officials are likely to believe that citizens support both their goals and their strategies. This means that it is important to study the psychology and interests of the men who authorize and exercise violence. For instance, Suu Kyi always emphasizes the importance of exacting no retribution when political change finally occurs. She understands that because of the fear of retribution, rulers find it hard to let go of the tiger's tail. Similarly, Balch always provided an economic analysis. Some of us will choose to work within a system that is largely directed by men, as did Addams, von Suttner, Myrdal, Ebadi, and (now) Maathai. Others will try to circumvent the system as did Jody Williams and Menchú. Still others will try to divorce themselves from the political, as did Betty Williams, Corrigan, and Mother Teresa. Each of us has different circumstances and different resources; nevertheless, each of us has the capacity to act. Each of us can be a champion for peace.

Questions for U.S. and Non-U.S. Readers

A Question for U.S. Readers

As an activist, what would your priorities be to make the United States a leader in peace?

(1) An end to all weapons sales abroad including small arms?

(2) Creation of a draft for all twenty-year-olds including women, those enrolled in school, and those with families? Or, alternatively, raising the age of enlistment to twenty-five so enlistees would be making a mature decision?

(3) U.S. participation in and support for the International Criminal Court?

(4) Reduction of the U.S. Department of Defense Budget to 2 percent of U.S. GDP, or to one-third of the world's total military expenditures?

(5) Vastly increased support for diplomacy by increasing the State Department's budget to one-third of the Defense Department's budget?

(6) Destruction of 9,950 U.S. nuclear weapons?

(7) Monthly reports of all deaths experienced by and inflicted by the U.S. military including deaths of civilians?

(8) Full access to all classified materials to every member of Congress; access to all documents twenty years or older to any citizen?

(9) Enforcement of UN Security Council Resolution 1325, which ensures women's participation in all peace negotiations?

(10) Closure of all U.S. military bases abroad beginning with the new bases in Iraq?

(11) Foregoing all vetoes in international organizations such as the Security Council and the IMF?

(12) Commitment of the United States to the rule of law including international law?

What other initiatives would *you* propose?

A Question for Non-U.S. Readers

As an activist, what would your priorities be to make your country a leader in peace?

Selected Bibliography

Chapter 1

Hamann, Brigitte. *Bertha von Suttner: A Life for Peace*, trans. Ann Dubsky. Syracuse, N.Y.: Syracuse University Press, 1996.

von Suttner, Bertha. *Lay Down Your Arms*. New York: Longmans, Green, 1914.

———. *Memoirs of Bertha von Suttner*. Boston: Gina, 1910.

Chapter 2

Addams, Jane. *Newer Ideals of Peace*. New York: Macmillan, 1907.

———. *Peace and Bread in Time of War*. New York: Garland, 1972.

———. *Twenty Years at Hull-House*. New York: Signet Classic, 1961.

Davis, Allen F., ed. *Jane Addams on Peace, War, and International Understanding, 1899–1932*. New York: Garland, 1976.

Diliberto, Gioia. *A Useful Woman: The Early Life of Jane Addams*. New York: Scribner, 1999.

Elshtain, Jean Bethke. *Jane Addams and the Dream of American Democracy*. New York: Basic Books, 2002.

Chapter 3

Balch, Emily Greene. *Our Slavic Fellow Citizens*. New York: Arno Press, 1969.

Randall, Mercedes M., ed. *Beyond Nationalism: The Social Thought of Emily Greene Balch*. New York: Twayne, 1972.

———. *Improper Bostonian: Emily Greene Balch*. New York: Twayne, 1964.

Chapter 4

Deutsch, Richard. *Mairead Corrigan, Betty Williams*, trans. Jack Bernard. Woodbury, N.Y.: Barron's, 1977.

Dixon, Paul. *Northern Ireland: The Politics of War and Peace.* New York: Palgrave, 2001.

Maguire, Mairead Corrigan. *The Vision of Peace.* Maryknoll, N.Y.: Orbis, 1999.

McKeown, Ciaran. *The Passion of Peace.* Belfast: Blackstaff, 1984.

McKittrick, David, and David McVea. *Making Sense of the Troubles.* London: Penguin, 2001.

Chapter 5

Cherry, Matt. "An Interview with Christopher Hitchens on Mother Teresa." *Free Inquiry* (Fall 1996): 53–56.

Egan, Eileen. *Such a Vision of the Street: Mother Teresa—the Spirit and the Work.* Garden City, N.Y.: Doubleday, 1985.

Muggeridge, Malcolm. *Something Beautiful for God.* San Francisco: Harper and Row, 1971.

Sebba, Anne. *Mother Teresa: Beyond the Image.* New York: Doubleday, 1997.

Spink, Kathryn. *Mother Teresa: A Complete Authorized Biography.* New York: Harper-SanFrancisco, 1997.

Chapter 6

Bok, Sissela. *Alva Myrdal: A Daughter's Memoir.* Reading, Mass.: Addison-Wesley, 1991.

Myrdal, Alva. *The Game of Disarmament.* New York: Pantheon, 1976.

Myrdal, Alva, and Viola Klein. *Women's Two Roles: Home and Work.* London: Routledge & Kegan Paul, 1956.

Chapter 7

Aris, Michael, ed. *Freedom from Fear.* London: Penguin, 1991.

Aung San Suu Kyi with Alan Clements. *The Voice of Hope.* New York: Seven Stories, 1997.

Houtman, Gustaaf. *Mental Culture in Burmese Crisis Politics: Aung San Suu Kyi and the National League for Democracy.* Tokyo: Tokyo University of Foreign Studies, 1999.

Larkin, Emma. *Finding George Orwell in Burma.* New York: Penguin, 2005.

Lintner, Bertil. *Burma in Revolt.* Chiang Mai, Thailand: Silkworm Books, 2000.

Victor, Barbara. *The Lady: Burma's Aung San Suu Kyi.* Chiang Mai, Thailand: Silkworm Books, 1998.

Chapter 8

Arias, Arturo, ed. *The Rigoberta Menchú Controversy.* Minneapolis: University of Minnesota Press, 2001.
Menchú, Rigoberta. *I, Rigoberta Menchú: An Indian Woman in Guatemala,* ed. Elisabeth Burgos-Debray, trans. Ann Wright. London: Verso, 1984.
———. *Crossing Borders.* London: Verso, 1998.
Stoll, David. *Rigoberta Menchú and the Story of All Poor Guatemalans.* Boulder, Colo.: Westview, 1999.

Chapter 9

Cameron, Maxwell A., Robert J. Lawson, and Brian W. Tomlin, eds. *To Walk without Fear: The Global Movement to Ban Landmines.* Toronto: Oxford University Press, 1998.
International Campaign to Ban Landmines. www.icbl.org (last accessed June 8, 2006).
Johnstone, Ian. *Rights and Reconciliation: UN Strategies in El Salvador.* Boulder, Colo.: Lynne Rienner, 1995.
Popkin, Margaret. *Peace without Justice: Obstacles to Building the Rule of Law in El Salvador.* University Park: Pennsylvania State University Press, 2000.
Roberts, Shawn, and Jody Williams. *After the Guns Fall Silent: The Enduring Legacy of Landmines.* Washington, D.C.: Vietnam Veterans of America Foundation, 1995.

Chapter 10

Abdo, Geneive, and Jonathan Lyons. *Answering Only to God: Faith and Freedom in Twenty-first-Century Iran.* New York: Henry Holt, 2003.
De Bellaigue, Christopher. *In the Rose Garden of the Martyrs: A Memoir of Iran.* New York: HarperCollins, 2005.

Chapter 11

Maathai, Wangari. *The Green Belt Movement: Sharing the Approach and the Experience.* New York: Lantern Books, 2004.

General Sources

Abrams, Irwin. *The Nobel Peace Prize and the Laureates: An Illustrated Biographical History, 1901–2001.* Nantucket, Mass.: Science History, 2001.
Alonso, Harriet Hyman. *Peace as a Woman's Issue: A History of the U.S. Movement for World Peace and Women's Rights.* Syracuse, N.Y.: Syracuse University Press, 1993.

Breines, Ingeborg, Dorota Gierycz, and Betty A. Reardon, eds. *Towards a Woman's Agenda for a Culture of Peace*. Paris: UNESCO, 1999.

Foster, Carrie A. *The Women and the Warriors: The U.S. Section of the Women's International League for Peace and Freedom, 1915–1946*. Syracuse, N.Y.: Syracuse University Press, 1995.

Harris, Adrienne, and Ynestra King. *Rocking the Ship of State: Toward a Feminist Peace Politics*. Boulder, Colo.: Westview, 1989.

Kelly, Colleen E., and Anna L. Eblen, eds. *Women Who Speak for Peace*. Lanham, Md.: Rowman and Littlefield, 2002.

Reardon, Betty. *Women and Peace: Feminist Visions of Global Security*. Albany: State University of New York Press, 1993.

Stiehm, Judith. *Nonviolent Power: Active and Passive Resistance in America*. Lexington, Mass.: Heath, 1973.

———. "The Civilian Mind," in *It's Our Military Too! Women and the U.S. Military*, ed. Judith Hicks Stiehm. Philadelphia: Temple University Press, 1996.

———. "The Protector and the Protected," in *Women and Men's Wars*, ed. Judith Stiehm. Oxford: Pergamon, 1982.

Swerdlow, Amy. *Women Strike for Peace: Traditional Motherhood and Radical Politics in the 1960s*. Chicago: University of Chicago Press, 1993.

Index

Note: Page numbers in *italics* refer to illustrations.

231

~~

About the Author

Judith Hicks Stiehm is professor of political science at Florida International University, where she served as provost and academic vice president. She has taught at the University of Wisconsin, UCLA, and the University of Southern California. She has been a visiting professor at the U.S. Army Peacekeeping Institute and at the Strategic Studies Institute at Carlisle Barracks. Stiehm earned a BA in East Asian studies at the University of Wisconsin, an MA at Temple University in American history, and a PhD in political theory from Columbia University. Her books include *Nonviolent Power: Active and Passive Resistance in America*, *Bring Me Men and Women: Mandated Change at the U.S. Air Force Academy*, *Arms and the Enlisted Woman*, *It's Our Military, Too! Women and the U.S. Military*, and *The U.S. Army War College: Military Education in a Democracy*. Stiehm has served on the Defense Advisory Committee on Women in the Military, and as a consultant to the United Nations Division for the Advancement of Women and to the Lessons Learned Unit of the Department of Peacekeeping Operations. She is a member of the Council on Foreign Relations, holds the U.S. Army Distinguished Civilian Service Medal, and has been honored by the University of Wisconsin as a "Distinguished Alumnus."